THE AUTOBIOGRAPHY OF WILLIAM SIMPSON, R.I.

THE AUTOBIOGRAPHY OF WILLIAM SIMPSON, R.I.

(CRIMEAN SIMPSON)

EDITED BY

GEORGE EYRE-TODD

GYAN

Published by

Gyan Publishing House
5, Ansari Road
Daryaganj, New Delhi-110002
Phone: 011-47034999, 9811692060
E-mail: books@gyanbooks.com

Distribution Network
gyanbooks.com
India, USA, Canada, UK, Australia, France

ISBN : 978-81-212-9250-4 (PB)
First Published, 1903

2nd Impression 2023

Printed at: Gyan Press, Delhi.

THE AUTOBIOGRAPHY OF WILLIAM SIMPSON, R.I.
Author: GEORGE EYRE-TODD

THE AUTOBIOGRAPHY

OF

WILLIAM SIMPSON, R.I.

(CRIMEAN SIMPSON)

William Simpson

THE AUTOBIOGRAPHY OF WILLIAM SIMPSON, R.I.

(CRIMEAN SIMPSON)

EDITED BY

GEORGE EYRE-TODD

AUTHOR OF "THE SKETCH-BOOK OF THE NORTH," "BYWAYS OF THE SCOTTISH BORDER," ETC., EDITOR OF "THE GLASGOW POETS," "THE BOOK OF GLASGOW CATHEDRAL," ETC. . .

ILLUSTRATED WITH MANY REPRODUCTIONS OF SIMPSON'S PICTURES FROM THE COLLECTIONS OF HIS MAJESTY THE KING, THE DUKE OF NEWCASTLE, THE MARQUIS OF BUTE, THE EARL OF ROSEBERY, THE EARL OF NORTHBROOK, THE BRITISH MUSEUM, SOUTH KENSINGTON MUSEUM, THE PALESTINE EXPLORATION FUND, ETC. + + +

LONDON: T. FISHER UNWIN
PATERNOSTER SQUARE. 1903

To

MY DEAR DAUGHTER

ANN PENELOPE SIMPSON

I DEDICATE THESE

NOTES AND RECOLLECTIONS

THAT WHEN SHE GROWS UP SHE MAY THROUGH

THEM LEARN SOMETHING OF HER

FATHER'S LIFE

PREFACE

IN his last years William Simpson occupied the hours of his enforced leisure in writing an account of the memorable circumstances of his life. His career had been eventful and varied far beyond that of most men. He had taken part, as an observer on the spot, in nearly all the great wars and historic events in which his country was interested during a period of forty years. As the earliest of war artists he had gone through the campaign of the Crimea, and this with such distinction as to earn for himself the soubriquet thenceforth of "Crimean Simpson." India after the Mutiny had also been studied and wrought over by him during two years of painstaking travel. Probably no artist before or since has investigated its ancient interests and remote regions with such thoroughness and sympathy. Among his later campaigns he followed Napier to Magdala, and took part in bringing the son of King Theodore home. He went with the Germans to Paris, was arrested as a spy, and passed through the dangerous episodes of the Commune in the French capital. And he took a brilliant part in the Afghan war, was shot at in the Khyber Pass, and by the merest chance escaped assassination with Cavagnari in Cabul. Among more pacific episodes of which he had intimate personal knowledge were the Kertch Expedition, the Duke of Newcastle's tour to Circassia, the opening of the Suez Canal, the examination of Warren's excavations at Jerusalem and Schlieman's at Mycenæ, the great Vatican Council of 1869, the Indian tour of the Prince of Wales, the Afghan Boundary Commission, and such royal marriages as those of the Czar of Russia, the Emperor of China, Prince William of Prussia, and the Princess Louise.

In all these events he took part as an eye-witness. Throughout his life he kept careful diaries, and his hundreds of sketches and pictures themselves formed an authentic record. His autobiography, therefore, constantly throws a vivid, and often an entirely new light on the living detail of the most momentous transactions of his time.

Even the more personal chapters in Simpson's life-story contain much more than matter of merely personal interest. The memories of early years afford a curious picture of the artist's native city of Glasgow as it existed two generations ago. The account of the relations between artist and publisher, and of the methods and resources of a great war artist, forms a narrative, valuable in itself, of the inner working of a peculiarly modern profession. And the details of his researches into the antiquities of India offer more than a glimpse of a most suggestive field of study in which Simpson had made himself an authority. On this last subject, indeed, Simpson had a claim to the highest regard. The library which he left contained a collection, probably unrivalled in private hands, of scarce books on eastern and primeval religions, the catalogue alone of which affords something like an education on occult subjects. And during the Afghan War, and later, he made excavations and special studies, under Government auspices, into the religious architecture of India. The unpublished volumes into which he gathered his studies of Buddhist archæology form a very valuable collection of original material. "Before this war," he himself wrote, "our knowledge of Indian architecture was limited to the mouth of the Khyber Pass. I extended that knowledge as far as the Jellalabad Valley and Gundamuck."

But perhaps the deepest interest of all will be found to lie in the personal life-story of the author himself. The bare facts of that life-story read like a romance. Simpson began his career in the very humblest circumstances in his native city in the north. He was without all the outside aids of education and influence which most men regard as the necessary levers of success. Yet he earned his way, by the fairest means, and by hard, real work, not only to high distinction in a profession he may be said to have created, but to association upon mutual terms with the most distinguished men who were making the history of his time, and was received with the regard of friendship and upon the footing of personal worth even in the closet of the King. Facts like these bespeak a character every chapter of whose story is likely to be worth study.

Throughout his career Simpson had a singular faculty for the making and keeping of friends. Possibly something of the secret of this is discovered in a letter written lately by one of his fellow-workers for the *Illustrated London News* who knew him well. "There was none of us," writes this correspondent, "who ever had such an interest as Simpson had in the deeper studies of archæology and history, of philosophy and religion, and I have never in my life known his equal for *truthfulness,* not only in the common sense—I wish it were our common practice,—but I mean his almost passionate zeal for the examination and inquiry to get at the truth, and to set it forth by pen and pencil. It was this high example of veracity, the virtue of the true scientific man, which is not always found in artists, for which I greatly honoured and admired him."

Behind all these qualities, however, as a means of attraction, lay the singularly human heart of the man. He married somewhat late in life, and the daughter who was born to him was the object of a singularly tender regard. Pasted into the manuscript of his life is an envelope containing a lock of hair, and on the outside of this is written, "A.P.S., 10th Sept., 1884. Sent to me in Central Asia.—W. Simpson." And by way of explanation is added, "This came to me in a letter from her mother which reached me on the 9th Oct., at Ahawan, in Persia, and from that it has been all through the present expedition of the Afghan Boundary Commission." Add to this the terms in which he dedicated the memoir of his life itself to that young daughter, and something more than lies on the surface may perhaps be understood of the personal charm which was Simpson's passport round the world.

Apart from his repute as an artist, William Simpson was an author of some consideration. When sent in 1872 by the *Illustrated London News* to attend the ceremonies of the Emperor of China's marriage, he undertook to act also as correspondent for the *Daily News*, and the direct outcome of that arrangement was his volume, *Meeting the Sun*, published in 1873. And in 1896 he was induced to publish *The Buddhist Praying-Wheel*, a collection of material, chiefly gathered from his Indian experience, bearing on the symbolism of the wheel and circular movements in custom and religious ritual. But perhaps his most valuable writings were those on Indian archæology and on primeval religions, contributed to the Transactions of the Quatuor Coronati Lodge of Freemasons, of which he was an ardent member, to the Royal Institute of British Architects, the Royal Asiatic, and other societies. His original researches and studies in India made him an authority on these subjects, his sane and unprejudiced habit of mind fitted him peculiarly for such work, and in his chosen fields he must be held to have advanced both the knowledge and the wisdom of mankind.

CONTENTS

CONTENTS

LIST OF ILLUSTRATIONS

LIST OF ILLUSTRATIONS

LIST OF ILLUSTRATIONS

CHAPTER I

A START IN LIFE

I WAS born in Carrick Street, Glasgow, October 28, 1823. My father was employed about the engines of the steamboats in that early period of steam navigation on the Clyde. He claimed to have made the engines of the *Robert Bruce*, one of the boats of that date. The Napiers were then only emerging from the blacksmith's shop in which they began. Tod and Macgregor both were fellow-workmen with my father for some time, or at least one of them was.* I cannot recall with certainty the succession of places we lived in during those early years. I remember we were at a place called Orbiston. This was an experiment of a co-operative or communal kind, of which a friend of my father called Alexander Campbell, was a leading man. The experiment failed, but how I cannot explain.† We returned later to Glasgow, and lived in a "land" or tenement in North Frederick Street, at the corner of Little Hamilton Street.‡

* [The firms of Napier and of Tod and Macgregor were long famous as shipbuilders on the Clyde.]

† [Orbiston Estate, in the parish of Bothwell, Lanarkshire, was in 1825 made the site of an establishment on the system of Robert Owen, whose social experiment at New Lanark, close by, was then attracting much attention. The land was purchased for £36,000, and a great building begun, to house 1,200 persons. Scarcely a fourth, however, was ever finished, never more than 180 persons were in residence, and the buildings which had cost £12,000, were finally sold for £2,000 for the sake of their materials. The establishment was named by its founder New Orbiston, but was known in the neighbourhood as Babylon.]

‡ [A series of interesting reminiscences of the Glasgow of that day, will be found in the Appendix, p. 325.]

WILLIAM SIMPSON, R.I.

I was sent to Perth for a time, to live with my grandmother. There were no railways in those days. Stage coaches were on the roads, but they were expensive. Goods were sent by carriers' carts, and these also at times carried passengers. The goods were piled on the cart, covered with a strong, thick blanket, and tied firmly with ropes. When a passenger was expected a framework which formed a low rail was strapped on the top, and some straw was laid down, on which the passenger could lie and sleep if necessary, without the danger of falling off. The Perth carrier started on Sunday night, at twelve o'clock, in strict observance of the day of rest, from the Carriers' Yard near the foot of Virginia Street, opposite the City of Glasgow Bank. I think there were three carts, and I must have slept on mine. But I wakened before morning, when there was a little moonlight, and I saw clothes hanging out to dry behind a house we were passing, the white articles looking to me like ghosts. I remember lying on my back as we went along, and learning the art of whistling. Some time on Monday we reached Stirling, where a long stop was made. At times I got down and walked a bit, and I have faint recollections of Blackford and Auchterarder, as well as of passing the bridge over the river Earn.

My grandmother lived in a small property of my uncle's in Shuttlefield Close, and kept a small huckster's shop. She was Highland. Her father's name was Hugh Maconnochie, and the family originally belonged to the Kyles of Bute. They had taken "Charlie's" side in "the '45," and lost their property. My great-grandfather was very young at the time. The family had to hide; and as a means of concealment he was handed to some gipsies. While travelling with them he learned to make horn spoons. Spoons made from the horns of cattle were the rule in those days. Metal spoons had come into use in my boyhood, but even then horn spoons were more plentiful. The making of these was one of the gipsy crafts.

I lived with my grandmother in Perth for about fifteen months. She had grand ideas, and sent me to the best writing school in the town. I believe it was at the end of December, 1835, that I came home again.

Up to this time my intention was to become an engineer. I often talked with my mother as to how I should get into some "shop," as engineering establishments were called. She considered, and reasonably, that I was still too young for that kind of work. There was a family of the name of Macfarlane that she knew, and one of the sons had a small lithographic office. He wanted a boy, and it was decided I should go there for a year or so, till big enough to begin engineering. This was the turning-point of all my boyish intentions.

David Macfarlane's office was at 14, Queen Street. He had only two rooms. In the one behind was his single press, with stones and other necessaries for printing. Sometimes a printer was employed, often Macfarlane printed himself. I polished stones, ground printing ink, and went messages. Occasionally I had time to practise—to draw, and do "lettering." I went to this employment in January, 1837, when just over fourteen years of age, and in a year's time I had become a fairly good hand at all the various branches of lithography. That is, I could design a ticket, do it on transfer paper, transfer it to stone, then print it. Further, I had to carry home the work, and afterwards call for the payment.

In one sense I received no education except the few months at the Perth writing school. In another sense my education has gone on all my life, and I hope is not yet finished. Frederick Street lay about midway between the Andersonian University in George Street and the Mechanic's Institute at the top of North Hanover Street. In both places there were courses of scientific lectures every winter, and the introductory lectures were "free." The introductory lectures to the chemistry and natural philosophy courses were naturally attractive to us boys on account of the experiments. I went to all these introductory lectures if possible, and it was a sore disappointment when the free lectures were given on the same night at both places. In the Andersonian I heard Thomas Graham, a professor there, who was a profound student and afterwards became Master of the Mint. At these introductory lectures I picked up scraps, at least, of knowledge which have been of use to me in after life. Another boy and I made hydrogen gas by means of water, iron nails, and sulphuric acid, in a bottle. But after some explosions, when I had burnt my hand badly and nearly set fire to the house with phosphorus, my mother put a stop to our scientific pursuits in this direction. One winter my father had a card for Dr. Hunter's lectures on anatomy and physiology at the Mechanic's Institution, and when he could not attend I went. This card also gave us a right to the library, and I began to read books on science. I was then looking forward to becoming an engineer, and although still a boy, I had the sense to wish to prepare myself. In 1837–38, Mr. Macfarlane, with whom I was at work, made me a present of a ticket for a course of lectures in the Gorbal's Popular Institution; the course was in Natural Philosophy, or Mechanics, by a Mr. Green. This also gave me the use of a library, of which I took advantage. Often we had no oil or candles at home, and I had to sit reading by the light of the fire. With the engineer idea still in view, I managed in the winter of 1838–39 to attend the architectural and mechanical drawing class of the Andersonian University. It was in the evenings, from eight to ten.

I was now close on sixteen, and beginning to think and act for myself. Accordingly, one Sunday I looked out the few specimens, or impressions, of work I had done in Macfarlane's, and on Monday forenoon I started early with them in my hand. My plan of action was made out. I had made some progress in drawing, and some in lettering. This last was then classed in lithography as "writing," in contradistinction to "drawing," or the draughtsman's department. The writing department included such work as circulars, invoices, &c.

At Maclure and Macdonald's, the foremost house in the trade, where I applied first, no one was required, and I retired, certainly relieved when I reached the stairs, and not quite disappointed, for I hardly expected success. The truth is that I felt as if it had been an effort to reach some Alpine height—for such had always been, from my position, the altitude and distance of these principal establishments in the lithographic business. The application was a bit of daring on my part, but it was part of the plan laid down at this turn in my life, and I have generally found sufficient determination when I have settled what was the right thing to do. In this instance the plan of action was rigidly carried out. I walked back along Argyle Street to Wilson's Court. The front house, in which Allan and Ferguson had their business, was one of the old mansions built by the "Sugar Lords," who had become rich from the trade with the West Indies. There were three such houses at that time in Argyle Street. The Buck's Head Hotel, next to Wilson's Court on the west, was the second. The "Black Bull," between Glassford Street and Virginia Street, was the third.

At Allan and Ferguson's, where the opening of the door was again an ordeal, I chanced to find Mr. Allan, whom I had seen once at least before, and whose appearance I knew. He was very kind, and after looking over my specimens declared himself willing to accept my services. I had to return next day to finally arrange, but I may say that before noon on that Monday I had accomplished my object, and the great change which gave a new purpose to my life had taken place. It so chanced that Mr. Allan had advertised for an apprentice, a thing I did not at the time know. It was the rule to work for the first two years without salary, but my previous experience made my case different, so I got remuneration from the first. This I need scarcely say was a necessity, else I should have been forced to go still further with my specimens. The salary at first was small, but my father and mother accepted the arrangement.

I should mention that I was bound by an indenture as an apprentice for seven years. Mr. Allan started me at first to "practise," this meant to copy something for the purpose of learning. I had always wrought before on paper, from which the work could be transferred to the stone, but in Allan and Ferguson's the plan had been adopted of doing the work directly on stone, hence the necessity at first for practice. In Macfarlane's, where I had to do such a variety of work, I never could have been good at any branch; but now I was limited to one, and being in one of the first houses in Glasgow, my chances of improvement were, I knew, of the best. It was not long before Mr. Allan entrusted me with something that was of use. An architectural work was in hand —folio plates, a large number of them, for a Mr. Alex. Hay. They included designs for houses, cottages, public buildings, churches, &c. So far as I remember now the plates were almost all geometric elevations. The first plate I did was so satisfactory that when Mr. Allan had a proof brought to him by the printer he came in with it in his hand and complimented me upon it. I also began to do plans, in which I was equally successful. I practised ornament, and tried my hand at designing in this branch, so that I could do tickets, of which large numbers were required in a manufacturing city like Glasgow. Chalk work was the highest department in my branch. I did not get anything of that kind to do at first, but I took a stone home and tried the work. Mr. Allan, seeing me anxious to improve, kindly lent me books, such as J. P. Harding's, to copy at home. So I made progress.

I also began to sketch from nature. This I did on summer mornings. The office shut early on Saturdays, so I was able to devote the afternoon to a walk in the country for sketching. Robert Carrick, a friend in the office, had practised water-colours, and had become very good at them. He, of course, had been able to get lessons. Carrick's productions, which I saw at times, fired me with the wish to do something in this line. But how was it possible? I had no colours, and they were expensive. The ordinary cakes cost a shilling, and some, such as cobalt, were eighteenpence. Such sums were out of the question with me. I might as well have longed for diamonds and rubies. Yet the determination to procure colours became so great that I at last saw my way. On certain days, when no dinner was being made at home, a penny was allotted me to supply myself. By taking a walk in the dinner hour, which I generally did by

Queen Street and Buchanan Street, where I could see pictures, water-colour drawings, &c., in the carver and gilders' windows, I saved my penny, and was able to buy colours in the colour shops. There was one man in Hutcheson Street who sold all colours in the "dry" state. A pennyworth of ochre, for instance, would make nearly a dozen cakes of colour. Cobalt and others cost more, but still they were cheaper a great deal than if I bought them as cakes in the artists' colour shops. I managed to get an old piece of lithographic stone in the office, to serve the purpose of a grinding slab, and a smaller piece I made into a muller. My first efforts at making colours were far from successful, but I persevered, and at last managed to produce such as I could begin painting with. This was the beginning of water-colour painting with me. I looked carefully at Donaldson's pictures, which were often in a shop window in Queen Street, and tried to do something like them at home. I also began to do portraits of friends, seldom getting anything for them. But in all this I had practice. My mother was so pleased that she would invite friends to come and have their portraits done.

After a time I was able to earn a little in various ways, and the first year or two being over in Allan and Ferguson's, things began to change for the better. Among my father's friends was Mr. James Mitchell, the brassfounder. He was a hard-working industrious man, and was able to start in business for himself. He often wanted designs connected with his work, and I was able now to do these things for him. I had many jobs from him, and he would always insist on some remuneration.

I soon began to be useful in the office, and Mr. Allan was not slow to appreciate this. Here was the beginning of a friendship which lasted while Mr. Allan lived; he died in November, 1875, when I was in India with the Prince of Wales. I could not tell him how poor we were, nor hint at the difficulties I had about colours, or I am sure he would have helped me—I preferred to act as I did. But he lent me books to work from at home, and one spring he gave me money to go to Edinburgh to the Exhibition of the Royal

Scottish Academy. This was a great treat to me, and I cannot express the gratitude I felt for such a kindness.

The year 1845, in which so many new schemes were proposed, was a noted period in the history of British railways. Engineers and others engaged in the work connected with these schemes afterwards applied the old phrase of being "out in the '45"—understood as relative to the "Charlie" rebellion—to their experiences. I may say I was "out in the '45," for the plans had to be lithographed. As the surveys have to be first made, the lithographing is left to the last moment. We had to work late nearly the whole of November in that year, and when we came to the end of the month—all plans must be sent in to the Board of Trade on the last day of November—we scarcely got any sleep at all! I had become very handy at this work; Mr. Allan could trust me with putting in the scales and other important details which required care, and at the end I received a present of £10 for my overtime. This was an unheard-of sum of money to me. If I recollect right a new silk dress, long promised to my mother, came out of this.

When Robert Carrick left in February, 1844, and went to London, I came in for the work he used to do. I had to go out and make sketches of places to be lithographed, often delightful spots in the country, all of which was very pleasant. This also gave me a better class of work; what was called "chalk"—the name given to lithographic crayons —was the higher branch of a lithographic draughtsman's work, and I came now into this.

There was not much demand in Glasgow for this description of lithography, but I was able to make some progress in it, and I knew that advancement in my profession depended on my proficiency in this direction. Mr. Allan sent me, when there was nothing pressing in the office, to make sketches on the Clyde and in the Highlands, which I lithographed, and these found a sale in various ways. He also caused me to make sketches of the old houses about Glasgow—anything that was of the past. These I put on stone, and they were all published in the form of a book, under the title of *Views and Notices of Glasgow in Former Times.* Robert Stuart, a stationer in Ingram Street, did the letter-press, and his name is on the title-page. It was not the custom in the office to put any name to work except that of the firm. Owing to this the book is now known as *Stuart's Glasgow.* In the preface Stuart states that he only wrote the letter-press to accompany the drawings. I mention all this because the work has already become rare and valuable, and it will be still more valuable in the future, as the drawings represent old houses, &c., which have almost all been since removed. Later books have appeared on Old Glasgow, and the so-called *Stuart's Glasgow* has been a sort of quarry from which illustrations have been taken.

I have another association of ideas connected with this book, as an influence affecting my life. The sketching of the old remains of Glasgow awakened in me the archæological instinct. The instinct was already there, for I well remember that when in Perth, which is an ancient city with many old houses, walls, &c., I was attracted to the crumbling stones of these places: I recollect looking at them, and wondering at them as witnesses of time. In the days I am writing about archæological works were scarce, and my reading was not given to them. My first reading had, as already described, been in scientific subjects. Theological books next came in my way, and I went through a pretty large course of them. This included polemical and metaphysical subjects, and ended in freeing me from any faith in the ordinary creeds of the time. Geology was then fighting its battle, the Church denouncing the new science as opposed to the Word of God; but geology went on, the Church had to change its tune, and ever since it has been "the harmony of Scripture and Science." Remembering the very dogmatic assertions that were made at first against science, in the case of geology, I have been inclined ever since to look upon the later pretensions as humbug. Of course this is not the case; but it is good evidence that declarations of this kind, either one way or the other, are not of much value. I gradually got out of this vein of reading, and drifted into poetry. Scottish songs became a favourite subject; but I did not limit myself to that. I also read the English poets, and Keats became a great favourite with me. I know he is not the greatest of poets, but I liked him better than all the others, and the place he then won in my heart he still retains. Books with literary criticism were also devoured at this further stage. There was a small society of young artists at this time in Glasgow, and I joined them. We met about once a fortnight, and showed our work for the benefit of mutual criticism. We had also a small library of works on art which were so far new to me, these I began to devour. Reynolds' discourses, Burnet, Fielding, and others, I began with. It was about this time I heard of the "Graduate of Oxford," as John Ruskin was at first named—no one then knew who he was. As there was a great demand for his book—the first volume of "Modern Painters"—it was some time before I was able to read it. The older men in our society had been expressing grave doubts about the "Graduate" as an authority, and my anxiety to know what he said was great. I remember the delight with which I read the book, and what a new world of thought it opened up. Reading the "Graduate," I felt almost no desire to read any other author on art.

When the Glasgow School of Design opened in 1845 I joined it. It was in Ingram Street, at the foot of Montrose Street, and I attended it for a good number of years. I forget the year in which I exhibited a picture in the Glasgow Exhibition. This was called the West of Scotland Academy, and it had an annual display. The subject of my picture was "Garscadden Gates," a picturesque entrance to Garscadden House, to the west of Kelvin Dock. It was a water-colour. In 1850 I sold my Exhibition picture in water-colour, called "The Braes of Lochaber." I had made a trip—a walking tour—with James Walker, an engraver in Allan & Ferguson's. We went in the steamer to Oban and walked to Ballachulish, then up Glen Coe, and by the old road to Fort William. From that we walked east through Lochaber to Dalwhinnie, visiting the Falls of Bruar; down by Killiekrankie to Dunkeld, where we got coach or train to Perth; and returned to Glasgow by train.

Another enduring friendship, which began about 1847 or 1848, was with Mr. Roger Hennedy and his family. I first met Mr. Hennedy at a botany class, and we used to make excursions together, he botanising and I sketching; but in these trips I picked up a smattering of botany which I have found very useful. Through Mr. Hennedy I made the acquaintance of Hugh Macdonald, author of *Days at the Coast* and *Rambles round Glasgow*. There was at that time a coterie, to which Hennedy and Macdonald belonged, called the "Eccentrics," and I had some acquaintance with most of them. Alexander Smith, the poet, was a friend of Hugh Macdonald's, and through this connection I knew him.*

One New Year time, a few years before I left Glasgow, I presented myself with a French grammar and dictionary. With these I made such progress in the language that a French book was nearly as good to me as an English one.

* [In a letter to Mr. Robert McClure, printed in the *Scottish American*, September 12, 1900, Simpson gave many interesting details regarding his three friends. "Hugh Macdonald," he wrote, "was a dear old friend of mine, and if you look up the *Rambles* you will find an allusion to me in the one on Robroyston."]

CHAPTER II

LONDON

AFTER having served four years with Allan and Ferguson, in addition to my apprenticeship, I determined, with Mr. Allan's advice, to move to London. I was now over twenty-seven years of age. I had been a constant attender at the School of Design, where I carried off a prize for drawing from the round; I had made some progress in water-colour, and done a little in oil. In the summer it was my custom to get up in the mornings. I rose early and painted. On leaving the office at eight o'clock in the evening, I went to the School of Design, getting home after ten to supper and bed. Sundays were devoted to painting, taking friends' portraits, or walks to the country with the object of sketching. By means of this constant work I had made some progress, but in Glasgow there was little doing in the higher branch of lithography, so no great advance could be made. I had to do plans and machinery, and design ornamental tickets. It was only in the metropolis that I could expect to find occupation at exclusively artistic work. If, in 1840, when I went to Allan and Ferguson's, it had been my fate to take to the "writing" department, there would have been no further improvement. London could not offer any advancement in that line. But for an artist a wide opening existed, and how far I might succeed time only could tell.

I left Glasgow on the evening of the 1st of February, 1851. It was the year of the great Exhibition, the first of all exhibitions of that kind. I arrived on a Sunday morning, or rather about midday, for the trains were not so fast then.

A friend who had been a writer in Allan and Ferguson's, but had left in 1844, met me at Euston, and I found lodgings in the same house with him, in Kentish Town.

On the Monday I went out to look about London—and I seemed to know it very well. On Tuesday I started to find work; I knew that Day and Sons' were the principal lithographers in London, more particularly for artistic work, so I settled to apply to them first. I had the example of two artists who had preceded me from Allan and Ferguson's. Day and Sons' establishment was in Gate Street, Lincoln's Inn Fields. I presented myself there and saw William Day, one of three brothers, the principal person in the firm. The father, the original "Day," had been dead some years. I was at once engaged to begin work next Monday. This reminded me of the morning on which I went out with my specimens in my hand in Glasgow. There I found a situation before noon; here I had done the same thing. On leaving Gate Street I went down to the Strand, and went into a place to have a chop, with the intention of writing a letter to my mother to tell her of my success. I found afterwards that the house was the "Cock," close to Temple Bar, which is the subject of one of Tennyson's poems. Mr. Day had asked me what salary I had in Glasgow; I told him two pounds a week; he asked if I would be willing to accept the same, and I said "yes." It was only a few months till this sum was doubled; afterwards it was raised to six, and ultimately to eight pounds.

Here, I may say, I had to learn my profession over again. The work was confined to "chalk"; that meant the lithographic crayon, and it also meant exclusively pictorial work. All I had learned at plans, ornament, and line work was in a certain sense useless; and my experience at "chalk" in Glasgow had been very limited. In Day's everything was so different, and theirs being the first house in London for pictorial lithography, a high style was the rule. To this superior standard I had to work myself up; but thanks to my constant practice in Glasgow, to painting in the mornings, School of Design at night, and constant sketching out of doors from nature, I was not long in establishing my position in the new field of action.

The pictorial work done at that time has now found other channels. Lithography had superseded copper-plate engraving. In the early part of the century it was a familiar phrase on the title-pages of books, that they were "embellished with numerous copper-plate engravings." Such illustrations were all done in lithography when I came to London, and I did a good many of them. This work was afterwards all done on wood. New churches and public buildings of importance were lithographed at that time; at a later period they appeared in the *Builder* or other architectural publication, as wood engravings. Many of these architectural subjects passed through my hands. Portraits of singers, dancers, actors, members of Parliament, &c., &c., were lithographed, and there was a large demand for this sort of work. Now it is all done by photography. New steamers, men-of-war, &c., were also done on stone. They are now photographed. Many public events were reproduced as lithographic prints; these now appear in the illustrated papers. Wars in India, the Cape, &c., were published in volumes of lithographs, Atkinson's *Afghanistan* being a good example. My Crimean book was perhaps the last and largest work of the kind. The startling thing is that it was a class of work which came into existence, lasted only about a quarter of a century, and has entirely vanished. Lithography is still carried on, but it is limited to such things as an auctioneer's view of an estate, or a window show-bill, few of which show any pictorial qualities.* When I came to London it was art, and good art. This will be understood when I mention the tendency among lithographers—such as Louis Haghe, Harding, Carrick, and many others—to become artists or painters, just as many of the draughtsmen on wood now do. As a rule engravers, whether on copper, steel, or wood, never became artists, or I should say painters, because

* [The pictorial poster has come into evidence as an artistic production since this was written.]

the work was mechanical, and merely copying. But in lithography, at least in the class of subjects I had to do, we had to work out rough material into pictures, and it is the same with drawing on wood. If a man has any stuff in him it finds development. It is from work like this that such artists as Sir John Gilbert, George Thomas, Herkomer, and Gregory, as well as others, have started.

Shortly after I went to Day's, Louis Haghe gave up lithography. The last work he did on stone was "The Destruction of Jerusalem," from a large picture by Roberts. It was a beautiful piece of work on the stone. I saw it when finished. But unfortunately it was rather under-etched. Nitric acid and water have to be poured over a stone before it has the printer's roller applied, and owing to this all the darker work has a tendency to fill up, and want clearness. Haghe was the President of the Institute of Painters in Water-Colours—what had been previously known as the "New Society"—and he devoted himself wholly to water-colour. After he left I used his room in Gate Street. This had a bay window on the top floor, from which, while at work, I could see into Lincoln's Inn Fields.

Most of the artists wrought at their own homes, but I preferred to work in the office. A Pole named Joseph Bielski, who was my assistant, had been in one of the insurrections in his own country, about 1830. In Brussels he had picked up lithography and French. He was very handy, obliging, and obedient, characteristics which I now attribute to his Turanian blood, for he had features of a strong Tartar type. He belonged to Wilna, between Konigsberg and St. Petersburg, and I have been much interested in the question as to how much Turanian blood has penetrated to almost the extreme north-west corner of Russia, or how far Poland would be found to be Tartar if it were "scratched." As Bielski preferred French to English I arranged that we should speak the former. I found that reading a language and speaking it were two different things. I could do one but not the other. By the arrangement with Bielski I had two or three years' constant practice in speaking French, and attained a facility afterwards most valuable. When I went to the Crimea my French was far ahead of that of most of the officers I came across. Only the few who had been educated or had lived in France were as familiar with the language as I was. I seem to have been lucky in many ways in preparing myself for positions which the future had in store.

I think I should here give a list of the principal artists connected with Day and Sons while I was there. I have already mentioned Louis Haghe, who had his brother Charles as assistant. Haghe was a Belgian, born in Tournai, and I consider him the best lithographic artist, not merely of this country, but of Europe. Born with a defect in his right hand, he had to work with his left. We ultimately became great friends, and he was one of the finest men I have had the luck to know—generous and good in every way. It has been my fortune to meet in life many worthy friends, but Louis Haghe had so many good qualities, that I cannot place him second to any.* Robert Carrick was mostly at work painting, but he did lithography at times. Edmund Walker worked mostly at home. He did a good many of the drawings of the great Exhibition which were then published. He had been originally a miniature painter, and was good at figures, and a fair general hand. George Hawkins wrought at home. He was almost wholly employed by architects, to tint their perspective drawings, and his lithography was of the same kind. He was particularly good at this class of work. T. G. Dutton did shipping—new clippers to Australia, or the last great steamer for the American passage. We called him "Admiral." A nice cheery man he was. Lynch was the best hand at elaborate portraits. Vintner also did portraits, and subjects with large figures. Ed. Morin, a Frenchman, who came over in 1851, did a good deal of work in connection with the great Exhibition, and remained some years in London. He did some of my Crimean subjects, but returned to Paris, where he was connected with the *Journal Illustré*. He was a very pleasant fellow. Needham began

* [Simpson contributed an account of Haghe's life and work to *The Printing Times and Lithographer* of 15th October, 1877.]

to do work after I came to London; he was a pupil of Harding's, and good at trees and landscape. William Butler, who had been brought up as an architect, was employed in doing architectural subjects—that is, drawing the outlines on stone. He was employed by architects to put their designs into perspective, and I had often to tint them, and finish them in colour, and more often, when they were to be lithographed, I had to finish them on stone. Butler did the outline, Bielski then put in, under my instructions, the flat tints, and I had only the artistic finish to give. This brought me a good deal into contact with Butler, and we were great friends. He died suddenly of apoplexy, and left his widow with six young children. There were others beside Butler who did outlines. Bedford had a staff of artists, and did a large amount of work in connection with the volumes Day published on the great Exhibition, as well as of others that followed. These were of art objects, and they were done in colours, and might be called ornamental art. Mr. Thomas, Mr. Day's brother-in-law, was also an artist, and did architectural subjects. George MacCulloch came at a late date.

The summer of 1851, owing to the Exhibition, was a busy one for me. At that date the illustrated papers did not occupy the position they have since reached, and photography was still in its infancy, so there was a great demand for prints of such a new and wonderful place as the "World's Fair." Day and Sons published great views, both of the outside and of the interior. There was a number of pictures published of the opening ceremony, and numerous views of the various courts. No such pictures are now done. No publisher, with the illustrated papers and the photographer as rivals, would risk the publication of a lithographic print. This shows what a great change has taken place since 1851. Every publisher was then anxious to do something, and I, as well as others, was kept hard at work. The summer was well over before I could be allowed a couple of days' holiday to visit the Exhibition. I spent one day in the place, but the second day I went to the country, and found that much more pleasant.

WILLIAM SIMPSON, R.I.

My first lodgings on coming to London were with a Mr. and Mrs. Gamble, but there were "family jars," and my friend, James Walker, and I left. Shortly afterwards I brought my father and mother from Glasgow to 1, Orchard Street, Kentish Town, to live. There my mother died in August, 1854 ; she is buried in Highgate Cemetery.

CHAPTER III

THE CRIMEAN WAR

THE war with Russia began in 1854. The illustrated papers were still in such a condition that lithographs of events connected with the war found a ready sale. Colnaghi's people had sketches sent to them from the Baltic, and I put some of them on stone. When the news of the Battle of the Alma came home I made a sketch, principally from the newspaper accounts, and put it on stone. This was published by Lloyds, publishers in Ludgate Hill at that time. It was such a great success that Lloyd gave me a commission to get ready a Fall of Sebastopol, and to have it so that it could be brought out a day or so after the news arrived. To carry out this it was necessary to have some material to work from, and I hunted everywhere for pictures of Sebastopol, but nothing of the kind could be found in London. Ackerman's people let me look over all their portfolios. The truth is that Sebastopol was an out-of-the-way place, which travellers never visited, and no sketches of it existed. Some one had procured a map of Sebastopol, published either in Russia or Germany, and it had, round the margin, some slight outlines of the public buildings. From these a view of the city had been published. This was the only material, and the chances are that I should have utilised it but for a sudden change in all my plans.

The news came of the troops making the trenches before Sebastopol. A siege in form was all so new after such a long peace, that every one was excited and anxious about every detail. I read the papers carefully, and used to talk to Mr. Day about it, and say I wished I were there. "Here they are making 'gabions,' 'fascines,' 'traverses,' &c. What are these? No one knows. If I were there I could send sketches of them, so that every one would understand."

I had a bad tooth, and it troubled me, so I had it pulled out one morning before going to the office. When I got there, I was queer about the mouth, and I had had a bad night's rest; so I spread the morning paper I had been reading on the floor, and laid myself upon it. I was in this position when the door opened, and Mr. Mackay, of Colnaghi's, came in. He put his glass up to his eye, and looked at me suspiciously. I got up, and he asked if I would go to the Crimea. Mackay has since confessed to me that his first impression on seeing me on the floor was that I had been out all night, and that the effects of that kind of performance had not quite left me. I need scarcely say that my answer to Mackay's inquiry was in the affirmative. I told him I had often explained to Mr. Day what could be done by an artist if he were on the spot and saw the siege operations. He said he had just heard all that from Mr. Day. Colnaghi's people wanted an artist to go, and Day said I was the man. It was only a question as to when I could go. This I could only answer by saying I should start as soon as things could be got ready. It was arranged that Day's people should help to prepare what was wanted—portmanteaus, clothes, paper, colours, &c. All was put in order in my room in Gate Street, and Colnaghi got letters of introduction for me. I took letters to the Duke of Cambridge, Lord Raglan, Sir Edmond Lyons—afterwards Lord Lyons—Captain Peel, R.N., and others. I wrote a few notes to friends, and I went off the next night.

When the packing of my portmanteau was nearly finished, about half an hour before I started, some one came into the room to say that Lloyd was below wanting to see me, as he wished to know how I was getting on with the "Fall of Sebastopol." Colnaghi's folk did not wish it to be known that I was going off, and Lloyd particularly, being a publisher, was not to know, so some one went down and told him something—what it was I never heard, but he did not come upstairs. It was on the evening of the 26th of October I left London for the Crimea. The trains for Paris at that time started from London Bridge, which meant the station at the south end of the bridge.

At Constantinople I got a passage to Balaklava on board the P. and O. steamer *Colombo*, Captain Methven, a well-known officer of the company. Lord Burgeshe was on board; he had been home with the despatches about the Battle of the Alma, and was returning to headquarters, as he was on Lord Raglan's staff. We arrived in sight of the Crimea on the evening of the 15th of November, and could hear at times the sound of the guns in the batteries. It was too late to enter the harbour of Balaklava, or even to communicate with it, so the *Colombo* slowly cruised about in the open sea till next morning. As soon as daylight permitted we neared the entrance to the harbour. There, to our surprise, we saw about half a dozen vessels at anchor, all of them dismasted and looking like wrecks. This was our first indication of the terrible storm that had swept over Sebastopol on the morning of the 14th. The storm had passed over Constantinople on the 13th. It had blown down a minaret there, but was mild compared to what it had been at Balaklava.*

* *Copy of letter from W. S. in Crimea, dated November* 16, 1854:

"Whichever way you looked you saw paddle-boxes, bows, sterns, many funnels, and gangways of the various injured vessels floating about in the water. None seems to have escaped. Lord Cardigan's yacht has her gunwale smashed in. It is difficult to conceive how so much mischief could have occurred in such a snug little harbour; but it would seem the ships were all lying so close together that they ground one another to pieces. Eight ships are reported to have sunk here, and about four or five hundred men were drowned. All the warm clothing for the Army is lost, and a great quantity of provisions. The late storm has blown away tents, and the poor soldiers have just to do without them—and what miserable-looking beings they are, covered with mud, dirt, and rags. The rains, too, have left all the roads a sea of mud, about two feet deep, through which supplies must be drawn to the camps. In the service are employed our soldiers, the Turks, the natives, and the sailors, with horses, oxen, camels, and mules, with every variety of cart. These with every description of costume and character, and the wild, uncertain kind of life, make it a scene which I cannot describe."

After breakfast Captain Methven went into the harbour in his gig to report his arrival and receive orders, and he took me with him. On our way we passed many dead bodies floating, besides wreckage, and pieces of ration pork from barrels of meat that had broken up. On landing I at once turned my face towards Sebastopol, and walked on till I found myself in a position to see the place. I called on no one, and spoke to nobody. My only desire was to look upon Sebastopol. I passed camps, and I must have been close to the Woronzoff Road, in front of the 3rd and 4th Divisions. I did not know that then, for I knew nothing of the ground or of the camps. It seemed to me, as it did to many afterwards, that I might have walked on and into Sebastopol. I stood there looking at the place all alone. At last I sat down and made a sketch. Just as I finished it a couple of soldiers came past. I had noticed cannon balls lying around, but thought little about them. It occurred to me that they might have been dropped by our people taking ammunition down to the trenches. I asked the soldiers what balls these were, and they answered, "Them's the Rooshians' balls, sir." "What!" I said, "do you mean that the balls from the guns of Sebastopol come up here?" I began to think that the sooner I was away from the spot the better. Here I had been sitting for nearly an hour where I might have been shot. Such were my ideas on this first experience, and I felt amused at them afterwards when I became familiar with the trenches. I had done my sketch, and had no reason to remain longer in such a dangerous spot as this appeared to me, so I turned my steps and walked back to Balaklava.

I remained some days on board the *Colombo*, but as she was a transport, and had to leave, I moved into the *Orient*, a sailing ship, which lay at the head of the harbour, and which remained my quarters all the winter. This vessel was the office of Captain Christie, the principal agent of transports, who had a staff of agents under him, a secretary, and a doctor. These all belonged to the Royal Navy. Mr. Pritchard was the secretary. He sat writing at the cuddy table, and I had a seat at the same, where I used to finish my sketches. Sitting there I heard all the business going on—captains coming, some to report their arrival, and others to receive orders; and I was soon well up in matters connected with the transport service. At times when Pritchard was not there I have given captains the information they wanted. Pritchard belonged to the Paymaster's service, and it may be worth mentioning as a curious connection, that a brother of this secretary, who had been a surgeon in the navy, left the service, and set up in Glasgow as a doctor. He married and had a family, and was reputed to have been a flashy, talking man, a great boaster, who earned such a reputation that no one believed him. His wife and mother-in-law died, and he was tried in Glasgow as a poisoner, found guilty, and hanged in front of the jail.

I delivered my letters of introduction; the one to the Duke of Cambridge was delivered to him on board the *Retribution*, a paddle-wheel ship, commanded by Captain Drummond. She had been outside Balaklava in the storm, which she managed to weather, with the Duke on board, and she was now going home with him. As he was himself leaving the Crimea, he kindly gave me introductions to some of the officers of the Guards.

My first experience in the trenches resulted from the delivery of my letter of introduction to Captain Peel. Under him I received my "Baptism of Fire," a fact of which I am rather proud, as he was one of the bravest of the brave. I found that he had already earned at Sebastopol a high reputation for pluck: his contempt of danger was the talk of every one. He was the son of Sir Robert Peel, so well known in connection with the Repeal of the Corn Laws. He commanded a small ship, called the *Diamond*, which lay in Balaklava, and he commanded the sailors in the "Right Attack," also known as the "Twenty-one Gun Battery," and "Gordon's Attack." The Gordon in this case, although an engineer officer, was not the "Chinese Gordon," of celebrity at a later date. The engineer of the "Left Attack," was Colonel Chapman. Captain Peel invited me to put up with him in the camp of the Naval Brigade, and the visit was my first experience of camp life. Captain Lushington commanded the Brigade.

I was always welcome in that camp, which was the most comfortable in the Crimea. This was owing to the handiness of the sailors. In the wet weather the soldiers' camps were a mass of mud from the men's feet walking about. There were twelve men in each tent, and no door mats or scrapers, and from the walking in and out all day, the mud was not much less inside the tents than it was without, and the men had to lie down at night and sleep under these conditions. In the naval camp it was altogether different. Jack had managed to pave a path through the camp to every tent, and had contrived to make himself comfortable under canvas. At night he had a light, and you could hear music and laughter going on. Some had rigged up a little mast on the top of the tent, and had miniature flags to represent the number of the tent, so that if a mate came up on a visit from the fleet, he could find the tent he wanted. The camp was in a slight hollow, and when the wet weather came on, there was a marshy place below which was difficult to cross. Jack managed by means of the staves of commissariat meat barrels, some ropes and poles, to make a complete model of a suspension bridge, strong enough for a man to cross. Captain Lushington had his flag flying, as if on board ship, and a bell, on which the sentry struck the hours exactly as if afloat, and all in camp could tell how many bells it was. When Jack's clothes got torn, he could mend them, and if he wanted a piece of cloth to fill up a hole, the sand-bags in the trenches were made to do service—some even made whole suits from them. The broad arrow is stamped on the cloth of the sand-bags, and I have often seen a sailor with a great patch on his trousers, where the broad arrow told how the cloth had been procured. The soldiers, on the contrary, could be seen going about "all tattered and torn," often with a large opening behind in the trousers, from which their linen, or whatever may have been beneath, projected, as if desirous of being taken notice of, but not producing what would be considered a military appearance.

In the matter of health the contrast was equally striking. The soldiers sickened and died, or went off to Scutari. One regiment, I think it was the 63rd, arrived in the Crimea over one thousand strong, and one day in the winter it had not above twenty men fit for duty. The duty in the trenches also told on the health. When the rain came, trenches became mud. Let any one dig a trench in a field, and have a multitude of people to walk along it in wet weather, and he will realise what it must be in a siege. Such a trench becomes simply a wet ditch. In this the men had to do duty for twenty-four hours at a time. They had no cover from the rain; the parapet of the trench is only intended to give cover from the enemy's fire. When the soldier wanted to rest or sleep in wet weather, he had to find the place he thought least muddy. If he had to go from one place to another he only added to the mud in the trench, which I have seen myself more than ankle deep. In the winter I have seen the reliefs going down in the evening, just before dark. This was considered the best time to change the troops. In the trenches it would be raining; before midnight the rain would change to snow; and before morning, it would be a hard frost. The men must have been first wet through and then frozen into icicles. This kind of weather was very common during that terrible winter, and the wonder is that any one was able to survive. The winter might have been said to begin with the terrible storm of November 14th. It not only wrecked ships which had brought supplies of winter clothing—the *Prince* was one—but produced a general disorganisation, the results of which were more or less felt during all the winter. It was not till spring came that things were made more comfortable.

On my first visit to the trenches I went down early in the day with Captain Peel. We had to pass the Woronzoff Road, which had been christened "the Valley of the Shadow of Death." It came from Sebastopol along one of the deep hollows which cut up the plateau on which our camps stood. It separated our left from our right attack, and as it was in rear of the right attack, a large quantity of the shot and shell fired from the Malakof and Redan rolled into it. These missiles lay in large quantities along the road, and made it a rather dangerous place. After passing along the "Twenty-one Gun Battery," with Peel as my guide, I sat down to sketch a gun belonging to the Naval Brigade. Peel recommended this gun as it was a favourite. A shot had come in before the battery was first opened, and knocked away a piece of the gun carriage, which was of wood from one of the ships, but it did not in any way disable the gun. This had often had special duels with a particular gun in the Malakof, in which it had generally come off with success. This gun, I may add, fought afterwards all through the siege till the fall of Sebastopol, and was never again struck. I not only sketched the gun, but the sailors I introduced were rough portraits, and Peel stood with half his body above the parapet of the battery while I sketched. The portrait was recognised by every one—as also was that of Captain Burnet, the other officer in the picture. The gun was pointing to the Malakof; there had been no firing that day, at least at this part of the attack, and nothing had been fired at us. Just as I was finishing my sketch, I said something to Captain Peel about having seen nothing that day of active work. He replied, "If I order that gun to be fired, two guns will be fired back at us in return, and you will have some experience." I said all right, and the gun was fired. Very soon after, as Peel had predicted, a gun from the Malakof returned the compliment, but the missile went wide of us. This was followed by another, a shell, that struck the outside of the parapet, then burst, throwing up in the air a great quantity of earth and stones, which came down in a shower upon us. I had sat all the time where I had been sketching, with my portfolio on my knees, and it was covered with earth. I, at the moment, remembered having read of Junot, who was at one time during a siege writing to Napoleon's dictation, when a shell covered his paper in the same way as mine, and he remarked that it would save him the use of sand to dry his writing with. This was my first experience, and I cannot say I was quite so calm as the Frenchman. Captain Peel suggested the title

A Quiet Day in the Battery.

to the sketch, "A Quiet Day in the Battery." This title led me afterwards to do "A Quiet Night," and by a natural induction, after I had seen a bombardment, a "Hot Day," and a "Hot Night" in the batteries. In each case the subjects were done from sketches made under the conditions indicated by the titles.

The sailors were so cool and unconcerned in the trenches that one could not help feeling cool also, and in my visits I soon became as indifferent to danger as themselves. I often went into the works, and began to think nothing of doing so, becoming, indeed, so well acquainted with them, that I was often asked to be a guide to strangers.

I was introduced to Dr. W. H. Russell, shortly after my arrival, in the mud of Balaklava. While I write this, 1889, I believe that he and I are the two oldest "Specials," he in his line and I in mine, at present living.

I think that my next visit to the "front" was to the camp of the Guards. This resulted from the introduction I had from the Duke of Cambridge, but it might be stated that I would have been made welcome, in my capacity as an artist, to any of the camps. At the time of my first visit, the Guard's camp was close to the Inkerman heights, and I wanted sketches connected with the ground of the battle. It was the camp of the Grenadier Guards in which I was a guest. Prince Edward of Saxe-Weimar was in that battalion. There were Colonel Hamilton, and his nephew, a lieutenant, with Lord Balgonie, Sir Charles Russell, and Sir James Ferguson. The last-named, expecting to be elected M.P. for the Ayr Burghs in place of Colonel Blair, who had been killed at Inkerman, had sent his address to the electors, dated "In the Fields of Inkerman." He was of course elected.

At the time of my visit it was rather surprising to find the condition in which such officers lived. Mess pork fried, and commissariat biscuits soaked in water, fried with the pork —this was about the full extent of the menu for breakfast, with tea or coffee, I forget which. The menu for dinner I have now no recollection of, but it was not much different from the breakfast. Sir James Ferguson was looked upon as a good caterer; when he went to Balaklava, he boarded the ships to see what he could buy, and generally returned laden with pots of jam and other delicacies. A tent had been put up for Lord Arthur Hay, eldest son of the Marquis of Tweedale, who was expected from England. I slept in this. A bench of stones had been built up for a bed, and an air mattress was laid on it for me. One of the nights was very cold, and almost all the officers insisted on sending their great-coats to cover me in bed. One of them had to go on duty some time after midnight to inspect the sentries round the Inkerman, and as he had lent his coat, not thinking of his midnight duties, he sent his servant to find it in my tent. This was not very long after the Battle of Inkerman. A possible attack by the Russians was looked upon as not at all unlikely, and I went to bed thinking what I should do if such an event took place. I was certainly in a position to make sketches on the spot. On that night I wakened in the dark, and found a man carrying off my bed-clothes. I felt sure we were attacked and that this must be a Russian, and in an instant I was up, and suited the action to the thought. I collared the man by the throat. This caused him to speak English, and mention his master's name—and something about a great-coat—when the whole case became clear, and it became necessary for me to apologise, and explain the mistaken motive under which I had so suddenly acted. The man returned to his master, and told what had taken place, and I earned a reputation for pluck where it chanced there had been no danger. Next night I arranged to go with the officer and inspect the outposts. In this I carried out what I had determined in my own mind to do, to see war in all its phases, venturing even where there was danger, but reserving to myself the right to avoid going where I thought the chances of shot and shell might be too plentiful, and where it would be foolishness for a non-combatant to trust himself.

I began to see, from the experience I had gained, that coolness and a little judgment were of some value. I had learned to keep a good look-out, and Peel's sailors had shown me that if a shell is coming to you, it becomes instantly visible, as a black speck against the white smoke of the gun which fired it, and before it reaches you there is plenty of time to go under cover. If you do not see this black speck, you may conclude that the projectile is not coming in your direction. Even if you see it at first for a second or so, it may be going sufficiently wide to be out of danger, and will soon cease to be seen. There is no saying where shells may burst. They may even pass you, and if they stop before the explosion takes place, pieces may come back. One day in our trenches I saw this happen, a fragment of the shell came hopping back into the trench. It passed me and went against a gabion where a young soldier was sleeping, and in passing it just touched the skin of his cheek, taking away a bit about a quarter of an inch in size. Had it come half an inch more on one side, it would have smashed his face, and killed the young fellow.

The only occasion on which I can recollect having been on a horse, before that time, was when my uncle met me in the Carse of Gowrie, and I rode behind him from Perth to Dundee. So when in the Crimea I had to put my legs over pigskin it was a new experience. One day Captain Woodford, of the Rifle Brigade, insisted on lending me a great, black charger, as I was going somewhere to the front. Somewhere about Kadikoi, as far as I recollect, the horse's feet got among some tent ropes, which frightened him. He kicked the ropes loose, and went off at a gallop with me. I noticed that we were galloping over the Balaklava plain, and that a very few minutes, at the rate we were going, would take us into the Russian lines, where the horse would have been a most acceptable prize. I felt that to stop the animal in his career would be out of the question, but I slowly gathered up the reins, to have a firm grip, and then gently pulled him round to the left, and before long he was galloping in the direction I wished to go. Had this powerful black horse carried me over to the Russians, my work in the Crimea would have come to a sudden termination.

My letter of introduction to Lord Raglan brought me in contact with Headquarters, where I found friends among the staff. Calthorpe, A.D.C. to Lord Raglan, became a special friend. Captain Maxse, R.N., who was naval A.D.C., also became a friend.

I was in the habit of taking my sketches up to Headquarters on mail day. Calthorpe took me in to Lord Raglan, to show the sketches, and I was always invited to lunch. Lord Raglan kindly allowed me to send my sketches home in his letter-bag, thus ensuring an extra security to them. At times I met General Canrobert, Commander-in-Chief of the French Army, at lunch; and Lord Raglan was evidently rather pleased at being able to show him my sketches, for the enterprise which had prompted my appearance at the seat of war had no counterpart in the French army.

I also met Sir Edmond Lyons, the Admiral, at Headquarters, and as I had brought a letter of introduction to him, he invited me to pay him a visit on board his flagship the *Agamemnon.* The fleet lay at Kamiesch, or rather at Kasatch Bay, near the south-western corner of the Crimea, where the French landing-place was. The French had Kamiesch, and our fleet had Kasatch Bay. As I wished to get sketches from that side of Sebastopol it suited me very well to accept the admiral's invitation, and I spent nearly a month with him. If I recollect right, I went round by sea in a gunboat. Admiral Dundas, who had been naval commander-in chief, had just gone home, and Lyons had become Commander-in-Chief of the Black Sea fleet, but had not moved on board the *Prince Albert* when I arrived. He changed his ship during my visit, and I changed with him. This gave me an entirely new set of experiences. I had had almost no knowledge before of military life, and I had less knowledge still of the navy. All was new and interesting to me. My berth on board the *Agamemnon* was a cabin, large and roomy, but it had a 32 lbr. gun in it. Rather a curious companion it seemed to me at first to have in one's bedroom.

The admiral has a mess of his own, to which the captain of the ship, the "flag captain," his secretary, flag-lieutenant, &c., belong. The other officers of the ship had their mess in the wardroom, and the middies had a mess of their own. The admiral has to entertain, so we had dinners at which the captains of the fleet were invited. This enabled me to make acquaintance with most of them. At times the French admiral and captains were the guests. These were grand dinners, and I could only appear in mufti. I had brought no dress-clothes with me, not calculating on having to join such company. There were regular invitations to the officers of the wardroom. The middies were only invited to breakfast. The admiral was always very gracious to them, often telling them stories about himself when he was a middy. I remember one morning there was a very small middy, I think they said he was the youngest and the most diminutive officer in the fleet, and the admiral told him a capital story. It was when he first joined the service. As is often the custom, his father had taken him on board the ship, and when his father left, the captain called Lyons into his cabin to have a chat with him. This is a regular custom, as it enables the captain to see what sort of stuff is in the boy, and to give him what he may consider good and useful advice on entering the service. On this occasion, at the end, the captain wound up with what he considered the most important counsel of all—not to allow any one to give him a nickname—a custom very common on board ship. "No," said the captain, "never allow anything of this kind. That is one of the things I never would stand. All through my life I have been determined on this point, I never had a nickname on board any ship I served in, and I advise you above all to be particular in this matter." On returning to the middies' berth, young Lyons was at once surrounded, every one wanting to know what "old Blueblazes" had been saying to him.

Sir Edmond was a great favourite with every one, he was so kind and genial in every way. To me he was particularly agreeable. I remember the first night on board the *Agamemnon*, while we were at dinner, at eight o'clock, a gun was fired. On board a wooden ship—men-of-war were all of wood then—a gun makes a great reverberation, particularly if one is below. As I had had no expectation of such a thing, I gave a visible start. The admiral noticing this, asked if I knew what the sailors called it. On my expressing my ignorance, he said, "They call that the admiral overboard."

After being about a fortnight on the *Agamemnon*, the admiral changed to the *Royal Albert*, a three-decker. There was a rule in the service that the admiral must fly his flag on board a three-decker. The *Agamemnon* was only a line-of-battle ship, a two-decker. The officers of the *Agamemnon* manned the boat, and rowed him to his new quarters. It was arranged that I was to stay on the *Agamemnon* till next day, and the wardroom officers looked after me. I was an object of special interest to the midshipmen, and I received an invitation one day to dine with them. I was amused at one of these very small gentlemen, from the manner in which he promised a glass of first-rate sherry when I came. The admiral never assumed the consequential air of this diminutive officer.

A cordon of ships was placed round the entrance to the harbour of Sebastopol—three French and three British. These were changed every week. The ships were at anchor, but ready at a moment to let go, and the fires were kept lighted, but damped, so that steam could be got up at command. At night one watch lay at their quarters ready for action, on the chance of a vessel coming out from Sebastopol, and making a sudden attack. It was part of the duty to watch the arrival of troops or supplies at Sebastopol, and signal them to the flag-ship. Captain Goldsmith, of the *Sidon*, a paddle-wheel steamer, was ordered to take his turn at this watching. Goldsmith was fond of sketching, so he asked if I was willing to go with him for the week, and I would get good sketches of the town from the sea. I had to take a week at it, for generally there was no communication with the fleet, which lay at some distance. I have not the date of my visit, but it must have been in the winter.

The first evening on board the *Sidon*, I remember, as Captain Goldsmith and I were sitting below, the officer of the watch came down and said, "Eight bells, sir." "Well, make it eight bells," was the captain's answer. As I looked curious, Goldsmith said, "Perhaps you are not aware that it is not eight o'clock on board ship till the captain orders it to be so." He then explained that "eight bells" meant the changing of the watch, and other movements on board, and it might be awkward to do this at times, particularly if it should chance that a Russian ship were bearing down upon us.

Next evening after dinner I had a block of paper out, and was putting my sketch of Sebastopol upon it. I had got well on with my composition, Captain Goldsmith watching the operation. While thus engaged we heard a rapid foot coming down the stairs, and the officer of the watch burst in almost breathless, to say that a vessel was bearing down upon us from Sebastopol. Naturally Captain Goldsmith made a sudden exit. I followed, but could see very little, for it was rather dark. But no guns opened on us, and after about ten minutes the captain came down from the bridge and explained matters. In the dark something had been seen coming towards us, and the order was about to be given to fire on it. All was ready, when some one suggested that it might be a French transport being towed out of a creek, where some of the smaller craft were sheltered nearer to Sebastopol than Kamiesch, stores landed here requiring less carriage. The place was so close to the enemies' batteries that such transports could only be taken in or out after dark. The guardships were always warned when one of them was to pass, but on this night the warning had not been sent. The result was a very close shave; transport and tug were very close to the *Sidon*, and the destruction of both would have been all but certain if she had opened fire.

I ought at an earlier part of this history to have given an account of one or two interviews I had with Lord Cardigan, the hero of the Charge of the Six Hundred. The Battle of Balaklava and the Battle of Inkerman had taken place before I arrived in the Crimea, but it was necessary for me to give pictures of them. I could easily make sketches of the ground, but I had to trust to those on the spot for a description of the events. Here, I may mention, I had my first experience as to how men who have been actors in an event will differ in their descriptions. Two officers, I think they were both on the staff of the cavalry division, were giving me details of the light cavalry charge, but at one point they differed widely. One, as evidence that he ought to know, claimed that he was in the charge, but the other made the same claim. One then urged that he had advanced a certain distance into the ground, but the other urged he had been equally far. Each evidently, so far as I could judge, had as good a right as the other to claim accuracy, and yet they could not agree. My function has since brought me into contact with many illustrations of this sort of thing, and my conclusion is that there must always be some slight uncertainty in details of important historical events, even when we have the accounts of them from eye-witnesses.

When I came in the *Colombo* from Constantinople there was a Captain Maxse on board — brother to the naval A.D.C.—a cavalry officer, and, I think, on Lord Cardigan's staff. It was through him I was introduced to his Lordship. Calthorpe first took me over the battlefield and explained the ground to me. I then did a sketch and took it to Lord Cardigan. He had his yacht in the harbour of Balaklava, and lived in it, his division being at Kadikoi, not far away. I went on board the yacht, and presented my sketch. He gazed at it with a vacant stare, and pointing to something, asked, "What is that?" On being told, he said, "It is all wrong," and gave expression to one or two remarks of a critical kind, objecting to the picture. I returned to my quarters and made another sketch, in which I tried to avoid the points objected to. On my taking this to the yacht next day sketch and artist were treated much in the same way as on the first occasion. I felt rather nettled at the cold, haughty style of his lordship, but I was anxious to be able to send home the sketch bearing with it the approval of the principal hero. So I determined to make another effort at the battle in which the light cavalry made themselves so glorious. At the same time I had settled in my mind that it should be the last attempt, whether Lord Cardigan approved of it or not. I went on board a third time, and on placing the drawing before him, I was rewarded with the .warmest praise, and was able to send it home with the expression of Lord Cardigan's highest admiration. The real truth was that in the last sketch I had taken greater care than in the first two to make his lordship conspicuous in the front of the brigade.

I may here mention that I did this with all my sketches. I made it a point to submit my picture to the officer, whoever he was, connected with the place or the event. All those of the trenches were submitted to Sir John Burgoyne and to Sir Harry Jones. And Cowell, now General Sir John C. Cowell, looked over and corrected all my sketches of trenches and works in Sebastopol. In addition all my sketches were submitted to Lord Raglan before they were sent home. There was at one time some complaint about special correspondents telling in their letters more than they ought, and thus conveying information to the enemy. To prevent all complaints of this kind being made against me I told Lord Raglan that if any of my sketches had better not be published he had only to say so, and they should not appear. My sketches all went home in Lord Raglan's bag. On their arrival in London they were first submitted to the Duke of Newcastle, who was War Minister, and then sent to the Queen for her inspection. After that they were placed in the hands of the lithographers. The Queen allowed the work to be dedicated to her.

Sometime in the early spring John Scott, who was the leading man in Colnaghi's, enclosed a letter from Miss Skerritt, the Queen's private secretary at that time, with a commission to do a picture for her Majesty. It was to be Balaklava, and I was to introduce the Guards' Camp, and sketches of Prince Edward of Saxe-Weimar, Lord James Murray, brother to the Duke of Athole, and Col. Seymour. This, of course, I did and sent home. I need scarcely describe how pleased I was when I received this commission. I felt rewarded for many years of hard work. My only regret was when I thought of my dear mother, so lately passed away. If she only could have lived to know that her son had painted a picture for the Queen.

I found then, as I have since, that the "Special Correspondent" of a daily paper is a far more important personage than a "Special Artist." Words are more direct and specific than a picture. The correspondent appeals to a larger number of persons, and what he says may have also a political bearing, which brings him more prominently before the public than the artist. So the special correspondent receives a greater reputation than the artist. But at the seat of war the artist is in a more pleasant position than the other. If the correspondent blames any one, or any body of men, in the performance of duty, he is hated. If he praises any one there are always others who consider they have done equally well with the one complimented, and they abuse the correspondent for not noticing their merits. Of course those who are praised are very friendly to the correspondent. The result is that the correspondent is much courted and much hated. I escaped all this. Every one was friendly to me, and I was welcomed wherever I went.

When the spring weather began to appear what a contrast the Guards' Camp at Balaklava displayed to what it was at Inkerman on my first visit! Now they had a large marquee tent for their men, and a cask of claret and another of sherry in the corner. Cooks even had been imported from Constantinople. One night I dined with Prince Edward, who had a cook to himself, and during the dinner the Prince gave me a hint to praise the dishes, as he wished his cook to know that his art was appreciated.

The Cavalry remained at Balaklava, or rather at Kadikoi. Lord Lucan was in command, having succeeded Lord Cardigan. He lived in a house at Kadikoi. I was in the habit of going there when I carried my sketches up to Headquarters, and letting him see them, and he encouraged me to do this, by letting me have the use of a pony to ride to the front. I had two or three friends who were kind in this way, but I think it was Lord Lucan's pony that amused me from its peculiar character. The pony was a lazy brute, and I had the greatest difficulty to make him move along. He soon found out that I did not belong to the Cavalry, for I had no spurs, and he cared nothing for the heels of my shoes, though I tired my legs hammering his flanks with them. Neither had I a whip. When I should have reached Lord Raglan's I could not calculate, but the almost total absence of progress to the front, led me to keep an eye on the road for the chance of a piece of wood to use as an influence. At last I saw a broken wand on the way, and I got down and lifted it. It so chanced that I flourished it before the pony's eyes, accompanied by some prophetic remarks. When I again got on his back, I was astonished to find that he went all right, without any application of the weapon, which I was really afraid to use, for a good blow would have broken it, and it was too slight an instrument to have touched his hide. If I had used it, he would at once have found out that it was more harmless than my heels. I only flourished the wand so that he could see it, and he went along capitally. The next time I went up on this pony, he repeated this old game. I tried the heels, but to no purpose. I looked out for a stick on the road, but none appeared, and I began to be very tired of my beast's Fabian performances. But a means of changing his manners did not seem at all likely to turn up. At last I saw some straw on the ground, and recollecting my former tactics, I at once descended. I selected the largest and most formidable straw I could see, and I got on his back again without crushing my weapon. This required some management, but once I was on his back, with my straw in my hand, he became my obedient slave, and went along in splendid style. My straw was typical of much that goes on in the world—there are many men of straw who get their fellows to believe they are great and important.

The sufferings of the troops during the winter roused the feelings of the people at home, and all sorts of things were sent out. But nothing could make men comfortable in the trenches, or even in the camp, while rain, snow, and frost continued. Great improvements had been made in the camps, the roads, and every detail; but the real improver of everything was the spring, which brought the sun, and fair weather. The first herald of the spring was the crocus coming up, and it was very striking to see it on the ground about our batteries, where the shot and fragments of shell lay—a strange combination. I did one subject of it, and called it "Spring in the Crimea." This subject led me afterwards to do the other three seasons—but I think these were not done till after I came home. Winter in the Crimea —chronologically the first of the series—was given with guns, big guns, covered with snow, even the muzzles being blocked up. This suggested, with other details, that the war was at a standstill—winter had suspended operations. Spring has been already described. The crocus suggested the returning animation, hope, and promise of action. Summer brought the action, and in it I introduced a live shell, somewhere in one of our batteries, with a butterfly fluttering over it, and a frightened lizard on the ground running away. Autumn might be supposed to be the inside of a Russian battery. The principal object was a sword, and the dead hand only of the person who had fallen was shown. In the background was the burning city, and in the ruined battery were the smashed guns, and dead bodies. These were the harvest of this autumn, and the sword allegorised the sickle of this crop which war had produced.

On the 26th of April, I went down to our right attack, and passed through the zig-zags to what had been named Egerton's Pit. Rifle pits had begun to be an important feature of the siege, and a few nights previous our people had driven the Russians out of some advanced pits in front of the quarries. A sap was made into them, and they were now part of our advanced works. Colonel Egerton died from a wound received on the night they were taken. I wished to make a subject of this, as it was a rifle pit, and also because it was our most advanced sap towards the Redan. I made a sketch, and the soldiers stood for it. One of them said "put 41 on our caps, so that we will know it again when we come home." One or two pits had been destroyed, as they could not be wrought into the sap. I asked the soldiers if it would be possible to take a peep over the parapet to see them. They said, "Yes, but be quick about it." I looked over for just a second or so, long enough to see the gabions and sand-bags scattered about, and then brought my head under cover again. I had scarcely done so when ping—ping—ping came the rifle bullets, which my appearance had drawn from the enemy.

It so chanced that when I submitted this sketch to Lord Raglan, Sir George Brown was with him. The men in the pit, as shown in my sketch, were not quite in perfect uniform—one or two had red night-caps on their heads. Sir George was a soldier of the old school, to whom all irregularities were a crime, particularly in such a matter as regimental uniform. When he saw the red night-caps, he pointed to them, and asked if the men wore "these d——d things on their heads?" Lord Raglan smiled and replied, "Yes, anything that is comfortable."

CHAPTER IV

THE EXPEDITION TO KERTCH

WHEN I called at Headquarters with the sketch of Egerton's Pit, it was to ask permission of Lord Raglan to accompany an expedition which I had learned was about to start for Kertch. Naturally I felt anxious to go with the expedition, but I was afraid that I might be away when the Fall of Sebastopol occurred. In this dilemma I met General Estcourt, the Adjutant-General, and told him my difficulty. "It will not do," I said, "for me to ask questions, which might involve secrets you are bound not to divulge, but as you understand my objects, tell me would you advise that I should go with this expedition?" His answer was that he thought I should go. Lord Raglan did not hesitate about the permission, and as Sir George Brown, who was present, had been ordered to command the force, I may say I had the permission of both these officers.

A large flotilla started for Kertch, including a considerable portion of the French and English fleets, transports, &c. We got in sight of the Straits of Kertch, the Cimmerian Bosphorus, when a steamer came post haste to order us all back. This was owing to the French. Kinglake has declared in the last volume of his *Crimean War* that Napoleon III. had ordered that nothing was to be done, as he himself intended to come out and be present at the Fall of Sebastopol that he might cover himself with the glory of the event. Accordingly, the Emperor not being ready, the bombardment of April was made into a farce, so that nothing came of it. Ultimately, after a number of delays and humbug, the Emperor found he could not appear, and Sebastopol had to be taken without him. The first expedition to Kertch was part of this farce. Our Admiral, on being ordered back, is reported to have retired to his berth, using language which is only to be found in a forecastle dictionary. We all returned to Kamiesch, where we remained some days. It was not till the 22nd that the expedition made a fresh start.

The second expedition was planned to arrive and land at Kertch upon the Queen's birthday, the 24th of May. On this occasion I think the *Orient* was towed by the *Valorous*, a paddle-steamer something like the *Sidon*. We were all close to the Straits of Kertch on the morning of the 24th, and early in the day we passed Cape Takli, which forms the western corner of the entrance to the strait. At this point a troop of Russian horse artillery was visible on the high ground. They galloped away north, and I believe they watched our movements with the intention of opposing us when we tried to land. But when the landing took place a few shells from some of the ships of the fleet sent them off. We sailed up the Strait to a place called Kamish Burun, on the west side of the channel, and at once began to land the troops. I went on shore after some of the troops had landed. The spot was a small bay, with a flat beach and a fishing village. The people of the village had all run away, and evidently they had done so in a very great hurry. In one house I saw a pot on the fire with food in it; the fire was still red, and the liquid in the pot still simmering. At one house the owners had bolted so hurriedly that they forgot to loosen the dog, who was wildly doing his duty, barking at every intruder that came near, running in every direction as far as his tether would allow him. It was sad to see the havoc in this quiet little spot, its peaceful homes so suddenly desecrated by war. As the inhabitants had left, stragglers of all kinds prowled about and destroyed things in mere wantonness. I met a boy who had come with one of the transports; I saw him afterwards in Balaklava, and am under the impression that he was Irish. He had wrought himself into a state of madness. In the village he had picked up a long stick—a wooden hay-fork formed by the natural branches of the tree. With this clenched in both hands, and his eyes staring wildly out of his head, he was rushing about exclaiming, "I smashes whatever I sees;" and whatever could be smashed with the hay-fork was destroyed by this maniac. Glass windows were special attractions to him. I saw him chase a very small fowl, and each time he failed to catch it he became more excited. At last the miserable chicken, exhausted with the chase, fell into his hands, and when this took place the wild fool did not know what to do with it. In an incoherent way he expressed himself as wishing to know what could be done, and at last, grasping the bird by the neck and squeezing it with all his strength, he said, "Die! die! die!" He was like a devil let loose.

The troops were all disembarked during the afternoon, and camped for the night on the higher ground north of the village. There were some Turkish troops, a French corps, a Highland brigade, the marines of the fleet, with transport corps, etc. As the force was not to move till next morning I slept on board ship.

On landing and finding my way, amid sundry adventures, to the town, I was told by a sergeant that the troops had passed through Kertch and gone on to Yenikaleh. I should be quite safe, he said, to go on, but he offered to be an escort to me if I would wait. He was in charge of a party of the Land Transport Corps with mules and blankets. These Land Transport fellows had been drinking, and they could not tie the blankets properly on the beasts' backs, so as soon as they began to move, the loads fell off, and had to be put on again. The Land Transport Corps was, I think, a new organisation got up in a hurry during the war, and the officers and men had been sent out before they were properly trained. The Kertch expedition was a first trial of their quality, and they showed a great want of discipline. I noticed empty bottles on the road, and other evidences of neglect and carelessness. It turned out that the men had made free with the medical comforts, which included brandies.

I afterwards told what I saw on the way to my friends of the medical department at Yenikaleh, and I very nearly had to appear as a witness either at a court-martial or a court of inquiry, which was afterwards held there to investigate what took place on the march that day.

The road brought me into Kertch, on the south, and close to the sea. Here I found a French sailor with a couple of goslings in one hand and his cutlass in the other, in a state of excitement. The mother of the goslings was in the sea, equally excited on account of her offspring. His dilemma was this—he had the goslings, but he wanted to have the old goose as well. He would have been quite content with what he had, and I saw him turn to go off, but when he did this, the mother came out of the water to follow her young ones, and the Frenchman was then tempted to come back; but the sea, as a place of refuge, being at hand, the bird retreated, causing a large expenditure of "sacres," and words of a similar, or even worse, signification. Time after time the Frenchman went off, and was attracted back by the chance of catching the devoted mother. Every time he flourished his cutlass at the bird in the water and called her many bad names. I left him going on with this see-saw, and did not wait to see the final result.

I went up to the Museum, a Doric building, and the most conspicuous structure in Kertch, as it stands high above the town, on an eminence called the mountain of Mithridates. It was empty, but a large amount of broken pottery was scattered about. I believe that all the really valuable articles had been removed to St. Petersburg, and that only a few trifling specimens of pottery had been left. Some of these were looted, and some smashed by the troops. What troops did this I do not know. Most of the men in the condition of the common soldier were given to smashing things. The authorities, and many of the better class, had run away from the town, and there were no guards left to protect anything. The criminal class finding this out, began to make depredations. We had rumours of Turkish soldiers cutting off women's breasts, and other atrocities. Sentries were placed at some points, but I think this was not done the first day or so. We did not occupy Kertch. Yenikaleh, at the entrance to the Sea of Azoff, was the place occupied.

On the road to Yenikaleh I came upon a couple of French soldiers at the door of a house, as if anxious to enter, while the inmates stood to prevent them. I asked the soldiers what they wanted, and the answer was, "Il y a une tres jolie fille dedans." A man and a woman within the door were offering the soldiers *vodki* to induce them to go away. The only influence I could use was to advise them to leave the house. The men did not seem excited, nor very determined, so my impression was that they would not push matters to an extreme.

On reaching the camp I found my medical friends, and as tents are part of the medical stores, I had one, or a share of one, that night—an advantage few in Yenikaleh had for the first night. One of the empty houses was allotted to the medical staff, so I came in for a share of this also, and found myself very comfortable.

In a day or more the *Orient* was brought up as close to Yenikaleh as the depth of water would allow. The straits are very shallow, and the *Orient* had only about eighteen inches below her keel; but as there was a couple of feet of mud at the bottom, the captain was not so much afraid of a sea that might make the ship pitch. The object in bringing the *Orient* close to Yenikaleh was on account of her being the hospital; it was necessary to have her as near the camp as possible for receiving the sick on board. As soon as she appeared I went on board again. The hospital attendants were a party of the Grenadier Guards under Lord Balgonie. When a death occurred, the body was sewn up in a blanket, with a shot or two in it, and as we had no chaplain Lord Balgonie had to read the funeral service. The body was put into a boat and rowed about half a mile from the ship, where it was dropped into the water. I often went out with these funeral parties. Two or three times we visited Kertch. Balgonie acted as interpreter. He could speak Italian, a more useful language in Kertch than French. Italian had been the language of the Levant before French, and Kertch being an out-of-the-way place, the Italian influence still lingered in it. There was a number of Germans, or at least people of German descent. I only met one person who could speak French.

I was at Kertch for perhaps three weeks. The old mounds with which the ground round the place is covered, and which form quite a feature in the landscape, interested me, but at that time I had not sufficient knowledge to understand them. I made notes of some, and have seen them since, and I have seen the objects found in them, as well as those found in tombs on the other side of the straits, which are in the Hermitage at St. Petersburg. At a later date these tombs assumed a considerable interest to me, particularly after I had been to Mycenæ, and seen the so-called Treasury of Atreus, and others of that place. I have seen the wonderful groups of mound tombs of Sardis, which include the tomb of Alyattes, of which the construction is described by Herodotus; and when in China I was able to visit the tombs of the Ming Dynasty, north of Peking. These are also mounds, and are only a variety of the same ancient type of sepulchre.

Captain Drummond, already mentioned as commanding H.M.S. *Retribution*, in which I presented my letter of introduction to the Duke of Cambridge, had changed into the *Tribune*, a thirty-one-gun frigate, and it was with him I returned home from the Kertch Expedition. He had taken me on board to dine, and was obliged to carry me off with him as the fleet were ordered to return to Kamiesch. I remember that he had to supply me with a brush and comb, and how my traps got back to Balaklava I do not now remember. We first visited Anapa, which the Russians had evacuated. In passing west, Captain Drummond took his ship in as close as he could to the coast off Woronzoff's Villa. Prince Woronzoff had been the Governor in that part of Russia, and the road to Yalta, from Sebastopol, which passed by his palace, was named after him, perhaps because he had made it. His villa, or palace, was magnificent, standing on the south coast, near Livadia and other palaces of the Russian nobility. I was anxious to sketch this grand residence, and had a special advantage on board the *Tribune*.

CHAPTER V

CAMP LIFE IN THE CRIMEA

WE got into Kamiesch on the evening of June 15th, and I slept on board the *Tribune*, intending to go off to Balaklava next morning; but at breakfast Captain Drummond was signalled to go on board the Admiral's ship, and I remained till he should return. When he came back he told me that a number of the ships had been ordered to go in that night and bombard Sebastopol, and the *Tribune* was to be one of them. On my expressing a wish to be on board and see the action, Captain Drummond gave me permission. We received an invitation to dine on Lord Clarence Paget's ship, the *St. Jean d'Arc*—a line of battleship—called by the sailors the *Jeanie Dacres*. At dinner Lord Clarence explained the difference between his going into action and my doing the same thing. He would be doing his duty, and if a shell struck him he would be a "hero," whereas, as I had no business there, if a shell struck me I would be called a "fool." This was all so good-naturedly put that I could only laugh at it and say that I was willing to take the risk, and the chance of being called by any name people chose to give me.

It may be explained that the plan was to attempt to take Sebastopol on June 18th. This was the date of the Battle of Waterloo, and the idea was that a victory by the combined forces, with the fall of the great stronghold, would wipe out all remembrance of the old conflict. There were to be two days' bombardment, and the ships were to go in after dark, one at a time, about every half hour, till daylight in the morning, and thus keep the troops in Sebastopol on the *qui vive*. Lights, not visible to those in Sebastopol, had been arranged on shore, and the ships were to steer into a position by their guidance and then open fire—each vessel to deliver three broadsides. The *Tribune* was to go in first, and when the captain and I returned to her she was under way. On going below for a moment, I found to my astonishment that my berth and all the berths had vanished —the deck was cleared from stem to stern. Here I realised the phrase about "clearing decks for action." All the bulkheads that formed the berths had been removed. This was the reason that Lord Clarence had invited us to dinner—it saved dining on board the *Tribune* while the clearing was going on. In addition to this all the upper rigging was taken in, so that there would be less to come down on deck if a shot should strike the masts.

It took some time to sail to our place, and when near it to get exactly into the position marked out by the lights. By this time it was quite dark, so that we were not seen by the enemy. I had selected the bow as my point of observation, and at last I heard Captain Drummond, after asking if all were ready, say "One—Two—Fire!" A thirty-one gun ship has fifteen guns on her broadside, and the pivot gun, making sixteen guns in all. Every one being at his post, all silent, except the captain, every one ready, the sixteen guns went off like one gun. The crash was terrific. The tympanum of one's ears felt as if it were utterly demolished, and at the same time, with the sudden flash of light in the darkness, one's eyes felt rather astonished. It was a second or so before I came to myself, but I was able to hear the hissing sound of the shells as they flew through the air, and then heard them bursting. Where they burst, or what damage they did we could not know. The guns were soon loaded again, but before they could be fired the Russians returned the compliment. We delivered our three broadsides and then steamed back to our quarters in Kasatch Bay. The Russians kept firing at us, but nothing touched the ship. Only one shell came very near, it whizzed over our rigging. None of the ships were struck that night, but next night the same performance was repeated, and Captain Lyons, of the *Miranda*, son of the Admiral, was wounded, and ultimately died from the injury. The *St. Jean d'Arc* went in next night, and a shell killed and wounded some of the men. I am not sure but the *Sidon* had a shot on board of her.

Next morning, the 17th of June, I left the *Tribune*, and instead of going to Balaklava, I went up to the front to see what was going on there and be ready for events. My friend Woodford had left Balaklava and joined his battalion of the Rifles at the 4th Division, on Cathcart's Hill. I remember the evening. I suppose I dined with Woodford. We all knew of the assault that was to be made next morning. Officers were writing letters, under the impression that they might be the last; some made wills. It was understood that there was to be an hour or so of bombardment after daylight, before the assault. I had arranged to sleep in Woodford's tent, but Colonel Somerset, who commanded the Rifles, came in from Headquarters, and he brought the news that sentries would be placed all round the rear, to prevent stragglers and people from Balaklava from getting near the trenches. To make sure, I determined to secure a place in front in due time, and instead of going to bed, I went out, and walked down to the ground in rear of our right attack. I was just a little to the north of the Woronzoff Road, and I found a snug kind of a hole in the darkness, and lay down in it as my bed for the night. As I lay I could hear the sound of the troops moving down the road to the batteries, to be ready for the business of the morrow. My recollection is now very indistinct, but I must have slept, and slept well. I was within range of the guns of Sebastopol, much nearer than I had been on the first day when I walked up to the front, but I had learned a good deal since then, and seen enough of shot and shell to trouble myself less about them. Did I sleep soundly? I cannot now say. But very early in the morning, in the grey dawn, I was wakened by a terrible noise in front. The roar of artillery and the rattle of musketry could both be heard. It was deafening. The number of guns in action produced a rolling rumble, from the one following so close on the other; and at times there seemed to be a number of these rumbles, growing into and out of each other. I have heard thunder in the Himalayas, that went on without intermission for hours, with this rolling and rumbling in it. It reminded me of the morning at Sebastopol, only the thunder in the Himalayas was not so loud as the noise of the guns. The sharp rattle of the musketry was quite distinct amid the grander roar of the artillery.

I could not understand what was going on, for I had almost direct information the night before that there was to be about two hours' bombardment before the assault was delivered. It turned out that at a late hour on the previous evening the French sent in word that they would not be able to conceal the troops in the trenches after daylight, and that the attack must begin at dawn. From the point where I was I recollect I could see a flag in the smoke of battle on the Malakoff, which hung down in a very listless way. That flag is quite distinct in my memory. As the light increased, and I wanted to get a better view, I came up the hill towards the camp of the Light Division, and found myself among those who had come to look on. I remained there most of the morning, till we learned that the attack had failed.*

I then made for Balaklava. Though a non-combatant, I felt a heavy depression at the failure. My own feelings that morning explained to me afterwards how the failure must have told on those at Headquarters. I have not the slightest doubt now but it was the depression of spirits that affected the health and caused the death of General Estcourt and of Lord Raglan, Colonel Vico, the French A.D.C. with Lord Raglan, and others. Colonel Vico and I had become great friends, and I had promised that when Sebastopol fell, I was to do my picture of it in his room at Headquarters. I chanced to go up there one day shortly after the 18th and I was told he was breathing his last, and was taken in to see him. It was sad. What a change it made at Head-

* [A full account of the combined attack, of the French on the Malakoff, and of the British on the Redan, on June 18th, is furnished both in Kinglake's "Crimea" and in "The War," by Mr W. H. Russell, the *Times* Correspondent.]

quarters. A new Commander-in-Chief. Almost every one was changed. Most of Lord Raglan's staff went home with the dead body. In one sense it made no change to me, for I was still as welcome with the new men as with the old. General Simpson, being a namesake, always made me welcome. Colville of the Rifles was his A.D.C., and he being an artist we had been friends all the winter at Balaklava, where he had been stationed with his battalion. Colonel Wyndam was chief of the staff, and I had also known him, so my position at Headquarters was as good as ever. Still, I had been on such good terms with the old set, that I regretted the change.

On the 23rd of June I went down to the most advanced approach in our left attack, Chapman's. This attack did not lead to any of the Russian works, for it was on a spur formed on the right by the ravine of the Woronzoff Road, and on the left by one, if not two, ravines, which separated us from the French attack on the Bastion du Mat. This spur ended in a steep descent, the top of which overlooked the end of the Man-of-War Harbour, at which was a twenty-one gun battery. I made a very careful sketch of this, and when it went home the people at the War Office copied the drawing. It was the most advanced picture that had been made, and gave information the authorities had not before received. There were other Russian batteries, and among them a small one, with two guns, could fire up the Woronzoff Road. Behind these I noticed some boards fixed on two posts. On looking at them with my binoculars I found that they displayed a caricature, the figures being more than life-size. The picture represented a Russian soldier, with a Zouave on one side and a British soldier on the other. Of course the Russian was in a heroic fighting position, while the other two were represented in rather a funky state. Moral—The single Russia could fight France and England. It was caricature under very strange conditions. The defenders of Troy, if caricature had been then known, might have indulged in something of the same kind, and they had a much stronger case on which to found such a picture.

The drawing I made showed many details of the proper left of the Bastion du Mat, and of the many batteries behind it, known as the town batteries.

The parallel was guarded or garrisoned on the day of my visit by the Rifles. One of the men offered me his rifle to have "a shot at the Rooshians." I took the rifle and fired it, but took care not to run the chance of touching any of the "Rooshians." I fired at Sebastopol, and struck it. I selected an open space on the ground sloping down on the east side of the town batteries, and I saw the dust knocked up from the ground where it struck. I might, if I had liked, have fired one of the big guns—the sailors knowing me would have been delighted to let me do so—but I could not tell where a shell might go and what it might do, and as I had not taken "the shilling" I felt that if it might chance to kill any one it would be "murder." Captains and mates of transport vessels were in the habit of taking their guns up to the trenches to have "a pot" at the enemy. I thought such conduct abominable, and I told some of them my opinion. I think this was the only time I ever fired a musket. The Russians fired at me oftener than I at them. More than once they had seen me, and supposing I was an engineer officer with new works and batteries in view, thought it necessary to pay me special attentions. One day in the Right Attack I was sketching from the first parallel. I was standing with rather too much of my body above the parapet when a couple of shells were sent rather uncomfortably near. One of the sailors said, "They see you, sir. You had better come down, and I will arrange for you." Trusting to his greater experience I took the advice, and he fixed something for me to stand upon, so that I was only sufficiently high to see over the top of the work, and I finished my sketch without further hindrance.

The chances of good or ill fortune with shells were in some cases very striking. Glastonbury Neville, R.E., who was on Chapman's staff, had to go down to the Left Attack every day, at times oftener. His marks at the end of the siege far exceeded that of any one else. Yet he never got a scratch, though it is the going out and in to the trenches which is the most dangerous. Afterwards, during the Indian Mutiny, he was appointed to Sir Hugh Rose's staff while the latter was chasing Tantia Tapi and fighting in Central India. Neville went out to Bombay, and hurried forward to join Sir Hugh, who was besieging an old fort called Ratghur. He reached that place—a tumble-down affair—with only a few small, rusty, worn-out old guns, and almost the first shot that was fired next morning killed him. A very striking instance of the fortunes of war!

Chapman gave a dinner-party one evening, at which I was one of the guests. I was to sleep in Neville's hut, and after dinner, while we were preparing for bed, we heard a shell coming. The Ruskis had invented a plan of firing into our camps. They dug a hole, and put any old used-up gun into it, breach downward, so that the muzzle pointed towards our lines at about an angle of forty-five degrees, and with a large charge of powder they used at times to fire shells. With this huge elevation the missiles took a long time to come, and they could be heard hissing in the air for some seconds. It was the sound of one of these we heard coming. They were tolerably harmless, but they had done some damage, though nothing to cause us to move the camps. Still, they were not pleasant to hear, and this one came nearer and nearer as we sat, all expectancy. To have run out to look for it would have been useless; we might have run to the very spot where it was destined to fall. So we remained looking at each other. Louder and louder came the whish, and at last, with a grand thud, the shell struck the ground and exploded. Where it alighted I could not say, but it was near enough to make the wooden hut shake and shiver.

I recall another curious instance of chance of this kind. Many visitors found their way to Balaklava, some on business and some merely as visitors. Various were their modes of looking at things. Some wanted to see the trenches, and I was at times asked to act as guide, or if I was going to visit the trenches for my own purposes, they asked to be allowed to go with me. But we had worldly-wise men, who did not see the fun of going into danger. "None but fools did so," etc., etc. When they went to the front they only looked on from a safe distance. Among the many who came out were the members of a sanitary commission: what they did I do not know. I have described the winter and its miseries, or at least I have suggested a few details by which any one may picture to himself what the fellows at the front had to contend with. A sanitary commission could have done nothing to improve things at that time; and when the good weather came, I don't know any better sanitary authority than it was. Well, the sanitary gentlemen did appear, and lived I think in Balaklava. One of them, when any one asked if he had visited the trenches, answered "No!"— he was not intending to be a fool. This was a matter regarding which he expressed himself in very decided language. It so chanced that he had a friend, a young officer in the Artillery, who invited him up one day to camp. He waited to dine, and after dinner the officer had to go to the trenches on duty. On leaving, the Sanitary Commissioner mounted his pony, and went a very little way with his friend. But of course, not being a fool, he was not going to risk any danger. So he was just on the point of returning, and had raised his hand to his cap by way of a parting salute, when either a shot or a shell came. It touched the pommel of the saddle, and would have carried off his right arm if it had not been raised at the instant. Whether it actually touched or grazed his haunch, or produced a concussion by almost touching, I am not certain, but the result was equivalent to a wound, and he was laid up with it, how long I do not now remember. This man had only gone once within the possible risk of danger, and this only for a second or so, and the above was the result. I heard afterwards that when he returned home he made himself a bore everywhere, repeating his account of the adventure, but I never could learn whether he described himself as a "hero" or a "fool." According to his own theory he had manifestly been the latter. However, he managed by telling his tale to be made a K.C.B

Nevertheless, on quiet days in the trenches, I do not

believe that the accidents, if I may use that word, were much more numerous than in the streets of London.

On the 28th of July I was invited to join an excursion to the Baidar Valley. If I recollect rightly it was got up principally by some of the officers in the guards, Neville and Higginson, and Glastonbury Neville, R.E. Altogether there were quite half a dozen of us, or perhaps more. I think we had lunch in Petrovski's Villa, which was supposed to be a shooting box on the way. That was on our going out, and we dined there on our way back in the afternoon. The Baidar Valley lies to the east of Balaklava, and we followed the Woronzoff Road as the way to it. This valley is said to be the Tempe of Russian poets, and we found it to be very beautiful. We went as far as the Phorus Pass, where the Woronzoff Road reached the top of the heights overlooking the sea, at a gateway with Doric pillars. Here the road descends among Tartar villages, villas, palaces, and vineyards, and passing Woronzoff's Villa, makes for Yalta. We had a very pleasant day, and I was able to make sketches—one, that of the Baidar Valley, appears in my book.

It was probably on the 11th of August that I had a little adventure. It was a Saturday, and I had gone to Headquarters with my sketches. That was the post day, and I continued my system of submitting sketches to Sir James Simpson, as I had done to Lord Raglan. The Sardinian Army, which had arrived during the summer, was stationed along the line of the Tchernaya, and I went in that direction to have a look at the village of Tchorgoun, and see the country. I was alone, and had crossed the Tchernaya, and passed through the village. On the heights beyond, I came upon one of the Sardinian piquets, and had a pleasant chat with one of the officers, who gave me a glass of wine. On leaving him I wandered south among the hills, till I thought it was time to turn westward, and find my way back to Balaklava, for it was getting towards evening. Just as I turned my steps a couple of Sardinian soldiers jumped up. So far as I can recollect, they did not seize me, but the process might be described by saying that I was surrounded by them. I think they were Bersaglieri. Communication in words was difficult with them, so they took me into the advanced piquet behind. There I discovered that the two soldiers were the most advanced sentries of the Sardinians at this point. Consequently I had been entirely beyond their lines, and had I chanced to wander a little farther I might have been caught by the Russian advanced piquet, which was quite close. To be found between the two lines of opposing troops is in itself a very suspicious circumstance. Add to this that I was not in uniform, and not particularly "swellish" in my outward appearance. I was as likely to be a spy as anything else. Fortunately I had a short note I had asked from the Sardinian A.D.C. at our headquarters. This went so far to explain, but it had no official stamp on it. I was sent in through all the piquets and posts, till at last I was brought before the General commanding at that place. I think either he or some of his staff knew me, but at any rate they were satisfied I was not a Russian spy, so I was allowed to return to Balaklava, where I arrived rather late.

On the Thursday morning, 16th of August, as I was finishing my breakfast on board ship, some one brought word that there was heavy fighting going on in the direction of the Tchernaya. Jumping up and cramming a sketch-book into my pocket I went off as fast as legs could carry me. When I reached the battlefield, the affair was just over, and I saw the dust rising in the distance from the heels of the retreating Ruskis. The point I made for was the Traktir Bridge over the Tchernaya. Here it was that the French part of the battle had taken place; the Sardinians had fought more to the right. The wounded French had been carried off to the hospitals, but the dead lay as they had fallen, and the wounded and dead Russians were still on the ground.

As the sea-weed thrown up by the tide tells how far the sea has come, so the dead and wounded Russians told how far the tide of battle had reached. The line was distinctly marked. I commenced to make sketches of those that lay around. The sketches were introduced into the picture I did of the battle, and I have been told by more than one soldier, familiar with such scenes, that I must have made sketches of the reality to give the exact character of the dead. One of the peculiarities is that most of the fallen seem to retain the position of the arms as they held their muskets. How to account for this I do not know. Instant death might explain it, but even in such a case, one would suppose that the arms would drop down. Any one might conclude that death would at once relax the limbs, and that all muscular action would cease. But no, all round I could see figures with the arms precisely as if the gun was being held in the hands. Even some who had fallen on their faces retained the attitude of holding the musket. Poets—few of them I suppose ever saw a battlefield—always use words bloody, blood-red, crimson, &c., with which to describe such scenes. This is far from being correct; it might be so in paved streets. I once saw a pavement in Paris, where there had been a butchery, and it was red enough. But that was an exception to my experience. A bullet hits a man, he falls and dies perhaps, and blood flows. A large quantity of it is absorbed by his dress, and through that it soaks into the ground below the man, and is not seen by those passing. I do not remember to have seen blood that morning on this battlefield. I noticed a French soldier, a piece of a shell, or it may have been a round shot, had gone through him carrying away some of his lumbar vertebræ, and yet the redness or appearance of blood was not a feature in this instance. There is at times another element which interferes with the "gory" appearance of battlefields, and it was present that morning on the Tchernaya. That is dust. I came upon a wounded Russian soldier. He was asleep, so I take it he was not very badly wounded. I could hear him snoring, but where his mouth or nose were, by which the sound came, I could not discover. I think his wound was somewhere in the head, and it must have bled freely. As the blood flowed, the dust must have been blown on it, and both had accumulated till the man's head seemed only to be a lump of earth. It was quite dry, not at all tinged with the blood. I could make out neither hair nor features; all I could make sure of was that the man lived, and was able to snore. In contrast with this man, there was a young Russian officer, who I think must have had an instant death. He lay on his back, with his face looking up to heaven. His blue eyes were quite open, they were perfectly clear, not glazed in death, and he had a most beautiful smile on his lips. The whole expression was that of a saint in a state of rapture. I have seen nothing in any picture equal to that face.

I was often asked on my return about Miss Nightingale; but she was always at Scutari. She once, for a day or so only, made a visit to the Crimea, but I never saw her. Mrs. Seacole, an elderly mulatto woman from Jamaica, was a well-known character in the Crimea, all the soldiers and sailors knew her. She had a taste for nursing and doctoring, but she added to this a business as a sutler. She told me one day that she had Scotch blood in her veins. I must say that she did not look like it, but the old lady spoke proudly of this point in her genealogy. She was a nice, good creature, and every one liked her. At Lord Raglan's funeral, and at such ceremonies as the investiture of the Bath, she turned out with the brightest of ribbons in her bonnet.

The miseries of the winter had so roused public opinion, that the authorities seemed to have lost their heads, and any and everything was sent out. Russell, or some other correspondent, put it very well, by saying that the men at last had so much, and so many, fine things sent out, that they were complaining, when they had to go to the trenches at night, that there were no white kid gloves to put on, nor perfumes for their pocket-handkerchiefs. "Generals January and February," not to forget November and December, were the worst foes our soldiers had to contend with. As soon as spring came round, and brought warmth and dry weather, things improved. But every man sent out after that—and during the spring and summer we were invaded with hosts of new schemes—claimed that he put things right in the Crimea. Among others sent out was M. Soyer, the celebrated cook. He came with new kitchens, to show what he could do with the ordinary rations, and as he lived in a vessel lying alongside the *Star of the South*, we of course became acquainted. He was a wonderfully good-natured man, full of talk. He told me of his wife, who was an artist, and only lately dead. And he described the wonderful monument he had raised to her memory in Kensal Green Cemetery. On passing through Paris on his way to the Crimea, Soyer met Edmond About. There was some chaff about shot and shell and the chances of being killed, and it was thought as well to prepare an epitaph. About accordingly suggested, as being not only short and sweet, but at the same time sufficiently expressive, the words, " Soyer tranquille." Being a Frenchman, although sent out by our Government, Soyer naturally went about a good deal with his own countrymen, and when anything was going on at the French Quartier-General, Soyer was sure to be there. He appeared on these occasions with a kepi shining with gold lace, a flowing burnous, and gold lace on his trousers. He was a short, round-faced, dumpy man; so was Pelissier, the French Commander-in-Chief, who also in the summer wore a burnous. Soyer often rode out with Pelissier, and it was not his custom to ride behind. My friend Colville made a sketch of the two, as I have described them, with the title beneath, "Which is the Commander-in-Chief, and which is the Cook?"

I recall here a touch of Soyer's humour. In August the grass in the Crimea was all burnt up; but he procured some paint from the ships at Balaklava, painted the ground round his kitchens green, and put up a notice-board, "Visitors are requested not to walk on the grass."

CHAPTER VI

THE FALL OF SEBASTOPOL

I FORGET now how I became acquainted with Major Welsford of the 97th Regiment. Colonel Handcock was the colonel of the regiment, and his wife had come out, and was on board the *Star of the South* for some time, and this may have led to it. Welsford was a particularly fine fellow, good in every way, beloved by the men of the regiment, to whom he was kind and attentive in all things. Hedley Vicars belonged to the 97th. He was taken up by the religious world, and made a great hero of, but he could not have been a better man than Welsford. About a week before the fall of Sebastopol I spent some days with the latter; and only two or three days before the 8th of September the Major, the Colonel, Mrs. Handcock, and myself rode round to a spot called by us, or rather by the French, the "Maison Rouge." It stood somewhere between the French left attack and our Greenhill Battery. Either there was nothing new at the point for me to sketch that day, or I was not in the mood for it, but I remember that Mrs. Handcock and Welsford sketched, and the artist was idle. It was a beautiful day, and I watched the bombardment going on—that which preceded the final attack, and which the Russians described as a "feu d'enfer." This day remains much clearer in my memory than the days that followed. Both the Colonel and the Major were killed on the 8th of September, only a day or two afterwards. The incident was terribly striking. To be out as we were, riding so pleasantly about, enjoying ourselves, and all so well and happy, and so soon what a sudden change—the two men dead, and the woman weeping in a tent beside her dead husband.

We all knew from the bombardment going on, that there would be an assault to follow, but it was impossible to know when. After spending some days with the 97th, I returned to Balaklava, and either that night or early next morning I learned that the attack was to take place. The 8th of September was a Saturday. I hurried up to the front. The attack began at noon. I was, as far as I remember, on Cathcart Hill, or on the ridge in front of the Light Division. Here I remained most of the day. We learned that the French were in, and held, the Malakoff. I remember a French officer who was an onlooker declaring that that was "le clef de la position." By and by the wounded began to come up from our trenches. They brought up word that we were in the Redan. Others confirmed this. But after a time came the news that our troops had been driven out of it. I remember some of the men of the 97th bringing up the body of Major Welsford on a stretcher, and I learned that Colonel Handcock was mortally wounded. I thought of Handcock's poor wife in the tent. She had been there all day, with the roar of guns going on. The 97th led the assault.

Next morning I started early for the front, and found that the siege of Sebastopol was finished. The Russians had left the place during the night. What a load this lifted from one's feelings! I pushed on till I reached the rear of our left attack, but a cordon of sentries would allow no one to pass into the town. I waited here some time noting the burning houses of Sebastopol, while occasional explosions took place. A long string of prisoners were marched up while I was there—men who had not escaped in the hurried flight. Seeing that I could not pass the sentries, I went back to Headquarters to procure an official document to enable me to do so. Here I found General Barnard, who said he was about to visit the city and would take me. A pony was found for me, and I accompanied the General and his A.D.C. We made first for the Redan. I had been into the Quarries while the siege was going on, and, even while it was being made,

THE FALL OF SEBASTOPOL.

into the flying-sap in front, which was our nearest approach to the Redan, and the cover from which our troops issued when the assault was made. We found two British flags flying on the Salient of the Redan, and we were surprised at the elaborate character of the works. Small curtains had been made between traverses, to protect the men at the guns from fragments of shells when they burst within the place. From the Redan we walked down towards the "White Buildings," and up into the Malakoff, entering it by the narrow gorge in its rear. The French were burying the dead Russians. They carried them from all parts of the Malakoff to the top of the parapet at the rear, and threw them into the ditch. It is upon this spot that the Russians have since built a commemorative chapel.

We found a small crowd of soldiers standing in the Malakoff round a Zouave, who was sitting at the side of a traverse. To our astonishment we found that the man was dead. He sat in an easy position, leaning his head on his hand, as if resting; but the pose was as perfect as if he had been sitting for a painter. No wound was visible, no sign of blood. The figure, if it could have been cast, would have made a perfect statue. It was this artistic appearance which evidently attracted the soldiers around him. He must have received a mortal wound, and afterwards had enough time to sit down; then the life must have fled, leaving him in the position he had assumed. There was no sign of pain on his features. The soldiers told us that his regiment was not in the attacking column, and that he had got leave—"Congé," to join.

In one of the batteries we looked at, we could see in a corner the place where a religious picture, a saint, had been fixed. The picture had been carried off, but the rude sockets where candles had been lighted were there, with the tallow that had run down still adhering to them. There were two Zouaves inspecting the spot, and they explained it to us, winding up by remarking that when, "Ces sacrés Russes—quand on tire, on prie que la balle attrape quelque un." The Zouave expressed himself in a tone as if the praying were taking an unfair advantage in war. My own notion is that the Ruski more probably looked on the picture of the saint as a kind of charm to save him from being touched by the bullets that came into the battery. I believe the Russians had many of these shrines in their batteries, and they present a curious feature of religion among that people. I think I was told that the priests came into the various works at times to bless them. Barnard's A.D.C. got one of these pictures that day, but there was a difficulty about getting it past the sentries on our return. I had my old grey plaid with me, and the picture was brought out very easily under the folds, which I spread out just a little to cover it.

Two or three incidents of this part of my work may be worth recalling. A French Division under General Bazaine, afterwards Marshal Bazaine, occupied the town, and I found his sentries a continual trouble to me. On the first day I was so bothered, that I called on Bazaine. He was very civil to me, and told me his wife was an English lady. I suppose he could not give me a pass, for next day I went to our Headquarters, and some one gave me a letter of introduction to Colonel Rose, the British A.D.C. at the French Quartier-General. At Pelissier's headquarters, Colonel Rose was out, but an officer, who turned out to be General Martempre, attended to me. On my explaining to him who I was, he asked me in, and produced some of the published plates of my drawings. He went out and brought in Pelissier, who was also very kind, and my passport received some additional touches.

This passport, I was assured, would make me all right, but I still had a good deal of trouble. Many of the young French soldiers could not read, and all they could say was that no one could be permitted to pass. The Russians kept up an intermittent bombardment from the north side, which was no doubt one of the reasons for not allowing stragglers into the town. The first day or so, I remember I had a pony, and when I wished to sketch I tied up the beast where he would be out of danger from the *things* coming from the Russians. The sentries, seeing me sketching, paid no attention to the artist, but walked off with the pony, knowing I was sure to follow. Of course as soon as I saw the officer in command, and explained, producing my passport, it was all right; but the next spot I chose for my sketch the same farce had to be gone through. This bother took another form. The sentry would come up to me, and after looking at what I was doing, would say—"Monsieur, vous prenez la carte?" As this way of putting the question did not appear to me so bad, or suspicious, as reference to a sketch, I on the first occasion answered "yes." This was enough; making a plan was not the harmless work I had supposed, so I had to go off with the soldier as a prisoner. One day, in the central bastion, I was arguing the point with a sentry, and trying to make him read what was written on my passport, which he would not look at, when a voice came out of a group of soldiers, who were playing cards close at hand. The words were in perfect English, and were a request to know what was the matter. I explained, and my interrogator told the sentry to let me alone. Naturally I now turned to the man who had befriended me, and asked where he had learned his English so perfectly. "Oh, sir," he said, "I am a Canadian."

One day, while sketching in the Malakoff, where I had to stand, I had not been long at work when I noticed that once or twice an itchiness about the ankles caused me to rub one foot against the other. But being intent on my sketch I went on with it. A French soldier passing began to grin, and pointing to the lower part of my extremities, he said, "V'la les puces." My trousers were of a light grey colour, but on looking down at my legs, I saw the lower part a deep, dark brown, which graduated to a lighter tint upwards. These were "les puces." I went off some distance, and picked up something with which I began scraping them off. I moved from place to place during the operation, so that those that were scraped off would not have a chance of returning; but it was impossible for me to get clear of all my friends. While I was at this I saw a French soldier not far from me, "sans culottes," with his red nether garments in his hand beating them against a Russian cannon. I thought at first that all the fleas in the Malakoff had congregated on my garment, but the action of the soldier showed clearly that there were a few that had not discovered my existence. How many insects of this kind were in the Malakoff I must leave to the calculation of those who are fond of statistics. The bomb proofs in which the Russian soldiers took shelter, and in which they no doubt slept, were filled with rags and old garments, and these I supposed were the strongholds, perfect Malakoffs, from which the hungry hordes issued to attack all who came within their reach. On arriving at my tent in the evening, I took Higginson's servant into my confidence, and he carried all my clothes to some distance, where he put them through a purifying process.

One day I was going along the main street of Sebastopol that led to the Admiralty of that time. I think the hotels are now in this street. I was stopped by a sentry, quite a young fellow, and evidently a raw recruit lately arrived. While I was arguing the point with him, two Zouaves came up, and he in a rather peremptory style stopped them also. The Zouaves took up my case, for I showed them my passport, which the sentry would not look at. The Zouaves were old hands, and could read, and they explained to the sentry that it was a "passe pour tout," or something of that kind. Our obstructor however stood perfectly obdurate, with a firm grip of his musket, looking in another direction, as much as to say, "You may talk as you like, but I know my orders and my duty." But a sudden collapse took place. A shell from the Russians on the north side of the harbour came with its wild shriek uncomfortably near, and the fellow at once bolted, and took refuge in one of the houses at the side of the street. The Zouaves and myself, as soon as the first whish of the shell was heard, directed our eyes down the street, and seeing that it was not coming our way, never moved, but the sudden retreat of the sentry excited the laughter of my friends, and as he did not venture out again—whether from fear of more shells, or of being laughed at, I cannot tell—we walked on our way free from obstruction.*

* Under the heading of "Grattez un Russe, et vous trouverez un

Tartare," Simpson contributed to *The Asiatic* of Sept. 15, 1869, a highly interesting paper, in which he put forward the theory that the war in the Crimea owed its decision to ethnological facts. The governing class, the brain, of Russia, he pointed out, is Aryan, but the mass of the people are Turanian. While, therefore, Russian diplomacy is singularly successful in Europe, Russian arms never can be, the Turanian soldier being inferior to the Aryan. The natural direction of Russian conquest he declared to be eastward, among the Mongolian races of Northern and Central Asia.

CHAPTER VII

CIRCASSIA

SOME time previous to the fall of Sebastopol I had made the acquaintance of the Duke of Newcastle. It occurred in this way. During the session of Parliament in 1855, the Aberdeen Government was turned out. That Government had begun the war, and incurred much blame for the miseries of the soldiers during the winter. The Duke of Newcastle had been Minister of War, and as he had been abused for what had taken place, he came out to the Crimea to see things for himself and, I suppose, to try and find means of defence by more direct knowledge gained on the spot. My introduction to the Duke was at Headquarters. He wished to see the ground of the Inkerman, and I was recommended to go with him, as familiar with the topography. When I went with the Duke I of course took him down the Quarry Ravine to the aqueduct, and into the old excavated church there. The front of this church has fallen down, but a stone wall had been built as a parapet, and some French soldiers were on duty there. Our visit had been noticed by the Russians, and they began " potting " at us. One of the bullets came in and struck the wall of the church. This we picked up and gave to the Duke as a souvenir of the visit, and he carried it off with apparent satisfaction, as a proof that he had been under fire.

On that occasion the Duke told me that he intended to visit Circassia, and that the Admiral had promised to send a ship round that part of the Black Sea with him; and he expressed a wish that I should accompany him and make a few sketches. A visit to Circassia was one of the objects

I had set myself. I had expressed my desire to the Admiral, and he had promised me a cruise in that direction, for we had one or two war steamers on the coast looking after the people there, and keeping an eye on the Russians, who had evacuated all the ports. I asked the Duke when he expected to go, as I could not with a clear conscience leave the Crimea till I saw the fall of Sebastopol. The Duke was not sure of his plans—perhaps it would not be till after Sebastopol was taken. I promised to go if it chanced that the place had fallen, and it turned out that the Duke waited till that event took place, and I managed to go with him.

I have still a letter from the Duke, dated from Cathcart's Hill, 21st Sept., 1855, telling me that Sir Edmond Lyons had appointed H.M.S. *Highflyer* to take us to Circassia, and she would be ready on "Wednesday next"—that would be the 26th Sept. This trip was a most pleasant after-piece to the grand drama, now finished, of the Siege of Sebastopol. I remember hearing some one at the time say that, previous to the Crimean War, the number of British who had visited Circassia might be counted on the fingers of one hand. One, from the earliest days, had notions of romance associated with the country. And the beauty of the women, was it not celebrated? A visit to such a land presented itself to me as a treat of the most interesting kind.

The Duke had a servant called Lucca whom he had brought from England with him. I think he was a Georgian. He had settled in London, where his wife had some kind of business. He could speak all the languages of the Levant—English, French, and Italian; Turkish he was quite at home in, and he seemed to be familiar with all the languages of the Black Sea, including Russian. I have seen him acting as an interpreter, standing in the centre of a circle of various races, turning round to each one as he spoke, replying to every one, and changing the language every minute, yet it seemed not to present the slightest difficulty to him.

Oswald Brierly, the marine painter, since Sir Oswald, was of the party; he had been with the Baltic fleet the year before. We picked up other notabilities as we went along.

We sailed along the southern coast of the Crimea, past Woronzoff's villa, and Yalta, and into Kertch, where we arrived on the 29th. I managed to make a few more sketches, but had none of the adventures of my visit in the May previous. Yenikaleh naturally interested the Duke, as the name literally means Newcastle—*Yeni*, "new;" *Kaleh*, "castle." There were jokes about a Duke of Newcastle visiting Yenikaleh as being very like bringing coals to Newcastle, etc.

On the 1st of October we were at Anapa. That place is the northernmost point of Circassia, and the Russians had fortified it all round, both on the land and sea faces, with numerous batteries. There were some Turkish troops in the place on our visit. The mountain country begins to rise immediately south of Anapa, but away to the north and east everywhere it is flat.

On the 3rd of October we started, with a large party of Circassians, and rode towards the east. We came to within a mile or so of the Kuban river. Here we were on low, undulating hills, the first beginning of the mountain region of Circassia. Along the base of these low hills, or at least not far from them at any point, the Kuban seemed to flow; it runs west or north-west, and into the Black Sea at the Straits of Kertch. This river, with the Terek (which flows east into the Caspian), formed at one time the boundary of Russia in this quarter. At the part of the Kuban which we approached there was a fort, or, rather, there were two forts, one on each bank, to support each other. We found a large number of Circassians gathered here who wanted to attack the forts, but our party were of opinion that they merely wanted to show off before us. The operations were very wild and might be called foolish. The forts had regular ramparts with embrasures and guns; the Tcherkess were on horses and had small rifles, pistols, swords, and the usual dagger; but the rifles were the only weapons they used on this occasion. They were brave, brave to the verge of foolishness. Mounted on their light horses they rode down to within range of the forts. A string of men following each other did this. When they got near the rampart they rode along rapidly in a curved line, and when on the point of the curve nearest the fort they, as is their custom, without stopping, fired their rifles, and then curved in a line away from the fort. Such practice was not likely to do any harm to the fort, or to any one inside of it. This was done once or twice, and in answer the fort fired some of its guns with grape-shot. The Duke advised the Circassians to give up the attack, for some of them began to come up wounded. So far as we saw no one was killed. One man came up to me with a bad wound in his hand, thinking, I suppose, that I might be a doctor. Another was brought up very badly wounded, with a bullet in the upper part of the thigh, and I was much interested in seeing a native leech operate upon him. The old Æsculapian produced what in Scotch would have been called a "speuchan"—an old greasy case, or bag, formed of skin with the hair on it. From this he produced an old "jockteleg," or jack-knife, and began to extract the bullet, which I saw after it was taken out; it had struck the bone, against which it was partly flattened. While the operation was going on some of those round held up one of their cloaks as a shelter from the sun. I noticed that the man was very pale, and the operation with such a rude instrument must have been a very painful one, yet he kept a smile on his face, and talked with those standing round. Wondering at his stoicism, and thinking there was something peculiar in it, I asked Lucca, the Duke's interpreter, to see what it meant. On inquiring he was told that if the man had shown any such marks of weakness as a groan or cry of pain, women's clothes would have been pitched at him as a symbolical mode of saying he was not a man.

We left the place, followed by the Circassians, and moved in a south-western direction. Next day—the 4th of October—we reached Soudjak Kaleh, where we found the *Highflyer*. Soudjak is in a bay forming one of the few good harbours on the Circassian coast. It is the first place south of Anapa, and on coming to it we struck an inland road connecting the two places. This road had been made by the Russians, and we passed on it a small fort, abandoned, made to protect it from the Circassians. Near this fort we were stopped and had to take our share in some funeral rites; it was not a funeral, but a ceremony due to some one not long dead. It would seem that for so many days, weeks, or even months after a death any one visiting the place has to partake of some entertainment in honour, or in memory, of the deceased. In this instance it was a drink called "Boza." It was a horrid kind of stuff; what it was made of I have no idea. Calthorpe declared that it was rough lime mixed with liquid indiarubber or gutta-percha! No mixture could have been more abominable to the taste. No matter what we thought of it, we had to drink: it was due to the manes of the deceased, whoever he was; and of course, in our present position, we wished to be on good terms with our hosts. We felt ourselves to be like the Circassian I had watched the day before under the operation: we had to smile while we absorbed the vile stuff—to have made a wry face would have been ruin to us. Our only relief was that we could freely express our opinions in English. And some pretty strong expressions were the result.*

We remained at Soudjak Kaleh on the 5th of October, and on the 6th we were at Ghelinjik, which is only a little to the south of Soudjak. The Russians had, of course, left both these places. Soudjak—or Novo Rossisk, as it is now called, from the fine bay—will some time or another become an important place.

The sequence of our movements after this becomes confused. From dates on sketches my impression is that we moved slowly south to Souchun Kaleh, visiting some of the evacuated forts as we went along, and that we came north again for an excursion into the interior. There was another of our warships cruising along the coast—H.M.S. *Cyclops*, an old paddle steamer. She was at times with the *Highflyer*. Mr. Longworth, of our Consular service, who had formerly visited Circassia, and published a book about the country, had been sent by our authorities to keep in touch with the people of that region, and to report on the political

* Longworth says "boza" is the Tartar name, "souat" is the Circassian. The stuff is a mixture of fermented millet seed and honey, thick and exceedingly nauseous.

feeling of the country, because if the war continued there was an idea of landing a British force, perhaps in the following year. The Highland Division under Sir Colin Campbell was talked of in connection with this campaign. My impression is that the *Cyclops* was employed to take Longworth to various places to consult with the chiefs. This gentleman joined our party, and was in some of our excursions.

Another man who joined us was Lawrence Oliphant, who has become of great note since. He chanced to have visited the Crimea just before the war, and managed to enter Sebastopol, and he published a book—"The Russian Shores of the Black Sea"—while the war was in progress. In the strange absence of information about the Crimea, and more particularly about Sebastopol, this book was a great success. He had come out again to the Black Sea, just to look about him and take his chance of whatever might turn up.

It was in an excursion north we had most experience of Circassian customs. We rode on horses provided for us, and I had to use a Circassian saddle. In this the strips of leather used as girths often gave way, and I went with the saddle. Luckily nothing serious happened. Oliphant wrote a small book some years afterwards, called "Patriots and Filibusters." The Circassians in this were the patriots, and he gave some of his experiences in our trips, and mentioned the frequent misfortunes of my saddle. The others had come provided with English saddles and were all right. Our way lay through a country without roads, only paths existed formed by those who passed along, and we had to go either up or down a hill, or along the stony bed of a river at times. The first night we enjoyed Circassian hospitality was a new experience. We had had a long and tedious day's journey among the hills, and reached a chief's residence. This consisted of a number of small huts, built of wattle and daub, with thatched roofs, one of which was the konag, or guest house. A separate house for strangers is a necessary consequence of Mohammedan ideas respecting wives and women folk in general. These konags were small places with mud floors and raised mud ledges, on which the rugs or sleeping carpets were placed. They were sofas by day and beds at night. Our repast was provided in this wise. Some one had to go and catch a sheep or goat, and it had to be killed and cooked before supper was possible. This took three or four hours, and the customs of Circassia were not spoken of in favourable terms as we waited. We could hear the women grinding corn for bread in the other houses, and the interest of our new position to me partly atoned for the trial of delay. It realised the old Biblical days, it was something to be going through experiences as old as the time of Abraham. The first indication of approach of our meal was the appearance of our host with a brass vessel containing water, a basin and towel. The basin was held out and the water poured over the hands. This was done to each. Immediately afterwards our host brought in the food. Tables, as we understand such articles, are not in use in Circassia, but the name is given to what we call a stool. This is circular, nearly two feet in diameter, and about the same height from the ground, convenient to eat from in a sitting position. Each of these was supposed to be a dish. A quantity of ground maize boiled was placed on the table, arranged somewhat like the crater of a volcano. In this hollow the meat in each case was laid, with whatever gravy belonged to it, the maize performing double duty of plate and part of repast, as it served the purpose of bread and vegetables. A number of these tables were brought in; not that there was any great variety in the dishes—boiled mutton had to do duty in each. Hospitality is reckoned by the number of tables, so it is necessary to make a show. According to Circassian ideas, the three great virtues are "a sharp sword, a sweet tongue, and forty tables." The first of these means bravery, the second eloquence, and the third hospitality. There are other instances in the East of "forty" as an expression of plenty, abundance, multitude, etc.

As Abraham stood by the tree and looked on,* so did our host while we were eating. We found the correct thing to do was to select a tit-bit and present it to him, when he retired to a corner and ate it with his face modestly

* Genesis xviii. 8.

turned away from us. Here again was a relic of the old world. Homer describes Ulysses at the feast of King Alcinous cutting off what was evidently a choice morsel for Demodocus the bard, who was standing at a column. The herald carried the piece to the bard. The description implies he had not a seat at the table. The tit-bits in our case were the fat of the sheep's large tail, and it was cut in stripes and laid on the dish.

On our first trip we overlooked knives and forks and found the want very awkward. When we had finished, our host came round again with the water as before, and we washed our hands. The necessity for killing a sheep now became obvious. The Duke had a firman from the Porte declaring his greatness. The Circassians at this time acknowledged the Sultan, for the Russians had not yet conquered this part of Circassia, and only held the ground round their forts as far as the gun's fire commanded. The result was that wherever we went we had a score or so of Circassians following us, and if I recollect right two or three chiefs among them. As soon as the dishes left us they were handed out of the door, and the chiefs had their turn. From them they went to the followers, and I question if one sheep would be too much for a hungry set such as they must have been. At the end the dogs got the bones.

While at these konags we had no chance of seeing the ladies of the establishment. We were in a land celebrated for the beauty of its women, and yet none was visible to us. We might catch the glimpse of a dress at times, but that was all. The Circassians are Mohammedans, and of course the harem system was in use. They are not reputed to be very strict followers of the Prophet, but we did not expect them to relax the rule about their female relatives. It was a subject regarding which it was difficult to make advances, and, above all things, we did not wish to give the slightest cause of offence. Knowing that we were in the East, we never expected to see the female members of the houses we lodged in. It was chance that made a change in this, and I had the luck to produce the chance.

At one of the places at which we were quartered I was

outside sketching the habitation of our host. I noticed portions of female dresses at the doors. By and by the younger women appeared, all evidently interested in what the artist was doing. The young ones at length ventured nearer to me, and when I had finished my sketch of the house I sketched one of the little girls. This produced great excitement. An older girl then stood to be sketched. This increased the excitement; girls older still now came, and the process went on till we had the whole household out. The proceeding had been watched by our party from the konag, and when at last I had attracted most of the women—had in fact broken the ice—the Duke and Lucca came out and joined us. The others of our party followed after a time. In a country where hospitality is such a great virtue it would be useless to offer money as a payment for entertainment, so the custom is to make presents. The Duke had brought a quantity of stuff with him for this purpose—pieces of silk, and leather of various colours, as well as knives, scissors, needles, and pretty cases with articles for sewing, commonly called "ladies' companions." Lucca produced some of these things, and the Duke distributed them, to the great delight of the girls. Once or twice afterwards I took to sketching the houses merely to bring out the natives. This served my own purpose at the same time, for it enabled me to make sketches of costume, which could not have been otherwise accomplished.

I cannot say that any of the girls it was our chance to see were particularly handsome, but our experience was limited, and it would not be fair to draw any general conclusion from it. The sketches in my sketch-books are all too hasty and roughly done to be taken as portraits. They were done more for the costumes than for the faces.

In one of these excursions we returned to the coast at a place called Ardiller, but found no ship waiting for us. We had to stay here for a day or so before our vessel turned up. The chief who lived at this place was away at Souchum Kaleh with Omar Pasha's force, and there was only his wife left to do the honours. Somehow food was scarce. There was the *pasta* or boiled millet, and *yughart* or sour curdled milk. The two combined were not unlike porridge and buttermilk. This was very nearly all that was to be had at Ardiller. Oliphant and I, from our Scottish origin, preferred this food to starvation; but the Duke and the others made but poor meals on such fare. The lady could not attend and wash our hands and do the honours, as there was very little to honour, but she got on a horse and scoured the country round for chickens and eggs. Bread, too, was scarce, the boiled millet being the substitute. Fowls and eggs were sent over to us by the lady as she could procure them. Oliphant and I, when we could get eggs, used to cook them by roasting in the hot ashes of the fire. On one of the days here I chanced to see a party of Circassians passing. The foremost man had a woman on the front of the saddle riding with him. I was rather attracted by the group, so I stood before them, holding up my sketch-book and pencil, a sign which was understood, for the man stopped and partly undid the cloak that covered his fair companion. I had just about finished my rough sketch when an elderly man, who either did not understand what was going on, or did not approve of what he saw, came up, and with indignation in his tone and gesture whipped the horse and made them ride off. I did not know at the time who the party were, but learned afterwards that it was a marriage party. In Circassia there are very distinct survivals of the old custom of "capture" in the marriage ceremony, and in this case I was lucky enough to see at least a part of this ancient rite. The bride had been captured, and the bridegroom was carrying her off.

It was in the northern part of Circassia that we one day came upon some very large tombs belonging to a past age. They were megalithic, and contained rudely formed, huge coffins with stone lids. The Tcherkess say there were at one time giants in the country and a race of dwarfs. The giants kept the dwarfs in these as prisons, and as there is a small hole in the end of each, it was through this that the giants fed their little prisoners. Looking at the monuments as tombs, the natural conclusion, judging from other examples, would be that the holes were for offering food, etc., to the dead.

There are two sketches of these tombs in my books, dated October 18, 1855. Longworth describes the opening by Bell—Yacoub Bey, as the Circassians called him—of a cairn or tumulus, in which was found a rude cist containing nothing but a few fragments of terra-cotta.

On the 26th of October I visited and sketched an old church at Ilori, a few miles south or south-east of Souchum. Some one took me to this place, and left me there with the priest, who was the only person I saw; and I remained a good part of the day. His name was Wassil Machateredsy. Wassil is Basil, the word used by the Russians for William. I made a sketch of him, and he wrote his name below in the sketch-book. "Proto pope" was the ecclesiastical rank he gave to himself. We spent the time very pleasantly together, and managed, out of a number of languages, to find a word or two which both of us understood. On entering the church he produced his brush and holy water, and expressed surprise when I avoided the sprinkling. The Georgian churches have the steeple separated from the church. In this case the gate of what might be called the churchyard went through it. The priest's house was a simple wooden structure outside. There were remains of frescoes on the inside walls the church.

After this we parted with Oliphant. He was to have gone on a mission to Schamyl, which was just one of those wild adventures that would have suited him. But in this he was disappointed, so made up his mind to follow Omar Pasha's force in its movement in the direction of Tiflis, and he was in the battle of the Ingour, where he took a part. From what I learned afterwards it was an incident in this battle that led Oliphant first into the region of spiritualism. As it was related to me, one of the European officers was wounded, and died the same day in Oliphant's arms. Years afterwards, when Oliphant visited New York, he went with some friend to a spiritual *séance*, and the medium made a reference to this event. The surprise was so great that Oliphant was attracted. How far he was a believer in this direction

I do not quite know. Years afterwards, when I was in 64, Lincoln's Inn Fields, one evening, as was often our custom, my next-door neighbour, Hinchliff, and I were sitting either at his fire or mine, and he related a curious episode that occurred in one of his voyages to South America. Some one, he said, was recounting this experience of Oliphant to a group sitting on the deck of the steamer. At the finish one listener said it was peculiarly strange for him to hear all this, for he was the medical officer who attended the dying man. When Hinchliff related this to me he was quite unconscious of my previous acquaintance with Oliphant, and that his narrative was almost as strange to me as it had been to the medical officer on the deck of the steamer, for I had parted with Oliphant only shortly before the battle of the Ingour took place.

We reached Batoum on the 30th of October, and were then on Turkish soil. We had visited Redoubt Kaleh; I forget now whether we called at Poti. These places are on the ground of the ancient Colchis, the scene of the story of the Golden Fleece. The Rion is supposed to be the ancient Phasis, from whose banks pheasants were first procured, and from which they were named. Batoum we found to be a very beautiful spot, and, for the Black Sea, a capital harbour. The only use the Turks seemed to make of it was as a receptacle for a few old and used-up vessels of war. Everything was dilapidated about the place, and yet it was a frontier harbour and town.

I went on shore in the afternoon to sketch, and met a curious-looking fellow with a most sinister face. Not quite that of a Mephistopheles—he wanted the brain for that, the expression was vile, wicked, and cruel. The costume was different from anything I had seen, and I managed to make him understand that I would like to sketch him. He appeared to be pleased at the proposal, and stood willingly. While I was sketching, the Duke and Lucca came on shore, and I asked Lucca to inquire of my model who he was. He was a Kurd, and had come down from the mountains on some business. On finding this the Duke began to take an interest in the fellow, so the conversation with him was continued. It was noticed that he had a gun, but no sword. On his attention being called to this he said he did not require a sword, it was not his way of doing it.

"Doing what?"

"Killing people."

"Who do you kill?"

"Travellers."

"How do you kill them?"

"I watch on the road, and when I see travellers coming, I hide behind a rock and shoot them as they pass."

"How many have you killed?"

"Thirteen, and five Russians."

He did not explain the reason why he made a distinction in the case of Russians. It may have been perhaps some patriotic sentiment. He was then asked what he was doing in Batoum?

To which he replied, "Some business."

"Where are you going when you leave this?"

"Back to the mountains, where, please God, I hope to shoot some more travellers."

While this was going on the brute was picking the skin off pieces of walnut and eating them with a pleased and satisfied smile on his countenance. The process of being sketched was soothing to his vanity, and hence the good nature that for the moment had touched his feelings. The sketches of him include one of his whole figure, then his face, full front, and a profile—which is that of a fiend. There is also a small sketch showing a back view of this human monster. Even this conveys an idea of a villain.

Trebizonde, which we reached on October 31st, is beautiful from its situation, as well as from the ruined walls and towers and old churches. There is an old St. Sophia here, an ancient Christian church, now a mosque.

I remember being struck, too, with the old and ruinous walls of Sinope, where we were on November 3rd. They had been built with fragments of former ruins. I noticed columns, fragments of marble, some of them friezes, others mouldings, showing that they had been the remains of temples or important buildings. The double harvest of decay struck me very forcibly. This was at one period the principal city on the Black Sea, or Pontus, as it was called.

From Sinope we sailed almost due north across the Black Sea to Balaklava, where we arrived on the 4th of November. This was a Sunday, and I have still a recollection of service on the deck of the *Highflyer*, which was very picturesque from the awning and flags. It was a bright, sunny day, and the sailors all turned out in their white summer clothes.

CHAPTER VIII

ARTIST AND PUBLISHER

FOLLOWING my experiences at the seat of war some account of the result has now to be told. At first the publishers announced one volume of forty plates. But the continuation of the war led to a second volume of the same size; and the whole work finally took the shape of two folio volumes, containing eighty plates, and dedicated by permission to the Queen. A small octavo edition of the letterpress was also published, in which the drawings were reduced to a size that would suit. The sketches I made after the taking of Sebastopol had all to be finished after my return. Most of these related to the fortifications, and I took them to Lieut. Cowell, R.E., who had come home. He looked over them all, comparing them with the plans of the place, and I corrected wherever he advised. From this I believe there is not an embrasure wrong in any of the pictures. Accuracy was a point I aimed at.

It was well enough known at the time that the publication had been a financial success. Except small wars at the Cape, in India, Burmah, or in China, there had been no great war since Waterloo. So, naturally, there had been a very strong interest in the Crimean War, and the interest was heightened by the miseries through which the soldiers had to pass in the winter. Owing to this the demand for the book had been great. It was also quite a new thing to have an artist at the seat of war depicting events as they took place. But it was not till about twenty years later that I learned what the publisher's success had really been. Mr. Mackay, who saw me on the morning when I was first asked if I would go to the Crimea, claimed the first suggestion of the idea, and on that account always took a great interest, not only in the work, but I may add at the same time in the artist. He had been at the trouble to look up all Colnaghi's business books, and work out the result, which he did, not only with my work, but also with all the other publications connected with the Russian War. According to the statement he made to me, they lost upon everything they published except my work, and the profit was still so large on it that, after allowing for all the other losses, the firm was still the gainer to the extent of £12,000. This left some unpaid debts, which would have made the total still higher. I think I was paid £20 for each drawing, but paid my own expenses of travelling, etc., etc. The publishers afterwards sold my drawings, and no doubt received as much as they gave me for them, so that they had the copyright for nothing. It was part of the arrangement that Day and Son were to have the lithographing and printing of the work. Some years afterwards William Day paid Colnaghi a sum, a kind of copyright fee, and they printed I think it was 2,000 copies of the work, and sold them by auction. How far this was a success to Day and Son I do not now remember.

Colnaghi exhibited the original drawings in Pall Mall, and sent them down to Manchester, Glasgow, and other places. One day when they were on view in Colnaghi's place in Pall Mall, Lord Elcho and some other member of Parliament chanced to come in, and one of them made the remark what a good thing it would have been for the nation to have had pictures of Marlborough's campaigns. This led to the suggestion that if the nation had no pictures of Marlborough's or Wellington's wars, here were pictures of the late war, and they would be equally valuable in the future as records. "Why should the nation not buy them?" The suggestion was accepted as a good one. Colnaghi's were consulted, and they consented to let the sketches go for a very low figure. This was rather less than they paid me, but the honour of such a finish to the whole scheme was tempting. They asked for letters vouching for the accuracy of the drawings from all the principal personages who had been in the Crimea—the Duke of Cambridge, Duke of Newcastle, Sir

Edmond Lyons, Sir John Burgoyne, etc.; these were printed in facsimile and circulated among the members of Parliament, and the thing was taken up so warmly, that we all thought it would be a certainty. If I mistake not, Sir Cornwall Lewis was Chancellor of the Exchequer, and he consulted Sir Charles Eastlake, who was at the time President of the Royal Academy. Colnaghi blamed Eastlake as the one who spoiled the whole affair. What the real reasons were I never learned; the avowed objection was that the pictures were "only water-colours," and were not permanent, and that they had been engraved. Lord Elcho stuck to his point, and brought the matter before the House. The price asked for the drawings, ninety in number, was only £1,400, but the Government did not accept the proposal.

I did a large drawing of the Retreat of the Russians across the bridge to the north side of the harbour on the night of the 8th of September. This was reproduced, and most probably would have been one of the set. The Duke of Newcastle bought the original for £60. After coming home and finishing the Crimean subjects, I did twenty or thirty pictures of Circassia for the Duke of Newcastle. The Duke invited me to visit him at Clumber, where I went and remained for a few days.

The success of the Crimean book placed me on a footing of great intimacy with the publishers, and a notice of them should be recorded. P. and D. Colnaghi, 13 and 14, Pall Mall East, was the title of the firm; the shop still exists with the old name, the first on the south side from Trafalgar Square. It was founded by Paul Colnaghi, an Italian who had been in Paris, and had come to London while the Revolution was going on. My impression is that he was in the print business in Paris, for he brought a stock of that kind with him to England, which made the first success of the establishment in London. It was only when the Crimean War showed our ignorance about Sebastopol and other places that the War Office started a Topographical Department. No such thing existed before, except in the Admiralty, which had a Hydrographic Department. This, of course, was for sailing charts, but in many cases hydrographic surveys included plans, &c., of forts. When the wars with Napoleon were going on in the early part of the century the Government had no knowledge, nor means of procuring it, about places which our soldiers had to besiege, so they could neither advise their generals nor form a correct judgment upon sieges or operations that were going on. Paul Colnaghi, it so chanced, had in his stock of engravings many pictures of places on the Continent. The authorities discovered this, and when a siege was contemplated they applied to Paul Colnaghi to ascertain if he had a print of the place. This brought the establishment into the notice of all the important official people, and made it one of the most flourishing businesses of the kind in town. It was frequented by all the upper ten thousand, who at that time collected prints. Paul was dead long before the date of the Crimean War, but I always heard him spoken of in terms of praise. There is an engraved portrait of him; the head is in an oval, a common feature of old engraved portraits. In this case Diogenes is represented outside of the oval, seeking with his lantern for an honest man. I believe he was a great favourite with all who knew him. His son Dominic, or "Old Dom" as he was called, was still in the business when I became acquainted with the firm. He would be perhaps about seventy years old. A little man, slightly bent, he had been brought up among prints, and it was said at his death—he was about ninety when he died—that a vast knowledge connected with old engravings and engravers went with him—a knowledge no one else could replace. He was consulted by all who collected prints, and often when I have been in the place I have found him with great people talking on such matters. One day I remember being told that it was the Duc d'Aumale, or Prince Loinville; at least it was one of the Orleans princes. They lived in England during the Second Empire. "Old Dom" had a room to himself, filled with portfolios and prints. There he was constantly arranging them, and he took little notice of the business beyond this. He was a most pleasant old gentleman, and had generally a good story to tell when I went in to see him. He was very deaf, and held his hand up to his ear when spoken to.

A characteristic story is told of the establishment which must be prefaced by the explanation that in such an old place the subordinates grow old as well as the principals. One day a "great swell" came in and addressed himself to the first individual he met. This was a man who had been long in the shop, and was old and deaf, and he raised the left hand to his ear to assist in hearing. The "swell" could not be bothered with that sort of thing, so he rushed past to another man. He when spoken to, raised the right hand to his ear. The impatience of the "swell" now excited him, and he demanded in loud tones to see Mr. Colnaghi. Some one led him into the sanctum of "Old Dom," and as he approached up went Mr. Colnaghi's left hand to his ear. The visitor, according to the tale, suddenly retreated, muttering denunciations, and was never more heard of. The title of "Old Dom" was the natural result of the existence of a "young Dom," an only son, who entered the consular service, and was in Constantinople during the war. He was for many years in Florence; I saw him at the opening ceremonies of the Mont Cenis Tunnel; and when the Queen went to Italy he was knighted, and became Sir Dominic.

Since John Scott's death his cousin, Andrew Mackay, has been the head of the establishment. Mackay's sister was wife to Dr. John Brown, of Edinburgh, author of "Rab and His Friends." While I write Mackay and his eldest son William are really "P. and D. Colnaghi," outwardly Italian, but inwardly Scottish. Knowing this, I was much amused, only about a year ago, when I discovered that the firm of Disderi & Co., photographers, near Hanover Square, apparently so purely Italian, was in truth a William Mossman—a Scotsman, with a broad Scot's tongue in his head.

On starting for the Crimean War my upper lip and chin were in the ordinary style of the period, but as my razors were intentionally left behind, I returned with a very long brown beard. It was so long that it could be buttoned up in my waistcoat. The beard movement had begun before the war. It was confined then to a very few, but the war completed the reform. Still, on my return to London, beards were not familiar to the people on the streets, and in some neighbourhoods young fellows on seeing me would call out, "Ma-a! ma-a!" imitating a goat. Others would call out "Door mats!" Among friends my common name was "Crimean Simpson," and, as a Crimean hero, I was introduced to strangers as "Mr. Simpson, from the Crimea." But Crimean heroes became so common after the war, that one day when I was introduced to a gentleman with the usual formula, he said, "Well, I am Mr. Smith, who has not been to the Crimea." These details about beards and Crimean heroes are now all but forgotten, but they are so intimately connected with the change of custom in shaving, that they are worth recording here. In my early days every man shaved, and any one with a beard was looked upon as a Jew or a foreigner. That fashion had existed for generations before me, and it might have existed still if the Crimean War had not taken place. Since then the War Office insists on two inches of the chin being shaved, and this military cut has led many to follow it. If it had not been for this I think that the natural growing beard would have been the fashion.

CHAPTER IX

ARTIST AND QUEEN

IT has been already mentioned that while I was in the Crimea the Queen sent me a commission for a picture. On the return of the troops to England, Her Majesty made a point of seeing almost, if not quite, every corps. That is, on its return each corps was paraded as soon after as possible, and the Queen, with Prince Albert and the children, attended the ceremony. When the artillery came home they were paraded at Woolwich, and I was commanded to attend and make a sketch of the event. This I did, and when the picture was sent in I received an order from Miss Skerritt to come to Buckingham Palace, as some alterations in the picture were necessary. No hint was given to me till I reached the palace why I was sent for. When Miss Skerritt came into the waiting-room she told me to remain there, as the Queen would see me herself. She was in the garden, and would be back in a little while. John Scott of Colnaghi's had come with me, and we were rather astonished.

In a few minutes Miss Skerritt returned, and led me to another room near the one I was in on the first floor. The Queen at that time lived in the north-east corner of the palace, the corner next to Sutherland House. The windows looked out on the gardens northward to the Green Park. The principal part of my costume was a big dark blue overcoat. At one of the windows I had just flattened out the drawing to be ready to have the corrections pointed out, when a door in the south-east corner opened, and the Queen entered. Her Majesty was very plainly dressed, and had a small white cap on her head. She came forward bowing and smiling, and stood at the window while the interview lasted. Miss Skerritt was on her left, while the artist stood on the right. The corrections were soon gone over; these were only a few details about the orders worn by some of the higher officers. The Queen then began to talk about Sebastopol, and one of the first things she said was to compliment me on going under fire. I learned afterwards that she had seen all the principal officers connected with the war. They had been invited to dine with her, and had to describe Sebastopol. In their descriptions my sketches had often been referred to, and the artist had been spoken of. I was rather astonished at the knowledge the Queen possessed about myself. She alluded to me having been made a prisoner by the French. It rather astonished me to discover that the Queen knew a story about me that had almost escaped my own mind. Her Majesty, I found, had acquired a very complete knowledge of Sebastopol. When I referred to any part of it she evidently knew the spot and its relative position to other parts of the town. This was more than any one I had found at home knew. Her Majesty seemed to take a great interest in everything connected with the Crimea, and particularly Sebastopol. The conversation lasted for about half an hour, when Her Majesty retired, and I rolled up the drawing and rejoined John Scott. The Queen was so easy and natural in her manner that I was not at any moment of the interview embarrassed in the least.

I did sketches of other corps coming home at that time, also of the laying of the foundation-stones of the hospital at Netley and the Wellington College, at which the Queen officiated. In these ceremonies my place was assigned near the Royal Family, and the children soon began to know me. This was the beginning of my acquaintance with the Princess Royal, afterwards Empress of Germany, and with the Prince of Wales, who was a boy at that date. Since then the Queen has often given me commissions to make drawings. Her Majesty had an album in which were placed drawings—not of the great events, marriages and the like—but of the lesser ceremonies. Many artists have been employed for these. Louis Haghe made some,

Sir John Gilbert, and others. The last I did was the christening of the third child of Princess Beatrice in St. George's Chapel, on June 29, 1889.

Miss Skerritt, a lady I had much correspondence with, and saw often at Buckingham Palace, is worthy of mention. She acted as the Queen's private secretary at that time. Her letters were scarcely readable, but she was a most methodical creature. The first time I saw her, her peculiar appearance struck me. Mrs. Noah, of the children's arks, was the first impression. It was the period when crinoline was the fashion, but Miss Skerritt evidently knew nothing of that peculiar costume. She wore a dark green dress, tight from hip to toe, and all round, as if she had just been produced from a turning lathe; a very small white collar, also turned in a lathe, and a small head with not much hair, also produced as suggested. She was about sixty years of age at the time, but did not look so old. With small, rapid steps she used to glide into the room, and without any waste of words begin direct upon business. The first occasion or so on which I saw her I naturally began with the usual common sentences, such as "How do you do?" "I hope you are well," or made a remark about the weather. But words of that kind might as well have been addressed to the blue paper on the wall of the room, and I soon ceased to utter any phrases of the kind. At first one felt rather snubbed, but by and by I began to like the lady, and from what I have heard from other artists who had to see her on business—I cannot conceive any one seeing Miss Skerritt on anything else but business—they all spoke favourably of her. She died in 1887, and her age was given then as ninety-seven. She retired in 1861 from the Queen's service, and lived with a sister.

Miss Skerritt was succeeded by the sister of Lord Elgin. I had little or no correspondence with her. She married Dean Stanley. Lord Elgin, who was Governor-General of India, died suddenly at Dharamsala in the Himalayas while travelling there. The news of his death came home just before his sister's marriage, and a message came to me from the Queen inquiring if I had a sketch of Dharamsala, and ordering me to make a picture of it. This the Queen gave to the Earl's sister as a wedding present. Sir Henry Ponsonby, who succeeded later to the post, had for years Edwards and Bigge as "assistant secretaries," and I often wonder how Miss Skerritt managed in former years to do the work single-handed. The duties may have increased since.

Towards the end of 1857 I began to be far from well. I noticed that many who had been ill in the Crimea were well on their return home; others who had been well all through the campaign suffered afterwards. I had luckily not had a day's illness while away, and it may be that I was now to have my turn. This may be the explanation, or it may have been the bother of two large pictures which I undertook—"The Defence of Kars" and "The Arctic Ship *Resolution*." These pictures were a considerable labour to me. At Kars General Williams and the officers with him had been taken prisoners, but released after the peace. It was suggested by the Colnaghi firm that I should paint a picture of this in oil. General Williams gave me a "sitting," as did his officers—Colonel Lake, Dr. Sandwith, and Captain Teesdale, now General Sir Christopher Teesdale. The latter and Churchill supplied me with details of the town of Kars, as they could sketch. I had not painted much in oil before, and found a picture of this size an arduous undertaking; but I managed to get it out of hand in a passable state. The subject of the other picture was one of our Arctic exploring vessels which had been abandoned and found by some Americans, who repaired and sent her home, manned by American officers and men. On her arrival in Portsmouth the Queen, being at Osborne, acknowledged the feeling of goodwill shown by the Americans, and visited the ship, being shown over by the officers. So I was started off to Portsmouth with a photographer to get particulars, etc. This was a larger picture than "Defence of Kars," and I worked at it in a spare studio at the artist Elmore's. It would be absurd to say either of these pictures was good, but they were engraved, and served their purpose at the time. Elmore was a splendid fellow, and we became great friends.

He caused me to be elected a member of the Garrick Club, David Roberts being one of my seconders, and Russell of the *Times* another.

When my health broke down John Scott insisted on taking me to Dr. Darling, who lived in Russell Square, and who, Scott said, had "brought him into the world, and kept him in it ever since." Dr. Darling ordered me cod-liver oil and tincture of steel—a prescription which evidently meant that I was weak and wanted strength. To this he added, "Get out of London, and keep out of it for a while." So in the autumn of 1857 I started for Scotland. Mr. Allan had a house at Kilmun on the Holy Loch, and he invited me there. As he had taken the house by the year, and as I did not wish to return to London, we arranged that I should live at Kilmun all the winter. I remained there till the spring of 1859. A sketching tent was procured from London, and I painted from nature in the summer. I had also my lay figure sent down, and, in spite of prophecies to the contrary, I spent the winter very pleasantly and happily.

In the early spring of 1859 I left Kilmun. I should have willingly enough remained, for I liked the place. My love for it increased with my stay. My first love in art was a Highland mountain. This affection had begun in my early rambles in the Highlands, before I went to London, and I should have been content to live among these hills and paint them. But the Crimea had opened up a new path for me, and I wished to go on again in work of that kind. My experience in the East had given me a longing to see more of it. In 1859 the war between France and Austria had begun in Italy, and my immediate object was to try and see the operations of this campaign.

CHAPTER X

INDIA AFTER THE MUTINY

ON coming to town I consulted with John Scott, of Colnaghi's, as to the feasibility of making a book of the Italian campaign. He was willing to take up the enterprise, and made some application to the Queen, but the idea was not at all received with favour. So far as I recollect, the Queen was afraid that I would be looked upon as a spy sent by our Government. The objection was not expressed exactly in this form, but this was our conclusion. It was enough, and the scheme was abandoned.

The great Mutiny in India had begun in May, 1857. The fighting which resulted continued for more than a year, and in 1859 this contest was only completed. Naturally such a momentous event had led to considerable attention being directed to India. The public were interested in the cause of the Mutiny, and in everything connected with the people of India. More interest had been excited in England about that country than had ever existed before. Mr. William Day and I talked all this over, and finally it was determined that I should go out with the purpose of making drawings for a large and important work that should do justice to such a subject. It was determined that we should take as a model for size the large work of Daniel Roberts on the Holy Land and Egypt. This had two hundred and fifty plates, and was published in four volumes, folio. But owing to the progress of lithography it was determined that the new work should be in colour, and that the pictures should be more or less reproductions of the originals. Roberts' work cost forty guineas, and that was the price proposed for the new undertaking. The Queen gave permission that the book be dedicated to her. This was unusual, the rule being that no work received this favour until it was published, and the giving of it on the first projection of the publication was a peculiar mark of confidence. Mr. Day suggested that Mr. William Walker, brother to Edmond Walker the artist, who was employed in the office, should go out with me to get subscribers for the work in India. As a sailor he had been in Calcutta before, and was supposed to know something of the country.

As summer was a bad time to reach India it was arranged that we should go with a sailing-ship round the Cape. The Suez Canal had not then come into existence. So passages were secured on board one of Richard Green's vessels, luckily a new one, called the *Newcastle*. In the meantime I looked out for letters of introduction, of which I managed to procure a large number, including one from the Duke of Newcastle to Lord Canning, the Governor-General. The term Viceroy had not then come into use. I also spent a considerable time in the library of the India House, then in Leadenhall Street, looking over books about India, such as Daniels', to see what had been already done, and to get hints as to places I ought to visit. I found afterwards that this time was well employed. As I counted on being able to sketch in the plains in the winter only, I guessed that my trip must last two if not three years. The last guess turned out to be the nearer, for I was away from England three years all but about four months. The travelling over long distances was what took time.

Mr. Walker and I landed at Calcutta on the 29th of October, 1859. We went to Spence's Hotel. I at once began work and made drawings of Calcutta. The site being flat, it is difficult to get an effective general view. This I managed by getting up to the maintop of the ship *Newcastle* as she lay in the harbour, and I obtained such satisfactory details, that I had to make a copy of this picture after my return for the Queen. Calcutta derives its name from Kali Ghat, a sacred temple on the river Hoogly. I went one day to see this celebrated shrine. Kali is one of the terrible forms of the consort of Siva, a

Hindu goddess. Kids are brought in front of the temple, where there is a forked piece of wood; the animal being fixed in this, the head is severed by a blow with a knife. It is said in former times human beings were sacrificed here.

Lord Canning, the Governor-General, had gone up-country, and with Lord Clyde, who was then commander-in-chief, was holding durbars on the ground where the struggle of the Mutiny had taken place. It was a sort of triumphal march to indicate the power of the conqueror; and the rajahs who had been faithful were received and rewarded by presents, grants, and honours, according to their rank and services. On this account I could not present my letters of introduction personally to Lord Canning. I found Colonel Mackenzie, however, an old Balaklava friend, in the Quarter-Master-General's Department, and he advised me to send my letters, and offered to enclose them when he was sending to Headquarters. I acted on this advice, and the result was a telegram requesting me to come and join the Governor-General's camp. This caused me to separate from Mr. Walker, who remained in Calcutta, and afterwards returned home.

The railway system of India had already been begun. There were parts in working order, and I had the train from Calcutta to Ranigunje, about 120 miles, as a first start. Before leaving Calcutta, I engaged a dak all the way to Delhi, and at Ranigunje I began my first experience of this mode of travelling. It was evening when I started. One sleeps in the gharry, or carriage. This is a roughly-constructed cab like our "four-wheeler," but the well for legs and feet is boarded over, bedding is spread out, and the traveller lies on this instead of sitting, so that it makes a bed, and one can sleep soundly. There are chokis, or stations, every six or seven miles, where the horses are changed. The first morning I wakened up at a place called Topechancee, where there was a dak bungalow, or post-house.

My constant travelling while in India brought me so often to these places of accommodation, that they ought to be described. *Dak* means "post," and *bungalow* means a building of not more than one storey. The Post Office of India has charge of the dak bungalows, and an inspector is sent round at stated intervals to report and receive any money the traffic may have produced. There is a native khansaman, a Mohammedan, in charge of each, who attends upon travellers and supplies food. Some travellers take a number of articles with them, and before I left Calcutta I had numerous suggestions about "your own tea," butter, preserved meats, etc., etc., from friends. The resources of a dak bungalow are limited, for meat will not keep in India, and unless the bungalow is in a town the only provisions to be expected are fowls and eggs. After I had learned a little of the language the following conversation would take place between me and the khansaman. My gharry would drive up to the front of the bungalow, and the khansaman would come rushing from his quarters, doing his best, as he ran, to fix on an outer garment in which to appear before me. I jump out of the gharry dusty and hungry. The khansaman salaams, saluting me with a high-sounding name. India is the region for high titles; any one wishing for honour of that kind can procure it at a cheap rate there, and nowhere better than in a dak bungalow. In ordering my breakfast, I have often been called "Huzoor," "Khodawand," and "Gharibpoorwa," this last meaning "Protector of the Poor," and the two first something equivalent to "Lord" or "Highness." I express to the khansaman, who is standing with his hands raised before him, the palms of both together, that I wish to have some breakfast. He answers, "Yes, your Highness." "What can I have?" "Whatever my Lord wishes." Knowing that fowls and eggs are all it is possible for him to produce, except tea, milk, and bread, you say, "Well, I will take a beefsteak." The closed palms go up and he says, "Your Highness, there are no beef-estiks." This spelling represents a peculiarity the natives have of pronouncing some words beginning with an *s*. "Well, give me a mutton chop, then?" "Oh, Protector of the Poor, there are no mutton chops." Other things may be asked for, but you know that the grilled "murghi" or fowl will be your breakfast. The fowl under these circumstances is known as a "Sudden Death." As soon as the khansaman leaves you a cackling is heard, and sounds of rushing about come on the ear. The catching of the victim is often the most serious part of the process. When the bird is caught a knife severs the head, the Mohammedan's rule of letting an animal for food bleed to death being thus followed. By putting the fowl into hot water the feathers are easily removed, and it is thus at once in order for cooking. So quickly is this all performed, that by the time the traveller has had his bath and has dressed, the "Sudden Death" is on the table ready for eating. These fowls are generally very small things, not so much as a good chop in them, and a hungry man can easily dispose of one, and can add an egg or two afterwards. Of course, when the dak bungalow is in a town, steaks and chops, as well as other articles of diet, can be supplied. After breakfast the khansaman produces the bungalow book, where each occupier of the bungalow has to write his name, and the sum he pays. For a breakfast and bath, which take about an hour, the sum is 8 annas or one shilling. If he stays longer, it is 1 rupee, which would cover a twenty-four hours' occupation. The book has a column for critical remarks as to the attention on the part of the khansaman. This is for the guidance of the inspector when he comes round. The price of the breakfast, or dinner, is settled with the khansaman, and is a separate matter from the occupation of the bungalow. There are charpoys, in other words, bedsteads in the bungalow, and as travellers bring their own bedding, the night may be passed in one of these, and the room may be occupied for any length of time, if no other traveller requires it. Now that railways have been extended over India there are hotels in all the large towns, and I expect that the bungalows along the principal roads must now be almost deserted, and that the crowds who visit India every cold season can have but small chance of the experiences I had thirty years ago.

Before Lord Dalhousie's reign as Governor-General it might almost be affirmed that there were no made roads in India. That which was called a road was only the track made by the feet of men and animals that had passed over it. The Grand Trunk road from Calcutta to the North-West was begun in Lord Dalhousie's time, and a very fine road it is. It was formed of kunkur, a kind of limestone, that was beaten down in a wet state, and when dry formed a road as smooth as one of asphalte. An officer was brought from the Madras Presidency to introduce the method of making roads, and at the time it was said he was like Cæsar, "He came, he saw, and he kunker'd." It certainly made a beautiful road, and at the time of my visit to India the great trunk line had been completed all the way to Lahore, and was in the course of making beyond, through the Punjab. It was ultimately finished to Peshawur. In our days transitions come quickly, even in India. Before this road was carried out the railway system was begun, and the grand kunkur road was to a certain extent superseded.

I reached Delhi on the 29th. The Governor-General's camp had arrived that morning, and was on the ground between the ridge and the town. I went off to it and found Sir Edward Campbell, who introduced me to Lord Canning. I slept that night in the dak bungalow, and here I may mention that I had started from Calcutta with a very imperfect outfit. One important detail, bedding, had been entirely overlooked. Every one of my advisers seemed to have assumed that I would have my bedding, but, being a "griff," I had no idea that this was more necessary in India than it would be in Europe. In Delhi at Christmas the nights are very cold, and a fire in the evening and morning is desirable. That night in the dak bungalow I had the usual charpoy, or bedstead, on which I lay with my clothes on, and a carpet bag for my pillow; and I still remember it as a most uncomfortable night. Next morning I started to find Major Fane, better known as "Walter Fane," who was quartered at Delhi, and he kindly invited me to come and put up with him. He was well known over the whole of the North-West for his ability as an artist. I have often said that he ought to have been an artist—Nature had meant him for that, and in saying so I meant no disrespect to his qualifications as a soldier.

Through him or his servants a man was found for me who was willing to travel about and do all that I required. On this account he had to be a Mussulman, as a Hindu would not touch meat or a plate on which meat was placed. His name was Jungly Khan, and he turned out to be a capital servant, remaining with me all the time I was in India. He procured bedding for me. This part of one's travelling luggage in India consists of two rezais. These are made of two pieces of cotton cloth, with about an inch and a half of cotton between, and stitched all over to keep the cotton in its place. One is below and the other above you when in bed. Chuddars, or sheets, with pillows, complete the outfit, and as charpoys, or bedsteads, are plentiful, you can make your bed anywhere and lie on it. The custom recalls Scripture, for you literally lift your bed and walk.

Fane lived in a native house. It was in the middle of the town, in a street called, if I remember right, the Lal Kooa. Delhi had been depopulated by the siege, and but a small portion of the population had come back. Many had been killed, and their houses were unclaimed. Fane belonged to the 4th Sikh Cavalry. I think he commanded the regiment at the time, and he was under orders to take his corps to China, where a war had begun. Probyn, who was then a captain—he is now Lieutenant-General Sir Dighton Macnaughten Probyn, K.C.B., V.C., and Comptroller of the Prince of Wales's household—was under the same orders with his regiment, and he came on a visit to Fane to consult about details. These two regiments, whose outfit I heard discussed in the evenings, became famous during the Chinese War as "Fane's" and "Probyn's" Horse. Probyn's Horse is now the 11th Bengal Cavalry, of which the Prince of Wales is Colonel. After dinner in the mess-room Fane at times made very clever and amusing sketches on the walls of "Fane's Horse Going to China." He retired at last with the rank of General, and died about 1883 or 1884. Sir Peter Lumsden told me he had twelve doctors to see him, and none of them could say what the disease was. He belonged to the Westmorland family, and was cousin to Lord Burghersh, already mentioned in this book as A.D.C. to Lord Raglan in the Crimea.

On the 2nd of January I received an invitation to dine with Lord and Lady Canning. The Governor-General was going to Lahore, and from there to Peshawur and Umballa, where the first tamasha, or important ceremony, would take place, and it was suggested I should remain until the camp reached that place. Delhi was in disgrace on account of the mutiny and siege, so no important ceremonies took place there. The Rajah of Bhurtpore alone was received one day.

I left Delhi on the 14th of January, and reached the Governor-General's camp on the evening of the next day at Shakabad, one march out of Umballa, where Lord Canning was to be met by the Cis-Sutlej chiefs.

It was the first experience I had had of a turn-out of the kind. An elephant had been set apart for me, and as I had so little practice of the language the Rev. Mr. Walters, chaplain of the camp, accompanied me, and directed the mahout in what direction we wished to go. The person on the elephant tells the mahout, who sits outside on the beast's neck, and the mahout, by means of a peculiar language composed of grunts and Hindostani, combined with punches from his heels, conveys the necessary directions to the elephant.

The principal native swells were the Rajahs, or rather the Maharajahs of Patiala, Jheend, and Nabha, whose territories are south of the Sutlej. These, with a host of smaller chiefs, were all waiting outside Umballa to receive the Governor-General. The Rajahs wore their most gorgeous array—khin-khob, or cloth of gold, and jewels in profusion—and each was attended by a numerous sowarie — mounted attendants, elephants, etc., etc.

A day or so afterwards a Durbar was held, at which these chiefs were received. As I cannot recall having met with a description of a Durbar, I will give an account of that at Umballa. The rajahs and chiefs who possess territory belong in the Indian Government to what is called the Foreign Office, of which Mr. Cecil Beadon was then the chief. This department has a list of all these rajahs, with the rank they hold. This means that in a ceremonial such as a Durbar they are entitled to so many guns of a salute, and to present so many gold mohurs, or coins, as their "nuzzars." It also decides their position or seat in the Durbar. The question of guns as the outward mark of rank is a most serious one among these native rulers. The Jheend Rajah had behaved, according to Government ideas, particularly well during the Mutiny, and he, as a reward, had a couple of guns added to his salute. This placed him above the Nabha Rajah, who had not shone so conspicuously during the time of trouble; and as no guns had been added to his salute he was reported as being in a very bad state. Bulletins of his condition were reported in camp. On the contrary, Jheend wallah was radiant with joy. Rank receives another outward mark of attention. When an important rajah is coming to a Durbar a sowarie is sent to meet him by the Governor-General. A rajah would do the same to another rajah coming to a Durbar, for it must be understood that the Governor-General's Durbar is modelled on the native ones. A sowarie includes elephants, in their best get-up of paint and gold trappings. If a rajah is of sufficient rank the Foreign Secretary goes on an elephant, with other officers and attendants, as far as the rajah's camp, and accompanies him all the way to the Durbar tent in the Governor-General's camp. To one of lesser position he only goes half way. To one smaller still he only advances to the outside of the Governor-General's camp. Some would be met in the camp. Some, again, would only be met by the Under-Secretary. In all this there is a scale of observance that has to be rigidly adhered to. On the rajahs' arrival at the Durbar tent their salutes are fired. With such a ceremonial it takes some time to get a number of chiefs into a Durbar. In this case there were about a hundred, but the great mass of them came in with none, or but few, of the attentions I have described. Most of them left their shoes at the door of the tent. The natives were ranged on the right hand of the Governor-General's chair, while the British officers were on the left, Lord

Clyde, as Commander-in-Chief, having his seat next to Lord Canning.

It is only when every one is in his place that the Governor-General enters the Durbar with his suite. While he does so, a royal salute is fired, and the band plays the Royal Anthem. On his appearing every one rises and remains standing till he takes his seat on the throne.

The proper business of the Durbar now begins. The Foreign Secretary first leads up the rajah, or chief, of the highest rank, in front of the Governor-General. The chief there makes a salaam, and holds out in his right hand his nuzzar. This is so many gold coins, the number being determined by his rank. The Governor-General merely touches them with his right hand, and then the tosh-khana wallah receives the money. This part of the ceremonial means that the inferior acknowledges the superior power. It may also be described as an act of homage by a feudatory. A soldier in Durbar offers the handle of his sword. I am not sure whether he offers money at the same time. The handle of the sword is touched in the same way as the nuzzar. This implies military service as due from the inferior to the superior. After all have been presented, each one receives his khillut. The khillut may be described as a dress of honour given by the superior to the inferior. The inferior having acknowledged his fealty, the superior accepts the fealty, and in return clothes him with honour. There is something like this in the account of Pharaoh clothing Joseph with a robe of honour; and perhaps the pallium is a survival of the same. In India the khillut, like the nuzzar, is determined by the rank of the recipient, and this is expressed by the number of "trays" each one receives,—each tray contains what may be looked upon as a dress, or part of a dress. I remember that when the trays with the Patiala wallah's khillut were brought in, they covered the central part of the tent from Lord Canning's seat to the door. If I mistake not, a rajah of his rank would be entitled to something like 200 trays. Perhaps they were not all brought in to the Durbar. The first tray might contain jewellery, such as an ornament to be worn on the head or arm, or a necklace. The trays following that would contain Kashmir shawls and khin-khob—cloth of gold. If I recollect aright, cloth of some kind was in each tray. In some of the last trays at a Durbar I remember seeing pieces of common muslin, the value of which could scarcely have been one shilling. The green and gold ticket on the muslin, such as I used to design in my early days, told me that the fabric had come from Manchester or Glasgow. It ought to be explained here that there is a department in the Government called the "Toshkhana," and every rajah has a toshkhana. This is the place—"khana," the last syllable of the word means house—where articles for presents, khilluts, etc., etc., are stored. With the Indian Government, this is, on account of the Durbars, and presents that have to be made, a large and important department. When the Governor-General goes on a series of visits, such as Lord Canning was making, the toshkhana requires a large staff of people. They bring in the trays, under the superintendence of the chief, and a note of everything, with its value, has to be kept. A large quantity of articles have to be carried with the camp, implying a considerable amount of transport. This, at the time I am describing, would be by bullock carts, for the railway had not then broken up the old system.

The khillut having been displayed as described, the rajah or chief receiving it is again led up by the Foreign Secretary before the Governor-General, and if there is a piece of jewellery, which is always the case with rajahs, the Governor-General ties it on the head or arm of the recipient, who then retires to his seat salaaming. The trays are then removed, and the trays of the person next in rank are brought in. This is repeated with every one who has been received in Durbar. It is only to two or three of the principal rajahs that a jewel is given by the Governor-General. Many of the lesser ones at the end of the Durbar are so low in rank that they are only entitled to one tray or so, and they act as their own khana wallahs, taking the piece of cloth under their arm, and carrying it back to their seat with them.

At the end, after each has received his khillut, the

Governor-General leaves with his suite the Durbar tent, every one present rising and remaining standing till he has disappeared, when each one leaves.

At the Umballa Durbar, as well as at others I saw, the Governor-General delivered a speech to those present. He spoke in English, and his speech was translated into Persian by the Foreign Secretary. In these speeches Lord Canning declared the future policy of the Government. The leading point of this related to succession. It had often been the case that when a rajah had no son to succeed him, the Government refused to acknowledge the adopted son, and this led to the territory of the rajah falling into the hands of the Government. This had become so notorious, and rajahs were so frightened about the future of their states, that it was thought it would strengthen the power of the Government if it was declared that adopted sons would be looked on as if they were real sons. It was at the same time a declaration that the red colour on the map of India would remain as it was. The meaning of the policy was that it would remove all fear from the minds of native rulers, and thus attach them to the interests of the Government of Calcutta. The safety of the rajahs being thus secured, it would be their interests to support the Government as their protector.

To rajahs of a certain rank the Governor-General made return visits. At Umballa he did so to the Patiala, Jheend, and Nabha wallahs. I accompanied these visits. They took place in the Durbar tents of the rajahs, where the Governor-General sat in the central seat—what I suppose would be the rajah's seat in Durbar. On one of the days during our stay at Umballa Mr. Beadon sent word to the principal rajahs that I would call and make sketches of them. I managed to call on Patiala and Jheend. A day or so before I had a curious adventure in the Nabha Rajah's camp. I had gone by myself for a walk, and took the direction of the native camps so as to pick up knowledge, and make notes in my sketch-book. At one place where I stopped to sketch some one invited me inside, and it turned out to be one of the Nabha Rajah's tents, and he himself came in. I rather think I had been recognised as belonging to the Governor-General's suite, and I learned afterwards that as I was with the camp of Lord Canning I was looked upon as his artist. On leaving I was asked to wait a little, and one of the attendants came in with a Kashmir shawl, which was offered to me. I stared, and would not hold out my hand to take it. I felt that I should be a sort of beggar to accept a present under the circumstances. I had done nothing to entitle me in the least to any gift. Seeing I refused the shawl, I was asked—some one I think spoke a little English—if I would prefer to have the price of it. This to my mind was worse in form than the shawl. On returning to camp, and recounting the adventure, I was told that my peculiar feelings would not be understood or appreciated by a native, and that I ought to have taken the shawl.

The camp of the Governor-General was a large town in itself. Lord Clyde, the Commander-in-Chief, had his camp going along with that of the Governor-General, and I was told there were about 20,000 persons altogether in the two camps. There were native as well as European regiments, and a battery of artillery, which is necessary to fire salutes. There were Government Offices, with all their secretaries, clerks, etc. The Commander-in-Chief had his Quarter-master-General and Adjutant-General—what in England might be described as the whole of the Horse Guards establishment. There were elephants, camels, and bullock carts, with their attendants, to move this large city of canvas. The Governor-General's great Durbar tent was so large, that the roof-part of it, which was all in one piece, required a very strong elephant to carry it, and if a shower of rain came on, from the extra weight of the water, the elephant could not carry it, and a day's halt had to be made till it dried. The Governor-General's tents and the Durbar tent were enclosed within a wall of canvas, in front of which was a pole, or mast, with the British flag on it. This was pitched at the head of a street of tents in which the principal officers were accommodated. Where the camping-ground permitted, the Commander-in-Chief's camp was placed in a line with the Governor-General's—Lord Clyde's tents formed the other end of the long line or street of tents. This part of the camp, with the exception of the Durbar tent, was double. That is, there were two sets of tents; one set was in advance, and put up the day before, so that when we left our tents in the morning, and got over the march, we arrived at what seemed to be the very camp we had left. Our baggage only was wanting. But that came up before we had finished breakfast. As I was the Governor-General's guest I messed with his suite. Lord and Lady Canning breakfasted in their own tents. Sir Edward and Lady Campbell did the same. Mr. L. Bowring, the Private Secretary, the A.D.C.'s, and Dr. Anthony Beale, breakfasted in the big tent. The other officers—Mr. Cecil Beadon, Mr. Charles Aitchison, Colonel Yule, who was then head of the Public Works Department, and the Chaplain, Mr. Walters, had a mess of their own. Captain Roberts, V.C., who has since become Lord Roberts, was Quartermaster. He had his wife with him, but he was generally a day in advance at the next camping ground, so we saw little of him. The camping grounds are generally about ten or twelve miles apart, and that would be the distance of each day's march. I had a fine large comfortable tent, about 12 feet square, in the main street of the camp, with a bedstead, table, chairs, and every necessary article. From Umballa I travelled with the camp as far as Lahore.

Life in the Governor-General's camp in India, with all its grandeur, was an experience worth recording, and naturally interested me in many ways. I found myself thrown among people I had never met before, and luckily found most of them to be of a good type. Lady Canning herself was devoted to art, having been a pupil of W. L. Leitch. She had no family, and to her the march of the camps was principally a sketching tour. She was a daughter of Lord Stuart de Rothesay, and she and her sister, Lady Waterford, had been Court beauties in the early days of the Queen's reign, and had appeared in "Books of Beauty" as "The Sisters." Lady Waterford, who is still living while I write—June, 1892—was also devoted to art, and had much greater power with her pencil than Lady Canning, and some of her pictures are on exhibition in London this season. Lady Waterford, to judge from works Lady Canning showed me, was a real artist, while Lady Canning would rank as a very clever amateur. In the morning after reaching camp, I generally took a walk to see if there was anything worth sketching, and reported it to Lady Canning, who went out almost every evening to sketch. She had a very large and docile elephant, and could sketch sitting in the howdah. In the evening after dinner I had to show any sketches I had made; Lady Canning produced hers; and any of the officers of the suite who had done anything also produced their work. On account of Lady Canning's interest in art, all who could use the pencil tried their hand, and from this it appeared at times as if the camp was merely a gigantic sketching excursion.

When we came to what is known in India as a "station," that is, a town where there was a civil and military establishment, we had all the principal people to dinner. We had a number of these big entertainments at Umballa. A grand dinner of sixty or seventy people in a tent made a wonderful scene, particularly when all the details were considered. Such dinners took place in the Durbar tent. Attached to this was a smaller, but still a large tent, which did duty as a drawing-room. Here the guests were received. The A.D.C.'s were in attendance in full uniform. They brought in the ladies, and presented them to Lord and Lady Canning. They also told each gentleman what lady he was to escort into dinner, this being a most important part of the ceremony owing to the rank of each person, which has to be carefully attended to in India. Lord Canning had to take in the Burra Beebee, or great lady of the station. Lord Clyde was always at these grand feasts, and he took in Lady Canning. At dinner parties in India the table servants, khitmagars, of the guests, attend their own masters and mistresses; but a dinner at the Governor-General's is an exception to this rule. A servant is provided for each guest, and as they are all in red, the colour of the Royal livery, and gold, they give a unity and richness to the tone of the picture. The military were all in full uniform, officers of native corps in various gorgeous colours. I remember an officer of 1st Bengal Cavalry—"Skinners' Horse," "The Yellow Boys"—with his bright yellow coat, sitting beside me one evening, and how I was afraid lest the servants should drop soup, or some of the dishes, on it, and spoil the beauty of the rich colour. Orders of course were worn on such occasions by all who had them. A band played outside during dinner. The ground was thickly carpeted, and the interior lining of the tent was a dull, deep yellow. The effect of the whole was therefore rich and brilliant. After dinner, conversation went on in the drawing-room tent, and at last the A.D.C.'s began to take the ladies to their carriages. During the night the Durbar tent was taken down, and moved on to the next camping ground, where we found it next morning, with breakfast ready in it. While we breakfasted the whole city of canvas would disappear from the spot it occupied on the night before, vanishing like a phantom city in an Oriental story. The carpeted ground on which lords, ladies, knights, and soldiers of renown had walked, would be a dreary, dusty maidan, or plain, with the pariah dogs sniffing about to discover if even a bone had been left.

The railways are changing everything in India, and the Viceroy now can go anywhere by that mode of conveyance, and does not require a camp when he travels, so such camps are already almost a thing of the past. My description is but a small part of what might be recorded, but it is enough in itself to convey some idea of the life I was thrown among for at least a couple of months in the cold season of 1860—January, February, and March.

One evening shortly after joining the camp I had an interesting reconnoitre with Lord Clyde. He was one of our dinner-party, and he came on these occasions, although in full dress otherwise, with only a forage cap. His custom was to take off his sword, and put it in a corner of the drawing-room tent along with the cap. I chanced to be standing chatting with a friend at the corner where the sword and cap lay when Lord Clyde was about to leave, and he came over to find his belongings. While he was buckling on his sword, I thought it would be an act of courtesy to such a great man to lift the cap and present it to him, which I did. This, however, he almost resented as a reflection on his years, for he said, "I am not so old yet that I cannot bend down to get my cap." I at once said something to explain that that was not the consideration under which I had acted. He then said, "You are a great swell, living here with the Governor-General. I am afraid to ask you to come and have a share of an old soldier's rations." To this I naturally replied I should be delighted to go, asking at the same time when I should come. He asked if the next evening would suit me, to which I answered "Yes," and added the inquiry, "When are the rations served out?" This question turned out to be a poser. He put his fingers through his ample crop of hair. That hair never seemed to have been combed or brushed. I noticed about a twelvemonth afterwards that Sir Hugh Ross, afterwards Lord Strathnairn, who succeeded Lord Clyde as Commander-in-chief, had also hair that appeared to know nothing of brush and comb, and I wondered if Commanders-in-Chief in India were in any way prohibited from possessing such articles. But to return to Lord Clyde. Putting his fingers through his hair did not help to solve the question. At last he called out "Alison!" This was his A.D.C., and a son of Sir Archibald Alison, a name that used to be well known in Glasgow.* Alison came, and the question of the dinner hour was answered by him.

At Lahore there was a very grand Durbar. About three hundred Sikh sirdars, or headmen, were received by the Governor-General. There were no great rajahs in the Punjab, but numbers made up for greatness. The sirdars were all gathered on horseback on the maidan outside the fort, with Mr. Temple, the Commissioner, in charge of them. They were got up in their finest costumes, in which all the colours were bright, particularly the blues and the yellows. When Mr. Temple, on the approach of the Governor-

* [Sir Archibald was Sheriff of Lancashire, and remains famous in the world of letters as author of "The History of Europe." His son has since achieved fame and knighthood as a military leader.]

General, waved his hat, and led them forward, it looked like a garden of flowers in motion. At the door of the Durbar tent I saw the shoes of those within, and the heap looked as if a cartload had been tipped at the spot. After dinner we all started on elephants to see the tamasha, or fête. Fireworks were let off as we approached. This frightened the elephants, so that the mahouts lost command of them. At one burst two or three elephants at once made for the gateway of the serai, with the result that the ladders for mounting, which hang on the side of the elephants, were broken to pieces in the crush, like lucifer matches. At the Hazuri Bagh there were more fireworks. Again the elephants were in a panic, and as my own brute rushed through the garden my head just escaped, by ducking down, from contact with the large branch of a tree. Officers said they would rather have gone through a day's fighting in a general action, and Lord Clyde declared that nothing less than the Victoria Cross would satisfy him for the dangers he had passed through.

We remained a week at Lahore. Arrangements for going to Peshawur had to be made, for the camp was to be left behind. I was one of the privileged few allowed to go with the party, and my conveyance was a mail cart. Before reaching the Jhelum the road came to a slight rising ground, which seemed to me to end the long plain of India. From Benares I could recall nothing but the Ridge of Delhi which had broken the flat surface. We crossed the Jhelum, the Hydaspes of the Greeks, on a bridge of boats. Alexander is said to have crossed at or near the same place to his battle with Porus. The march of this day brought me to the Manikyala Stupa, known at that time as the Tomb of Bucephalus, the horse of Alexander, which died and was buried near the Jhelum. I sketched the monument, and made notes of its details. I had been such a short time in India that I had acquired almost no knowledge of Hindu or Buddhist architecture, and I was perfectly unconscious of any question as to Greek architecture having reached the Punjab. In my diary, however, written at that time I mention that the mouldings "seemed almost pure Greek."

THE RAJAH'S ARTIST

At Peshawur I made the acquaintance of Captain Speedy. He had the gift of picking up languages, and could speak Pucktoo, the language of the Afghans nearest Peshawur. He went with me to the bazaar, and by his speaking powers got all sorts of fellows to stand to be sketched, Peshawur being a place with a wonderful variety of races and types from India, the Himalayas, Tibet, Afghanistan, and all parts of Central Asia. There was a Durbar here which the wild frontier chiefs attended, and a "burra tamasha" one evening with illuminations and fireworks.

The Governor-General and Lord Clyde went out to Jamrud, at the mouth of the Khyber Pass. Speedy arranged to take me on another day. For this purpose permission had to be got from the officer in command of the station. With this was given an order for a cavalry escort. Robbery or murder by some of the wild men of the Khyber had to be guarded against. I still recollect Speedy, as he came to my room to wake me. He was "armed to the teeth"—covered with weapons. I asked if I would have to go with as much stuff upon me. He said, "No, but it was as well to be prepared." All this suggested that the Khyber was not one of the safest of spots.

The Governor-General's visit to Sealkot was made to meet the Maharajah of Kashmir, who was received in Durbar. Next day the Governor-General made the return visit. I went to this and made sketches, and here a little incident occurred which illustrates the position of art and artists in India. As I wanted a sketch of the Maharajah and his son, I asked Mr. Beadon to request the Maharajah to sit to me after the visit was over. While I sketched, the Maharajah explained that he had his own artist in the Durbar tent endeavouring to get the Lord Sahib's portrait. The artist was in a curious position, he was in fact concealed. The Rajah asked if the man might be allowed to appear, so as to make his sketch under better circumstances. The request was of course granted, and the artist made his appearance by crawling out from under a kind of sofa, which had been placed as nearly opposite Lord Canning's seat as was possible under the circumstances.

To see this man squeezing himself out was like a scene in a farce, and produced something like laughter, which is scarcely appropriate in a Durbar. After the Durbar, I sketched a few of the Rajah's people. Some of them were in chain armour, and one was a Ladaki.

The Kashmir wallah pays every year to the Queen a tribute of two shawls, and, I think, two goats. The Maharajah took advantage of this return visit to present the Queen's shawls. I presume they were two of the best. I could see that they were woven, and long shawls, which, as I learned afterwards on my visit to Kashmir, are the most expensive. Shawls were afterwards presented to each of us, but all in the public service have to hand over their shawls to the Toshkhanah. I, not being in the service, could keep mine. From this I was able to say that the Queen and myself were the only two persons who could keep our shawls.

From Sealkot the camp was to travel by Kangra towards Simla. As I had not had time while in Lahore and Umritser, to do all the sketching I desired, I parted from the camp, and returned *viâ* Wazzeerabad to Lahore. Here I remained about ten days, and sketched all the principal buildings, including Jehangir's Tomb on the Ranee. Jehangir was the hero of Moore's "Lalla Rookh." Noor Mahal's tomb is at the same place.

From Umritzer I moved by dak gharry to Umballa, and thence by mail cart to Kalka, and by jampan, a kind of sedan chair, to Simla. I put up at the Simla Club, then a hotel. I bought a horse, and on my first ride one morning met Lord Clyde and Colonel Metcalf coming into Simla. The Governor-General and suite also arrived about the same time. Lord Canning and Lord Clyde only stayed about a month in Simla, when they had to leave for Calcutta. Simla had not at that time become the established headquarters of the Government as it is now.

When the club filled with men on leave from the plains there were often discussions on the character of the natives. These controversies arose from the manner in which the "Royal" officers treated their servants. This was 1860, only two years from the end of the Mutiny. The Mutiny was the turning-point of many changes in India, and one of these was the treatment of the natives. In the days of old John Company, when a young lad came out to begin his Indian career, he knew that he had twenty or thirty years of service before him, so he set to his work resignedly, learned the language, and became familiar with the ways of the natives, soldiers or servants, that were under him. The servant class knew that if they got into his employment he would be their "father," and they would be comfortable for these twenty or thirty years, so it was their interest to behave themselves and not lose their places. When a "Royal" regiment, on the other hand, had to serve its turn in India, the officers looked upon it as ten years of banishment. They hated the whole thing, and of course they hated the natives. They did not know the language, and made blunders in speaking, often blundered in giving orders to servants, and then thrashed the servants for doing what they had been told. A "Royal" regiment with its blunders and misunderstanding of things in India, had long been a subject of joke with the more experienced men of the Indian service. In fact the word "Royal" was often used in the sense of something stupid or ridiculous. When a "Royal" regiment arrived in India, the servants, at any rate the good ones, who knew the difference between "Royal" officers and those of the Indian Service, would not as a rule take service with them. Owing to this they often got bad servants, which unfortunately justified their opinion of the natives. In the club at Simla the old Indian officers and the "Royals" were pretty well divided as to numbers, so that there was not a majority on either side to bear down the other with mere weight of assertion, and on that account I look to the discussions I heard there as fairly representing the merits on each side. I noticed that without an exception, while the "Royals" abused the natives, the old Indian officers took their part. As to honesty, I remember a general officer saying that he had had about thirty years' service, and during all that time he had never seen his own money. It had been in the charge of his bearers, who received four rupees, that is, eight shillings, a month. He signed his order for his pay, the bearer went to the paymaster and received it, and the money remained in the bearer's custody, who paid it out again as required. That, he said, was the custom with officers in the old days, and he asked what would be the result in England if people trusted servants paid only two shillings a week in the same way. The case was unanswerable, at least it seemed to me to be so from the point of attack made by the "Royals." As to greater honesty on the part of the natives, I scarcely think it proved anything. "Dustoor," or custom, has great influence over the native mind. Under the old system, at military stations where everything went on with a quiet regularity, the idea of robbing a Sahib would not be thought of. This was "dustoor." It should be added that such acts would not pay. These servants would not run the risk of losing their situations. The Sahib was their "father," his house was their home, and to be turned adrift would be to lose all. So I think it was not so much honesty but the system, or "dustoor," which had produced regularity and routine. When I have been in the house of one of the old Company's servants, whether that of a single or married man, I always noticed how smoothly everything went on. No abusive language or scolding would be heard. The house affairs went like clockwork. In the quarters of a "Royal" the contrast was remarkable. The chances were that he used the very strong terms which Hindostanee supplies for abuse. Everything was wrong. At the club I noticed how this treatment of servants at table caused them to be nervous and flustered, and do their work badly. I have more than once noticed a khitmagar, or table servant, making a mess at drawing a cork. His master would scold him, call him a "pig," an "owl," and an "ass," making the man more flustered. My own servant I have seen on more than one of these occasions, being cool and good at his work, take the bottle and draw the cork. Whatever might be the real character of the natives of India, it became evident to me that the manner of treatment by the "Royals," was not the best.

I had chanced by good luck to get a good man in Jungley Khan, and so far as I can recollect, I never had occasion to scold him all the time I was in India. Naturally I should have avoided the "Royal" style of treatment, and my experience at the Simla Club confirmed me in the assurance that the other was the best.

I may here state that I have long held exceptional ideas about national character. Almost every one, in talk of the character of the people of the world, assumes the superiority of his own nation. In Scotland I heard of the character of the Irish, the English, the French, and the Americans — and the superiority of the Scotch. Before I was out of my "teens" I suspected these pretensions, and had thrown from my mind all such prejudices. I saw that each country remembered only its own virtues, and saw mainly the vices of its neighbours, and, by contrasting the good features of its own character with the bad of the others, reached what was to it a satisfactory conclusion. There are, no doubt, national characteristics, but these as a rule are little more than external; the difference of human nature that underlies them, among the civilised races at least, must be infinitely little. This will some day be realised, although very few believe it at present. I have seen the evil effects of this Philistine manner of believing evil of our neighbours. Politicians take advantage of it to serve their purpose by stirring up hatred against nations. Frenchmen are made to hate Germans, and Germans Frenchmen. When the great American War was going on, our statesmen and newspapers used every means that could be invented to make the people of this country hate the North. But this false hatred is not limited to separate nations. Politicians use it to set class against class. It has played a very prominent part in Irish politics; in the warfare between Conservative and Liberal, between Church and Dissent. It may be said, in fact, that wherever there is controversy, the rule is to attack the character of the opposite party. Bad feeling is thus produced, and malice is engendered. I have long looked upon all this as wickedness. Let men believe that as a rule bodies of men are much the same everywhere, that there is an average human nature in any collected mass of people—I speak not here of individual character, that is quite a different matter—and they would cease to be led by political humbugs. I could say a great deal, and give many illustrations on this subject, but enough is here said to indicate the conclusions I have reached. In my various travels this subject has often been brought before my mind, and the more I have seen, and the more I have thought upon it, the stronger my convictions have become.

CHAPTER XI

THE SUTLEJ VALLEY

I ARRANGED with a Captain Evans to go to Chini on the Sutlej—about sixteen marches from Simla. Chini is just beyond the first high range of the Himalayas, which stops the rain clouds from passing, and by going there we should avoid the wet weather of the rainy season. We had a shower or two at Chini; there was enough rain to produce trees, grass, and flowers; but on the second march beyond, this state of things ended, and the dry, barren country of Tibet began.

We started from Simla on the 9th of June, our route being along the Hindostan and Tibet Road, one of the works of Lord Dalhousie, who did things on a grand scale. In this case the high perfection of the road rendered it almost useless. He had commanded that the gradients were in no instance to exceed a certain figure, and the result was that in order to realise these conditions the road had to be made winding round the spurs of hills, making such long detours that the natives, and even Europeans, take the short cut over the hill. It was thought that this road would open up the commerce of Tibet, but there turned out to be little or no commerce to open up in that part of the world. The Tibetans bring in the pushim, or wool, from which the chuddars are made, and which is the principal article of traffic, to Rampore, on the Sutlej, on the backs of goats, and take back, by the same means of transport, the few things they require. On the road I passed droves of these goats with small bags containing the merchandise, in twos, placed saddle-wise on the animals' backs.

The view from Narkunda is celebrated. Here the high

ground overlooks the valley of the Sutlej, and one is nearer the high ranges than at Simla. Many go by Rampore, but that route is by native tracks and is hot. The Tibet road keeps along the upper part of the hills, and although longer, is more comfortable.

Chini is said to be about 10,000 feet above the sea. We found it very cool, and the climate delightful. It is on the right bank of the Sutlej, and about 4,000 feet above the bed of the river. The hills rise very steeply on the other side, and form a magnificent range of snowy peaks rising from 20,000 to 23,000 feet. The view is considered to be one of the finest in the Himalayas. Lord Dalhousie had built a house here, and we occupied it. The place was a rough structure, but it was a house. There was a native carpenter putting it in repair, and I instructed him to make a sundial, which he did with wood, and was very proud of. This enabled me to keep my watch nearly right, and my servant could see by it the hours for our meals. Captain Evans devoted himself to shikare, and that produced supplies for the pot. I made sketches of the place, and worked up the sketches I had previously done. I made friends with the villagers. They looked upon me as a great hakim, or doctor. On the first day of our arrival I found a man with a bad sore on his leg. It was on the front of the tibia; his rough wool trousers rubbed on it, and there was a mass of proud-flesh, about the size of half-a-crown. I made him expose the sore, on which I poured some raw brandy; this must have been very painful, but he stood it manfully. I then tore a white pocket-handkerchief into two, and put one of the pieces round his leg, covering the sore so as to keep the trouser off it. When this was done, I told him to come again next day. When he came I poured more brandy on the sore, and put on the other half of the handkerchief, making him go to the well and wash the half that had been used, so that it would serve next day. He came day after day till I thought the proud-flesh was gone. Then I applied some ointment, and made a successful cure. He turned up two months afterwards as one of our coolies when we left Chini, and he showed his leg all right, and said, "Brandy shrab bahut atchahai," or "brandy is very good." This cure brought people from the villages to me with all sorts of diseases. Many came with goitre, which is very prevalent in the Himalayas. To these I held up my penknife, as a sign there was no other medicine, and they understood.

Chini, being so high up, must be very cold in winter, and the people wear woollen clothes, which are seldom or never washed. One morning I was rather surprised to find numbers of them coming to the principal well, which was close to the bungalow, and undergoing the process of washing. I asked what it meant, and was told it was a "burra din," literally translated, a "great day" or "holiday." I asked when they had washed before, and they said "six months ago," and it would be six months till they washed again. One day I spoke to a woman with a child in her arms, and pointed out the dirt on herself and her child, which was so thick in some parts that it might have been scraped off. But she did not seem to think washing was necessary. She gave the usual answer, "Is moolk ke dustoor hai" ("It is the custom of this country"). The women's dress was composed of a large woollen garment, like a Highland plaid, which was wrapped round the body, and held on by a kummerbund, or waistband, and a large brass brooch. I bought two of these plaids to use as blankets, and one or two of the brooches. The younger women generally stuck bright-coloured flowers in their caps and hair, which gave them a very jaunty appearance.

The "pujah," or ceremony, mentioned above, of which the six-monthly washing was a preliminary, took place at the temple, which is a feature of every village. The peculiar object of worship in this temple is a structure which can be carried by two men with staves on their shoulders. The one at Chini was formed of a square framework—an office stool with the seat removed will convey a rough notion of its shape. This frame was completely concealed by pieces of silk of various colours which hung down all round, and a piece of red cloth hung over the staves on each side, covering them except where they touched the men's shoulders. Above the level of the staves were fixed some masks, of gold or brass. I understood they represented Devi. The central part was surmounted by a mass of yaks' tails dyed red. It may be presumed they were looked on as chowries, or royal emblems, and were placed there as a mark of honour. What constituted the sanctity of the object I never could find out. My supposition is there was something enclosed in the central part which endowed it with the character of a deity.

The ceremony was a peculiar circular dance, performed on the paved space in front of the temple, on which the dharmsalah, or guest-shed, stands. In this dance the Devi was carried round by two men with the staves on their shoulders, each facing the other. The drums and large trumpets were of course out, and in full operation. The villagers, both men and women, formed a large segment of a circle, facing the dharmsalah. Each person had his or her arms twisted into those of his next neighbour's behind their backs. The end man had his right hand free. In it he held a chowrie, which he waved in the air, keeping time to the movement of the dance. In the evening they lighted a fire, and kept up the holiday till a late hour. After going to bed I heard the instruments and chant still going on.*

The villagers seemed to be pleased with the interest I took in their pujah, for they told me of others, and even invited me to them. My regret now is that, owing to my very slight acquaintance with the language, I was unable to converse freely and get more details of their primitive worship, every scrap of which would be of interest in the present day. The details of village life and organisation would have been valuable. I understood that there was no caste among the people. The kate wallah owned the "kates" or fields, and there was another class who were merely cultivators. They said they had no thieves, no

* [A full description of "Pujahs in the Sutlej Valley," with a lithograph of the ceremony, was contributed by Simpson to the Journal of the Royal Asiatic Society, vol. xvi. part 1. He pointed out that much of the ritual—the offering of sacrifice, and sprinkling with blood—bore a striking resemblance to the Mosaic worship round the Ark, a fact tending, he considered, to support the theory of the Jewish origin of the Afghans.]

police, and no jails. I did see them punishing a man one day. The process was peculiar. They tied his hands behind his back with a rope; the rope was then thrown over the branch of a tree, and pulled till the fellow had only the points of his toes touching the ground. It was calculated to pull the arms out of their sockets, and must have been very painful. I got some native hill shoes made at Chini, and wore them. A pair disappeared, and I spoke to one of the villagers about it. His suggestion was that a dog had carried them off, the idea being that as the leather was untanned, the dog could eat such articles. This might have been the case, and it might not. A dog would scarcely carry off a pair—he might have carried off one shoe; but I put it in a different manner to this man. I did not wish to say he was telling me lies, yet I did not like that he should suppose I accepted his story. He had not explained the eating part of the dog-theory, so I put it that a dog had four feet, and there was only two shoes. A dog would have stolen four shoes. It must have been some one with only two feet that took them. The man grinned at this in such a manner that I rather think the dog was innocent.

Travellers often relate curious ways in which distance is measured. The Himalayan method is by "smokes," which mean so many rests—for in resting the coolies indulge in a smoke. To do this they have a plan which saves them the carrying of a pipe. They insert their two forefingers into the earth, first downwards, and then towards each other till they meet. The tobacco is placed in one hole, and the mouth is applied to the other. I remember passing a resting-place on the bank of a stream where the ground was hard, most of it rocks and stones, so that the usual pipe could not be extemporised. Here I noticed pieces of flat stones, on which some mud had been placed, and formed into pipes similar to what they made in the earth with their fingers. Each man carries his tobacco, with a chuckmuck, or steel, and a flint or pebble, and the dried leaves of a particular plant serve as tinder. One day at Coatee I took a stroll through the wood, and on coming back I noticed a number of girls, or rather young women, lying on a grassy spot, with all their heads in the centre, and their bodies radiating out like the spokes of a wheel. On seeing me they got up and ran away, so I went to find out what they had been doing. At the place where their heads had been I found one of these extemporised pipes, and concluded they had been having a smoke and a gossip.

On the 8th of August Evans and I started for a short trip beyond Chini. I wanted to see the Lamas, and when I was so near to them it would have been something to regret if I had not had a glimpse of these votaries and their doings. Our first march was to Punghee, a village beyond Chini. From that we went over the Oorung or Werang ghat, and thus left the Sutlej valley, and came down to a place called Leepee. Here there was some Lamas. The first indications I noticed of Buddhism were at Meru, a place one march to the west of Chini. At Chini there was a Lama, and he had a small temple. This man took no part in the usual religious ceremonies of the village, but a death occurred while we were in Chini, and two days afterwards there was a ceremony on the hillside called khana-khata, or food-eating, and this man figured in it. From this I concluded that the people of Chini were not Buddhists, but this Lama was a sort of missionary holding an advanced post of the Buddhist frontier. From Leepee we went to Kanum, passing Lebrung on the way, where there is an old killa, or fort, a very high building. At Kanum everything bore the evidence of Lamaism. I saw a monastery, and I saw a Lama nun. She wore a red dress like the Geelongs, or monks. The nuns are called chomos, or anees. I was taken over the monastery, but it seemed empty. It formed a quadrangle, the temple being on one of the sides, and the cells of the monks round the other three. I think it was two stories high. I sketched one of the cells, which was about 6 feet square. This arrangement of cells, in a quadrangle, I recognised afterwards in the plan of the rock-cut viharas of Western India. This visit, with my further experience next season in Tibet, helped me to grasp the meaning and purpose of the earlier rock-cut temples and the Buddhist monuments of India and Afghanistan.

A SERPENT-LOVER

On our return I bought at Leepee a praying machine, or mani, for two rupees, from a Lama who showed me how to use it, and taught me the mantra—"Om Mani Padmi, Hoong." We got back to Chini on the 15th of August.

A few days before our departure from Chini a Captain Mainwaring arrived from Simla. Mainwaring had travelled among the Lepchas in the Darjeeling district, and he told me a great deal about that race. The noted peculiarity of this man might be expressed by saying that he was a serpentphil. He seldom went out but he brought back a serpent in his hands, "all alive O!" He stroked them, expressed his admiration for their great beauty, and wondered how any one could kill such lovely things. He seemed to have acquired some manner of handling the serpents, and whether they were poisonous or not appeared to make no difference to him. Somehow he had the power of a serpent-charmer. We learned afterwards that at some station where he had been quartered he collected some hundreds of serpents, and when a change of quarters took place he could not carry off his pets, nor would he kill them; they were all set free in his garden, to the horror and fright of every one at the station, particularly of the ladies.

We had now been over two months at Chini, and on the 28th of August we began our march back to Simla. Mainwaring accompanied us.

At Serahn we got into trouble. On our outward march from the place, two months before, our coolie-mate did not make his appearance, my bedding was not forthcoming, and I had to sleep that night "anyhow." He turned up next day, and said he had been detained, but we had doubts about what he said, and did not know what to believe. The want of the language on my part prevented me from catching everything that was said. The mate of the bungalow now, on our return, said, "These are the Sahibs that did not pay for a sheep." He refused to provide anything, and was very rude and uncivil. As Mainwaring was not connected with the sheep transaction, the man offered to get whatever he wanted. Through this arrangement our servants found what was necessary for our food. So far as the sheep was concerned in the matter, I had a distinct recollection of putting down the money at the time, and saying, "That is for the sheep." Next morning we were up and ready for the march at 5 a.m., but no coolies appeared. Eight, nine, and ten o'clock came, and still no coolies. We had passed some of the time at breakfast. At last I proposed to have the bungalow mate in to see what was to be done, for without coolies to carry our things nothing was possible. The mate point blank refused to do anything, so, as I had seen the mode of punishment at Chini, which is peculiar to the locality, I proposed that we should tie the mate up to a beam in the bungalow, telling him he must remain there till the coolies were brought. We got a rope and did this, that is tied his hands behind his back with the rope, then threw the rope over a beam, and pulled it till the man only touched the ground with the tips of his toes. I took care that the rope was not pulled too tight, so that he never was very much hurt. As we tied him up I heard him give some order to one of the bungalow people, who instantly disappeared. Evans and Mainwaring believed he had gone for the coolies, but I suspected a different errand, so, to be ready, I got my revolver out, as well as a long bamboo stick that I carried in marching. The bamboo was in the right hand, and the revolver in the left. I calculated that the bamboo would be sufficient for my purpose, but should it fail, and real danger appear, the revolver would take a part in the proceedings. The Rajah of Bussahir has a palace at Serahn, and it was not long before a man, said to be a Wuzzeer, made his appearance with a number of followers, and one of them came forward and began to untie the mate. I went at him instantly with the bamboo, and sent him reeling towards the door. That was enough; none of the others manifested any desire to come forward. Evans and Mainwaring had gone for their rifles. However, my prompt action had settled the matter before the rifles came on the scene. The Wuzzeer was invited to take a seat, and I said, "Now that we have begun it is necessary to carry this affair out by decided action. Tell this Wuzzeer that if the coolies are not here in half an hour, he goes up with a rope round his wrists like the mate. I pulled out my watch while Mainwaring stated the conditions, and pointed to the hands. The Wuzzeer ordered some one away. There was a lot of running about, and I was really in fear that the whole thing would end in a fight. If the Wuzzeer had ordered every one to turn out, we three would have been outnumbered. The half hour came, but no coolies, and we tied up the Wuzzeer. This brought him to his senses, and he then gave orders for the coolies. But it turned out that all the people had gone to the fields to work, and as some were a long way off, it was impossible to call in a sufficient number. The final arrangement was that we were to wait that day and march next morning, when coolies, we were assured, would be forthcoming. Thus the whole difficulty was brought to a satisfactory end, which I ascribed largely to my prompt action. One difficulty I had, while the mate was tied up, was with his wife. She tried hard to get him loosened, and I could not apply the bamboo to her. We gave the mate some brandy afterwards, and we were very good friends. The coolies did turn up next morning, and we started. There were no further difficulties, and when we reached Simla I reported the whole matter to Lord William Hay, who was then Deputy Commissioner there.

CHAPTER XII

BENGAL

I LEFT Simla on the 9th of October, and made for Delhi, where Wagentreiber, editor and proprietor of the *Delhi Punch*, put me up. He had a large native house, and my quarters were in the inner quadrangle, which had been the zenana in former times. The pictures for the *Delhi Punch* were printed from stone, and the press was in one of the rooms below my bedroom. The lithographic printer, from old associations, naturally interested me. He was, of course, a native, with a very scant dhotie, or loin-cloth, as his only garment, excepting his pugree, or headgear. I think he had gum amongst his materials, but no acid. Everything was primitive. I gave him some practical hints, and he was rather astonished when he found I could use the roller.

Mrs. Wagentreiber promised that I should get sketches of a zenana. This, of course, was an important point to manage, for native life was to be a feature of my projected work, and the interior of a Mohammedan harem in Delhi would be a triumph. Mrs. Wagentreiber was a descendant of the well-known Colonel James Skinner, C.B., of Delhi, but the exact relationship I now forget. Colonel Skinner left a number of sons. One of them had a native wife, a Kashmiri, and it was arranged that she and her daughter should array themselves in jewels and finery for me to sketch. A bullock carriage came one morning to take me to the house, where I found the two ladies waiting, surrounded by the attendants of a grand personage. I was told that each of the ladies had about £4,000 worth of jewellery on her person.

The ladies were on visiting terms with the inmates of the

Imperial zenana, so I have no doubt the correct form in every detail was before me. I have often seen the "Light of the Harem" in pictures, but in no instance have I seen anything that had the slightest resemblance to truth in it. I may mention one bit of detail. Before the ladies there were on the floor two large, highly ornamented silver vessels, one about eighteen inches, the other about two feet in diameter. These were "pawn-dans," and contained the morsels of betel-nut, wrapped up with a small quantity of lime, in pawn-leaves. The "Light of the Harem" has some of this compound always in her mouth, and the result is a saliva of a bright-red colour, requiring the constant use of a spittoon, which article, in silver, and ornamented, stood at a convenient distance for the hand to reach when required. No picture of a harem would be complete without these objects. The costume worn by ladies of position in Delhi is very limited in quantity. A small silken vest, trimmed with gold edging, merely covers the breasts; the sleeves reach halfway to the elbow. The chief garment is a pair of pyjamas—literally "leg-clothes"—so wide and long that I never suspected they were not a skirt. Between the very small vest and the pyjamas there is a pretty large hiatus in the costume, which might rather astonish a European lady. To a certain extent this is covered by the "chuddar"; but the chuddars worn by the two ladies were so transparent that they concealed nothing.*

From Delhi I moved on to Agra, where I sketched the Taj, and the so-called gates of Puttun Somnath, and visited Futtehpore Sikri, Muttra, Bindrabund, Secundra, etc. About the time I was in India I read some articles in the papers which discussed the theory that a European had been the architect of the Taj. The articles in the papers caused me, when I was sketching, to notice the ornament on the Taj, and I came to the conclusion that a European must have designed it. Since then Mr. Keene has shown that the architect was a Venetian named Geronimo

* [Drawings of the costumes and jewellery worn by these ladies of the Delhi zenana were contributed with a description by Simpson to *The Watchmaker, Jeweller, and Silversmith* for October, 1886.]

Verroneo. For some years back I have noticed that there has been among visitors who go to India an ardent admiration of the Taj. It might be called "Taj-worship." Very few people pay any real attention to the details of architecture. If they did they would find that the Taj belongs to the decadence of the Mohammedan architecture of India. It is certainly a magnificent monument. But for real art it will not compare with some of the old fragments about Delhi. The work produced in Akbar's time at Futtehpore Sikri is far superior. I had seen the Mohammedan architecture of Delhi before I saw the Taj. I went one day to sketch the old musjid in the Killa Khona, or old Delhi, and I spent my time gazing at it. I did not attempt to sketch the Alai Durwaza at the Katub. I consider the ornament on the Taj poor in its design, and not well rendered. My conclusion is that the European architect was far from being a first-class designer, and the natives who reproduced the designs were new to the style.

I ought to record here what took place when I sketched the celebrated so-called gates of Puttun Somnath. When Mahmoud of Ghuznee destroyed the temple of Somnath, he is said to have carried off its gates of sandalwood to Ghuznee, and after his death they were put up as the gates of his tomb. At the end of the first Afghan War, half a century ago, the "avenging army" brought these gates back to India. That is, they carried off the gates found on Mahmoud's tomb, believing them to be the gates of Puttun Somnath. This was done as an evidence to the people of India that our soldiers had been victorious in Afghanistan. "Here are the gates the Mohammedans carried off, and we now bring them back." Such was the tenor of Lord Ellenborough's celebrated proclamation issued to the people of India at the end of the Afghan War. These gates are now in the Fort of Agra. I sat down to sketch them one day, believing what I was told, that these were the veritable gates of Puttun Somnath. But sketching leads one to notice details as well as to think. I soon began to realise that the ornament was purely Mohammedan; there was nothing Hindu upon the gates. Not a vestige of the Hindu mythology was visible. Before I had finished the sketch I said to myself, these are not the gates of Puttun Somnath. I spoke to two or three people about it—men of position; I also mentioned the matter to Lord Canning. But each and all assured me that there could be no doubt in the case, and every one referred to Lord Ellenborough's proclamation. It was not till my return to England that I could find any confirmation of my conclusion. I mentioned the subject to Mr. James Fergusson, and he told me I was quite right, and that the ornament was a perfectly sufficient guide, but to this he added, that the wood of the gates had been inspected with a microscope, and it was not sandal-wood, which the gates of Somnath were reputed to have been, but Deodar pine. This might be called an illustration of the "new criticism," where the evidence of an important historical document has to be thrown aside upon the evidence of a style of art. Since then I have come upon a further bit of evidence connected with this subject. In 1881 I was at Abergeldie—a guest of the Prince of Wales. Lord Colville of Culross was there at the same time. As his brother, Colonel Colville, and I had been great friends in the Crimea we took to each other. I was surprised to know that he had been A.D.C. to Lord Ellenborough, and still more surprised when he told me that he had acted the part of showman with the so-called gates of Puttun Somnath. He had gone with them through Rajpootana, and still possessed some fragments of the wood, which had to be sawn off in order to pack them for transport. On my expressing a desire to have a piece of the wood inspected, he complied with this request, and I handed it to Mr. George Murray of the British Museum, who reported to me that it was undoubtedly pine, but what particular kind he could not determine. The conclusion is, that if the gates were carried off, about which it seems there is a doubt, they must have been destroyed at some time, and new ones made for Mahmoud's tomb.

When Lord Ellenborough died in 1871 the newspapers in their notices of him all referred to the celebrated gates. At the time the gates were brought from Ghusnee Ellenborough had been caricatured as Samson with the gates of Gaza on his back. I mention this to indicate how notorious the event had been. But none of the papers seemed to have been aware that the gates were not the real ones. So I wrote a letter, which was published in the *Daily News*, giving my experience with the gates, with the conclusions based upon it. This letter was copied into the local guide to Agra, the author of which was Judge Keene, and I believe it still appears in that small work, where it is declared to be decisive on the subject.

I was about three weeks at work in Agra and the places near it. Thence I went by dak gharrie to Cawnpore, now Khanpur, where I sketched the Well, Slaughter Ghat, and other places connected with the events of the Mutiny. Major Mowbray Thomson was, if I remember right, one of the only three persons who escaped from Cawnpore. He was stationed at Cawnpore when I was there, so I called and saw him. I found Colonel Woodford's grave and sketched it. He was my old friend of Crimean times, of the Rifles, and was killed at Cawnpore in fighting under Wyndham. At the time of my visit—November, 1860—the Gothic screen had not been erected round the well. It was an ordinary well with a circular wall round the top of it, and the mouth had been closed up at the top with bricks and mortar. This original part of the wall, I understood, was not removed, but was covered over with marble, which forms the base on which the winged figure now stands. This figure was done at the expense of Lord and Lady Canning, by Marochetti the sculptor. The Gothic screen was designed by Colonel Yule, who was then at the head of the Public Works Department in India.

From Cawnpore I went to Lucknow. On arriving there I found that Bishop Cotton of Calcutta had arrived the day before, and was in a camp of his own. I called and found the Bishop sitting under a Shemiana, among some mango trees. He quoted the verse in Scripture about every man sitting under his vine and his fig-tree, which was his case at the moment, only instead of a vine he was under his own "mango tope." The various localities in Lucknow con-

ALLIGATORS ON THE GANGES.

From Simpson's water-colour in the Print Room at the British Museum. Reproduced by permission.

To face p. 129.

nected with the memorable defence, as well as with the siege operations for the relief of the defenders, required some time, so I was nearly three weeks at that place. While I was there Sir Hugh Rose, who had succeeded Lord Clyde as Commander-in-Chief, arrived at Lucknow. Having a letter of introduction to him, I went and presented it. With it I presented another letter, the circumstances connected with which were peculiar. When in the Crimea Sir Hugh was the English A.D.C. at the French Quarters-General. When I was bothered by the French sentries when sketching in Sebastopol after it was taken, I went to our Headquarters to see what could be done. Colonel Steele, Lord Raglan's military secretary, gave me a letter of introduction to Sir Hugh asking him to do something for me in the matter. As mentioned before in these memoirs, I did not find Sir Hugh, so the letter was not delivered. It came home with me and remained among my papers till I started for India, when I put it among my letters of introduction. This was the second letter alluded to above. Sir Hugh received me very kindly, and quaintly remarked that "he was sorry he could do nothing for me with the French." I was asked to dine with him in the evening, and did so almost every evening while I remained in Lucknow.

From Lucknow I returned to Cawnpore, and took the railway to Allahabad, where I remained about a week, and then went on to Benares, where I put up at what was then the Victoria Hotel. It took me three days to do all I required at the Golden Temple. Each day I noticed a fakir who came and danced at the temple. He was rather a stout, elderly man, so his dancing was only a sort of hobbling up and down, merely lifting one foot after another. But the thing that caught my attention was the phrase he kept repeating the whole time he danced, about twenty minutes or so. This was "Bum bum bo, Maha deo, bum bum bo. Bum bum bo, Maha deo, bum bum bo." Sometimes he raised his voice and at times he lowered it. I was not then familiar with Hindu mantras, and was, of course, very much struck with this manifestation of mumbo-jumbo. He seemed a good-natured sort of man, and I thought he turned his head slightly at times in my direction to see if I were noticing him. Some days afterwards I met him at one of the ghats, so I stopped him and said, "Bum bum bo." He smiled and looked very pleased, and it was evident that he felt a satisfaction in the fact that I had noticed his performance at the temple. A mantra, it may be explained, is a sacred sentence, of which there are many used by both Brahminical and Buddhist worshippers. A Brahman would call "hallelujah" a mantra.

At Benares I made the acquaintance of General Campbell, who was brigadier or general commander of the station. He told me he belonged to Loch Fyne, near Ardrishaig. That was the family place, but he was "Jock, the Laird's brither," so he had to become a sodger. I dined one night at his house, and saw a survival of an old custom. It was the only instance which came under my notice. As soon as the ladies rose after dinner a servant placed a big, handsome chillum, a native pipe, in which the smoke passes through water, on the table before the General. I assumed that a pipe of this kind must have been the rule in the earlier days of the Company. On Christmas Day I dined with a Mr. Smith, who was, if I recollect right, the Judge of the Sudder Ameen. After dinner, as there were some young folks, I introduced the game of "Gubbins," which amused them very much, and the word "Gubbins" had a special relish, as that was the name of one of the big officials at Benares, whose bungalow was either next door or across the road. I think it was Mr. Smith who took me one morning to see the making of ice at Benares, which was a surprise to me. He was chairman of the Ice Club, an institution at most stations. We went early in the morning and found a field in which some hundreds of small porus earthenware saucers had been spread the night before, with a little water in each. Even in the latitude of Benares a thin coating of ice existed on each in the morning, and a large number of women, girls, and boys were gathering this ice, and depositing it in an ice-house. At that time ice-machines did not exist, and I understood that ice was made in this way in most of the places in the North-West.

A HINDU NAUTCH-GIRL

One day at the ghats I saw the burial of a fakir. He was sitting as in life, with his orange-coloured cloth wrapped round him, and decked with garlands of orange-coloured flowers. His water-dish, and the one or two articles he required in life, were attached to the body, which was fastened to a flat stone, and placed at the end of a boat. The boat was pushed only a short distance out into the river, when the stone and the corpse sitting on it were dropped into the river. The whole disappeared beneath the water, the stone, from its weight, going first. No doubt it would settle at the bottom, where the holy man would sit exactly as he did in life.

I was lucky enough to be introduced to the Rajah Deo Narain Singh, and at his invitation went to make sketches at his palace. While there I asked some of his people if it was possible to make sketches of the inmates as well as of the palace itself. I had to be very careful in my manner of putting this lest a mistaken intention should be attributed to me. I was under the notion that the Hindus would not have the same strictness in secluding their women as the Mussulmans. But I was completely mistaken. We know that two thousand years ago the women of India did not hide their faces, but since the Mohammedan invasion all that has changed, and they have adopted the strict zenana system of the conquering race. Some one communicated my wishes to the Rajah, and he most kindly sent for a nautch-girl, who came with all her finery on, as I expect she had been ordered. Haidree was one of the most noted nautch-girls in Benares. She had at one time been a favourite of Jung Bahadur, Prince of Nepaul. Judging by the jewellery she wore—a pretty safe test in India, where this is the means of investment—this lady must have been prosperous. Probably the gems she wore were gifts from her numerous wealthy admirers, for I understood that Jung Bahadur was not the only one.

While I sketched her a light coming from a door at hand disturbed the process, so I rose and shut it. In doing so I moved a pair of shoes which stood in the way. When I returned to my seat I noticed there was a smile on her lips and that she was talking in her own language. I afterwards inquired of the person who had brought me what had tickled Haidree's fancy, and he explained that none but the lowest class of servants ever touched shoes, and that she was surprised a Sahib could condescend to such a thing. Even the shutting of the door was a service I should have given a "hookum," or order, to an inferior to perform.

CHAPTER XIII

CENTRAL INDIA

SIR EDWARD CAMPBELL wrote to me sometime during the cold season that Lord and Lady Canning were to visit Central India, and that a tent, with a knife and fork at the table, would be ready for me whenever I liked to join the camp.

The object of this visit by Lord Canning was to see the rajahs and chiefs of Central India. Holkar was received in Durbar, and the old Begum of Bhopal had a Durbar all to herself. She was a Mohammedan lady, and had been very true to the Government during the Mutiny. I went with the return visit which Lord Canning made to her camp. Here a curious bit of etiquette was observed. Lord Canning and the Begum sat at one end of the tent. Upon something being said, Mr. Bowring, the private secretary to the Governor-General, rose and walked to the other end, where there was a door with a purdah, or veil, over it. There he said to the purdah, "Lord Sahib bahut, bahut salaam detta hai," meaning, "Lord Sahib (or Governor-General) sends (or, literally, gives) many salaams." A voice within said something, and Mr. Bowring returned to the Governor-General and reported what had taken place. I understood afterwards that it was the daughter of the Begum who was within the purdah, or curtain. Technically she was thus present in Durbar, but being a married woman she could not be seen. Mohammedan ideas on this subject were illustrated by something I heard at the time. Some one asked the Begum why she did not keep the purdah. "Whose purdah should I keep?" she in return asked. She was a widow, and being so had no need to keep the purdah. But the phrase indicates the relationship of the curtain or act of concealment to the husband.

The Begum, whose name was Secunder Begum, Ranee of Bhopal, had with her two Christian ladies. They were of French origin, and belonged to a family that had been more than one generation in Bhopal. They were Catholics, but otherwise they had become natives. Deulin, I think, was the name, or a word like that.

On one of the days Lord and Lady Canning, and almost every one in the camp, went to Berah Ghat to see the marble rocks. We started early in the morning on elephants, and found tents at Berah Ghat, with breakfast ready for us. The boats were few and the party large, but at last Dr. Beale and I got one, and we managed to get sketches of the marble gorge through which the Nerbudda flows at this place.

There was at the time of my visit to Jubblepore an establishment connected with the department for the extinction of Thuggism. Many Thugs were apprehended, tried, and hanged, but there were many who could not be disposed of in this manner. These were informers on whose evidence convictions had been made. They were often women and children. The children might have followed the profession of their fathers, so the plan was adopted of keeping all these under confinement. There the informers, old men, would end their lives, and the children were let out when they grew up, one or two at a time, so that there would be no chance of them forming a gang and resuming their old trade. The place was walled in, and guarded, and they were employed in making carpets, tents, etc. I believe the establishment has now ceased to exist. It must have done so by automatic process of exhaustion. Colonel Hervey had charge of the place at the time. It was a curious sight to see these people, most of them boys and girls, the children of murderers. There were some old men who had no doubt used the roomal, the handkerchief with which the Thugs strangled their victims. I have in one of my sketch-books the portrait of one old man, the mildness of whose expression struck me very much. His eyes were soft and clear, as gentle in appearance as the eyes of the young deer, and it was hard to believe that such a man could have been an actor in the cold-blooded murders of the gang he belonged to. There was one young girl, sitting at a spinning-wheel, whom I was sketching. Colonel Hervey was with me explaining everything, and he chanced to say as an example that he expected that this girl would soon claim her release. "What will she do when she gets out?" "Oh," replied Colonel Hervey, "I suppose she will get married." "Ask her," I said, "if she will marry me." This he did, and said something about having a carriage for her to ride in. Her eyes opened wide, and she darted a look at him, then at me, glared wildly, and hid her face with a rapid motion, flinging her chudder, or sheet, over her head. I understood from what she said that I was rejected on the spot.

I was about twelve days at Jubblepore. The camp was to move eastward again, and I might have returned with it, and in pleasant company; but at Jubblepore I was well into Central India, and I wanted to see Chittore, Oodeypore, and Rajpootana. Sir Richard Shakespeare and other functionaries connected with that part of India had to be at Jubblepore, and so I was able to make arrangements for the tour I desired. I was provided with purwanahs or passports ordering that I should receive every facility in the States I should pass through. I bought a dooley, a light palanquin, and started with a very small quantity of luggage, sending my one attendant, Jungly Khan, back with the camp, so that he might go to Agra with my baggage, and wait for me there. The dooley and luggage required about ten coolies, four to carry the dooley and four more to change, one bhangy wallah, who carried my luggage in a couple of baskets by means of a bhangy or piece of wood on his shoulder, and a massalchi, to carry a torch. For the men carried me at night, while I slept in the dooley, which formed a sort of bed. They rested during the day, and this gave me the opportunity of sketching. I had by this time learned a little of the language—not much, but enough I thought, to manage with.

It was rather a wild thing to go off all by myself for some weeks in this way, but I thought it could be done, and as I should be able to traverse a large region, it was worth the risk. In this journey at times, for a week or so, I never saw a European. Most of the roads were only the trails which are called roads in India. Travellers were scarce in this region, and dak bungalows were few. Those I found on my way were miserable places. At times I had an empty house in a village, sometimes a shed. Often I had only the dooley as a shelter. One morning I wakened, and on looking out found myself on something very like a dungheap. The coolies had arrived in the dark, and put down the dooley at the handiest spot on their arrival. Often I had no food, but only a share of the coolies'. This simple diet they handed to me on leaves, which are much used in many parts of India as plates. So I may say I have done a little in the ascetic style of thing among my Indian experiences. This existence gave me many opportunities of seeing the real life of the people. The ordinary traveller who "does" India sees Bombay, Calcutta, Benares, Agra, and Delhi, but the vast spaces between these noted places he sees nothing of. It is in these spaces that the real India exists. That is where the 250 millions of people live their lives—a vast mass of simple folk that lead a simple existence among their fields and cows. They know nothing of Calcutta nor of politics. They go to bed with the sun, and are up with it again in the early morning. They pay their taxes, and possibly do not know who receives them, or how they are spent. I was chatting one day with a villager, who mentioned the Company Sahib. I wished to tell him that the Company Sahib no longer existed, but that was too much for my knowledge of the language, so I put it that the Company Sahib was morgia, or dead. He looked at me and smiled a smile of incredulity, and said "Nahin Sahib." I naturally thought of the clergyman in the Hebrides praying for George III. for years after his death. This journey impressed upon me a lot of vague notions about the village system of India. Wherever there is ground that can be cultivated these villages are dotted over it. Often I could see that some of them had been so long on the site, that in building and re-building the mud houses the spot had become a mound, and it stood up with the present village on the top, so that it was visible at a distance. They were there when we arrived in India, they were there when the Mohammedans came, and were probably on the same spots when Alexander crossed the Indus. To this it may be added that these villages will still be there when we leave India, whenever that may take place. You find no Mohammedans in these villages. It is even doubtful if the people ought to be called Hindus, because the simple and primitive rites celebrated in various forms by them can scarcely be identified with the recognised worship of Brahminism. I believe it is now recognised that such tribes as the Goonds, the Sonthals, the Kols, and others, are the descendants of races of the pre-Vedic period, and although they are now nominally Hindu, survivals of their old rites and ceremonies still cling to them.

Bhilsa was my second stopping-place, and there I made my first essay in the study of Buddhist architecture. I stayed some days sketching at the old Sanchi stupa, which is about four or five miles from the town of Bhilsa. The stupa was then covered with vegetation, and the whole place was in jungle condition. The south and west gates had fallen. The Department for the Preservation of Ancient Monuments did not then exist in India. This Department has put up the two gates, and it keeps the whole place in order. An old chuprassie, named Dildoor-khan, was placed at my disposal, and I told him to take me to the parana tope. "Ha, Sahib" ("Yes, sir"), he replied, and in pompous style marched before me as a beadle might be expected to lead some function in a parish. He led me into the town, to a spot where there was a large gun, about 20 feet long and with a bore of 8 inches. It lay on a sort of pedestal of mud, and evidently the Bhilsa people were proud of this fine old cannon, which from the ornament on it I took to be of Mohammedan workmanship. Dildoor-khan struck his long stick on the ground, and pointing to the gun said, "Purana tope, Sahib;" and he stood eyeing me and the gun with a look of pride and satisfaction. But he became disconcerted when I began to laugh. The word *tope*, as applied to a Buddhist stupa, is only used in the Punjab and Afghanistan. In Hindostanee it means a cannon, and a group of trees. Dildoor-khan had certainly brought me to a parana, or old tope, but it was not what I wanted. As tope is not in use as a word, I had considerable difficulty in making Dildoor-khan understand what I wanted.

Bhopal is about twenty miles further west. Notice had been sent by some of the Begum's people at Jubblepore that I was coming, and I was put up in a bungalow which is kept for visitors. It was called the "Mottee Bungalow," or House of Pearls. The place was very dirty. Food was brought to me, but no knives or forks, and I had to eat with my fingers in this House of Pearls. There is a fine lake at Bhopal, which has some celebrity in India, for there is a rhyme which says—

> "Tal, Bhopal tal, aur sub talingha,
> Ghur, Rotas ghur, aur sub ghuringa."

which might be freely translated :—

> "Lake, Bhopal lake, all others are pools,
> Fort, Rotas fort, all others are fools."

One of the Begum's people, named Nujeet Khan, took me on the lake in a small steamer, and drove me through the town in a carriage.

Indore, Holkar's capital, seemed a wretched place. I stayed a day there, and was quartered in the Residency. I had left Holkar, the Begum, and all the officials at Jubblepore.

From Indore my route changed northwards towards Rajpootana. At Neemuch I was put up in the house of Captain J. B. Dennys, who, with his wife, was very kind to me. They thought it absurd that I should travel as I was doing and feed on the dooley-bearers' khana. So they arranged that a sootar sowar, or man on a camel, should go with me. He was a very good man, and could cook a curry, so my meals were improved. From Neemuch my route turned westward to Oodeypore, the capital of the Rajpoot state of Mewar. The Rana of this place is looked up to by all Hindus as belonging to a family that can be traced farther back than any other in India. It is understood that his descent can be worked back to the Sun and the Moon. The Jeypore and Jodhpore Rajahs go very nearly as far back, but I understand that the Maharana of Oodeypore—I do not know whether it is only by a few weeks or a few thousand years—has the more ancient pedigree. The Resident was away, but I was accommodated in the Residency. Oodeypore itself is from its position a very fine place. There is a large artificial lake with two islands, on one of which is a marble palace. The town stands on a rising ground overlooking the lake, and the whole is surrounded with hills, making it most picturesque. Since I have seen this town I have always classed it, Malta, and Edinburgh as the three finest cities, from their surroundings and appearances, that I have visited. Rao Bakhut Sing of Baidla, better known as the Baidla Rao, called upon me. I understood that he was always attentive to Sahibs when they visited Oodeypore. The Baidla Rao accompanied the Maharana to Bombay, to meet the Prince of Wales on his arrival there in November, 1875. After the ceremony of receiving the Prince was over and most of the people had left, I was going about making notes of details, when I found Colonel Herbert and the Maharana, and was introduced. I told Colonel Herbert to tell the Maharana that I had a copy of Tod's Rajasthan in my possession, and that I had read it. From these words he would know that I understood who the Maharana of Mewar was. When Colonel Herbert told him this he looked pleased. The day before I left Oodeypore Baigrie and another man turned up. Baigrie belonged to the Bombay side and was a capital artist. He turned up again in Abyssinia, where both of us were for the time working for the *Illustrated London News*.

WILLIAM SIMPSON, R.I.

On leaving Oodeypore I had intended to visit Nathdwarra, celebrated for its magnificent Bund, or dam, but I began to find that time would not allow me to visit all the places I wished to see in Rajpootana, so I made straight for Chittore Ghur. This was the ancient capital of Mewar. A railway now passes Chittore, but at the time of my visit the place was quite out of the line of travellers, and difficult to reach. For this reason there are few accounts of this wonderful old city in books about India. If my memory serves me, this place was twice taken by the Mohammedans, and at the last siege, when it became evident that it could hold out no longer, a chosen band cut their way through the besiegers at night with the young Rana. Next morning a "Johur" was performed. A tank was filled with all the wood, butter, and oil that was left. This was set fire to, and all the women and children were thrown into it. Then the men sallied out and met death fighting with their enemies. The place was deserted after the last siege, some centuries ago, and is now partly in ruins, but many of the buildings remain pretty perfect, so it might be described as a deserted city. It stands on flat-topped hills, two or three miles in its longest direction. The walls and gates still remain. Within are towers, temples, and palaces, with here and there a village or two that has grown up among the silent streets. This place is all Hindu architecture. When I had seen the architecture of Old Delhi, Agra, etc., I had come to the conclusion that the Mohammedans were the past masters of this art in India, but after my visit to Chittore I found it difficult to say that they were better than the Hindus. The old Jain tower is perhaps one of the finest works in India.

Old Tower of Victory at Chitore.

From the original water-colour by Simpson, at South Kensington. Reproduced by permiss ion of the Secretary of H.M. Board of Education.

To face p. 140

The HIMALAYAS

It required nearly a couple of weeks to outfit ourselves for marching in the Hills. There are no Hotels after you leave Simla or Mussoorie. We required tents, kitchen things, and stores of various kinds. I, of course, employed some of my time in making sketches at Mussoorie. At last we started on the 19th April. Our course was up the Ganges to its source at the Cow's Mouth. This sacred river is supposed to have four sources. The Bhagirat'ha, the Aluknanda, the Jahnuvee, and the Bishenguinga. – All these sources are celebrated places of pilgrimage. Our route was that of the Bhagirat'ha, which is the one generally understood, at least by Europeans, as the source of the Ganges. – In 1874 I read a paper to the Alpine Club, entitled Gangootree, or a Journey in the Himalayas, to the 'Cow's Mouth', or Source of the Ganges. It is published in Vol. VI of the Alpine Journal. p. 385. – where many details will be found that I cannot give here.

At Deralee, which is only three marches from Gangootree, we found James Wilson who was well known in the hills as the 'Shikaree of the Himalayas'. He dined with us in passing up, and on our coming back, and he had an immense fund of knowledge. At Gangootree there is a small temple, and some hill Brahmins attend it in the summer months, for the spot is covered with snow in the winter and no pilgrims come at that season. This temple is about twenty miles below the Glacier, and there is no road or trail beyond it. We stayed a day at the Temple and then started for the actual source and encamped for the night some miles below it. Next morning we went up to the Glacier taking sufficient with us to have breakfast at it. The water flows out, a very small stream, of muddy stuff. As a bath at this Sacred Shrine is supposed to wash away all previous sin, that is according to Hindu notions, – [illegible] below the Glacier. – and I also drank a little of the water, – so as to complete

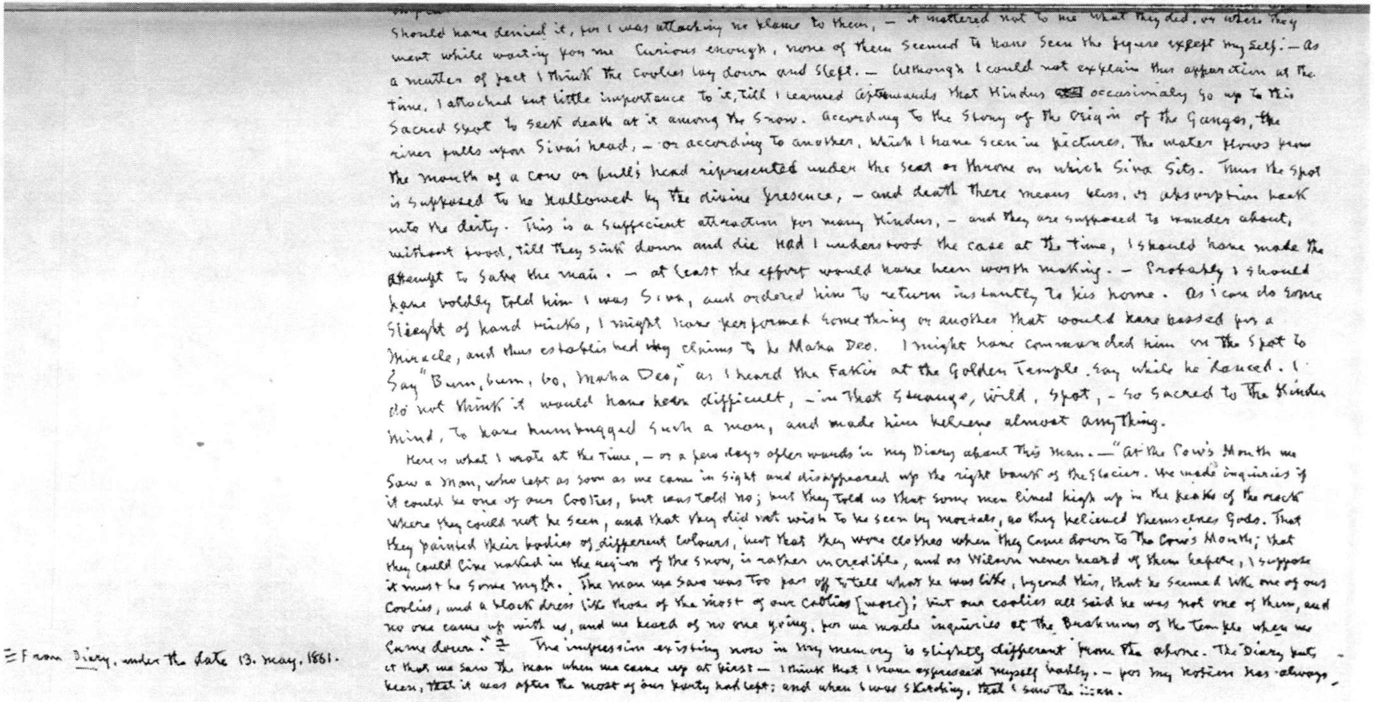

Should have denied it, for I was attaching no blame to them, — it mattered not to me what they did, or where they went while waiting for me. Curious enough, none of them seemed to have seen the figure except myself. — As a matter of fact I think the Coolies lay down and slept. — Although I could not explain this apparition at the time, I attached but little importance to it, till I learned afterwards that Hindus occasionally go up to this sacred spot to seek death at it among the snow. According to the story of the Origin of the Ganges, the river falls upon Siva's head, — or according to another, which I have seen in pictures, the water flows from the mouth of a cow or bull's head represented under the seat or throne on which Siva sits. Thus the spot is supposed to be hallowed by the divine presence, — and death there means bliss, or absorption back into the deity. This is a sufficient attraction for many Hindus, — and they are supposed to wander about, without food, till they sink down and die. Had I understood the case at the time, I should have made the attempt to save the man. — at least the effort would have been worth making. — Probably I should have boldly told him I was Siva, and ordered him to return instantly to his home. As I can do some sleight of hand tricks, I might have performed something or another that would have passed for a miracle, and thus established my claims to be Maha Deo. I might have commanded him on the spot to say "Bum, bum, bo, Maha Deo," as I heard the Fakir at the Golden Temple say while he danced. I do not think it would have been difficult, — in that strange, wild, spot, — so sacred to the Hindu mind, to have humbugged such a man, and made him believe almost anything.

Here is what I wrote at the time, — or a few days afterwards in my Diary about this man. — "At the Cow's Mouth we saw a man, who left as soon as we came in sight and disappeared up the right bank of the Glacier. We made inquiries if it could be one of our Coolies, but was told no; but they told us that some men lived high up in the peaks of the rocks where they could not be seen, and that they did not wish to be seen by mortals, as they believed themselves Gods. That they painted their bodies of different colours, but that they wore clothes when they came down to the Cow's Mouth; that they could live naked in the region of the snow, is rather incredible, and as Wilson never heard of them before, I suppose it must be some myth. The man we saw was too far off to tell what he was like, beyond this, that he seemed like one of our Coolies, and a black dress like those of the most of our Coolies [wore]; but our coolies all said he was not one of them, and no one came up with us, and we heard of no one going, for we made inquiries at the Brahmins of the Temple when we came down." ≡ The impression existing now in my memory is slightly different from the above. The Diary puts it that we saw the man when we came up at first — I think that I have expressed myself badly. — for my notion has always been, that it was after the most of our party had left; and when I was sketching, that I saw the man.

≡ From Diary, under the date 13. May, 1861.

FACSIMILE PAGE OF SIMPSON'S MANUSCRIPT, ACTUAL SIZE.

Insert opposite p. 141.

CHAPTER XIV

THE HIMALAYAS

IT was the end of March before I reached Agra, and warm weather had set in on the plains, giving me a touch of fever, so I pushed on for the hills, which I reached on the 6th of April. As I had been to Simla the year before, I went to Mussoorie this summer. My plan was to visit the sources of the Ganges and Jumna, then go over the high passes into Tibet, and come back by Kashmir.

It required nearly a couple of weeks to outfit ourselves for marching in the hills. There are no hotels after you leave Simla or Mussoorie. We required tents, kitchen things, and stores of various kinds. I, of course, employed some of my time in making sketches of Mussoorie. At last we started, on the 19th of April. Our course was up the Ganges to its source at the Cow's Mouth. This sacred river is supposed to have four sources—the Bhagiratha, the Aluknanda, the Jhanuvie, and the Bishengunga. All these sources are celebrated places of pilgrimage. Our objective was the Bagiratha, which is generally understood, at least by Europeans, as the source of the Ganges.*

At Deralie, which is only three marches from Gangootrie, we found James Wilson, who was well known in the hills as the "Shikaree of the Himalayas." He dined with us in passing up and on our coming back, and he had an immense fund of knowledge. At Gangootrie there is a small temple, and some hill Brahmins attend it in the summer months.

*[In 1874 Simpson read a paper to the Alpine Club, entitled "Gangootrie, a journey to the Himalayas, to the 'Cow's Mouth,' or source of the Ganges." It is published in vol. vi. of the *Alpine Journal*, p. 385, and contains many details of interest.]

The spot is covered with snow in the winter, and no pilgrims come at that season. This temple is about twenty miles below the glacier, and there is no road or trail beyond it. We stayed a day at the temple, and then started for the actual source, and encamped for the night some miles below it. Next morning we went up to the glacier, taking provisions with us to breakfast there. The water flows out, a very small stream of muddy stuff. As a bath at this sacred shrine is supposed to wash away all previous sin, according to Hindu notions, I had my morning dip a little below the glacier, and I drank a little of the water, to complete the pujah, or rite. When I chatted afterwards with Brahmins I at times told them this, and they said, "Sahib, these are great words."

I spent the early part of the day in sketching. Most of our party returned, but I arranged that a couple of coolies should remain with me. Here a strange thing occurred. While I was sketching, a figure appeared on the right side of the stream, at a considerable height above the snow. I took little heed of it at the moment, but I afterwards asked the coolies which of them it was that had gone up so far. They all said they had not been up among the snow. There was no reason why they should have denied it, for I was attaching no blame to them. It mattered nothing to me what they did or where they went while they were waiting for me. Curiously enough, none of them seemed to have seen the figure except myself. As a matter of fact, I think the coolies lay down and slept. Although I could not explain this apparition at the time, I attached but little importance to it till I learned afterwards that Hindus occasionally go up to this sacred spot to seek death there among the snows. According to one story of the origin of the Ganges, the river falls upon Siva's head. According to another, which I have seen in pictures, the water flows from the mouth of a cow's, or bull's head, represented under the seat or throne on which Siva sits. Thus the spot is supposed to be hallowed by the divine presence, and death there means bliss, or absorption back into the deity. This is a sufficient attraction for many Hindus, and they wander about without food till they sink down and die. Had I understood the case at the time, I should have made the attempt to save the man; at least the effort would have been worth making. Probably I should have boldly told him I was Siva, and ordered him to return instantly to his home. I do not think it would have been difficult in that strange, wild spot, so sacred to the Hindu mind, to have humbugged such a man, and made him believe almost anything.

We returned down the Ganges a few marches, and turned to the right, and in about eight or nine marches we came to Karsalie, the village nearest to Jumnootree. Two officers, named Dysart and Birket, arrived at the same time. The second morning after our arrival we and the other party all started for the hot-springs at Jumnootree. We went off early, taking servants, so as to breakfast at the spot. The Sahibs had their shikarees and their guns with them, and guides from the village, so we made a large party. We took a road over the hills, intending to come back by the bed of the river. The hot springs formed a curious contrast. The water was hot enough to cook our breakfast, yet round a corner of a rock, not many yards off, there was a mass of snow still remaining, underneath which the Jumna flowed. Behind this was a cascade, and higher up were the snowy peaks of Jumnootree.

If I remember right some of the servants with the breakfast things went back by the hill road, and got safely home; but the larger group of our party started on the return by the river. We had scarcely left when it began to rain, and in a short time the rain came down very heavily. We understood that there were about a dozen places where we must cross the stream. We had crossed three times, but when we reached the fourth bridge it was covered with a rushing torrent, and impossible. To make matters worse our guides deserted us; they clambered up the hill to find shelter under rocks, and would give no advice as to what we should do under the circumstances. We were on the right bank of the stream, and the passage on that side was barred by a large rock projecting with perpendicular sides. Some of our party tried to clamber round it in hopes that, if it could be passed, we might go on, but they failed. Then it was proposed to go back and find a way home to camp by the road we had come in the morning. While this was being discussed, I tried to get past the projecting rock, and I succeeded. Dysart then made the attempt, but he wanted my flexibility of body, and failed. A chuprasie, however, a Brahmin, managed to scramble over the rock to the spot where I was. Finding him with me I said, "Let us go on." We waded down in the shallow water by the bank, but at a short distance we found it necessary to get over to the other side. There was nothing for it but to wade. The water was up to our breasts, and we had to hold on to each other to avoid being swept away. In fact this very nearly took place, but we were so nearly over that I made a bold dash, got a grip of the rock on the other side, and was able to pull the chuprasie after me. We then climbed up the rocks, and I had a hope that we might pass along above, and thus avoid the stream. But there were so many bushes, with very prickly stems, that I soon saw it was impossible, so we descended again to the river, and came to the next bridge. "Bridge" is the word I have to use, but some of the fabrics were only a couple of small pine-trees laid across and held in their places with big rocks at each end. We managed, by desperate struggling and careful balancing, to get along till we came to one that looked so bad, I thought it would be madness to attempt a crossing. At first we could not see the trees, but the chuprasie noticed them. They were stems not above 6 inches in diameter. I was for again trying the hillside, but the chuprasie felt with his stick for the trees, and managed to cross. The risk here was from the fact that there was a fall of about 6 feet underneath the bridge, and if one slipped a terrible plunge into this fall and into the deep pool below was inevitable. The chuprasie made the attempt, and as he succeeded, I followed; but I look back still with a kind of tremor when I think of the risk we ran. At last we cleared the last crossing, and found a path that led back to our camp, where we arrived just as it was beginning to be dark. What I had feared was that, if we lost the daylight, we must have had to sit down and wait till morning. The other party found themselves in this very position. When they went back the third bridge could not be re-passed, and they could do nothing but wait. The rain ceased, the water fell again as quickly as it rose, and they were able to move at last down the stream. But it became dark before they cleared the bridges, they were forced to remain at the place where the light failed, and they did not reach camp till morning relieved them. As the chuprasie had behaved very well, I gave him some backsheesh, and insisted on his taking some brandy as "medicine," offering it to him in my own tumbler. This he refused, but brought his own lota, into which I poured the brandy.

At the village of Karsalie there is a large and important temple. They had a devi in it, which they carried about on staves, but it was different in form from those in the Sutlej Valley. Rainy weather kept us a day or two longer at this place; and we were bothered with our coolies, most of whom took fright on account of the snow, which we would now have to face in our marches. One night they nearly all bolted. They must have been really in a funk, for we owed them money for their wages, which they forfeited.

The first snowy pass we had to get over was the Manji Kanta, said to be about 13,000 feet. This pass, being on the Indian side of the Himalayan range, receives a larger deposit of snow than those beyond, and it was the worst pass we encountered. We had to march for hours up to the knees in snow. There was no path, as we were the first that season to go over. I used a bit of gauze to protect my eyes, but I found it inconvenient as I struggled along, so took it off. The result was that I waked early next morning and found my eyes in a bad state. They felt as if full of breadcrumbs. I got my brass basin and kept bathing the eyes in cold water. When the morning began to appear I heard voices outside my tent saying "Sahib," and when I asked who were there, they said "Coolie log." It was the whole of our coolies, and they said they were "blind, like night." I felt I could not march, so I told them we would remain where we were for that day. My eyes became well again before midday, and I think the others were the same. The whole of our day's march had been in snow, and when we came over the pass we encamped just a little below the snow-line.

Our next pass was the Roopin, said to be as high as Mont Blanc. It forms the dividing line between the rainy region and the dry region of Tibet. We found it an easier pass than the Manji Kanta. Others had crossed before us, so there was a beaten path, and we got over early before the sun began to shine, so there was no snow blindness.

Beyond this pass we came down into the Buspa Valley, the stream of which flows into the Sutlej near Chini. A march or two brought us to the Sutlej, where we had to cross on the joola, or rope bridge, below Chini. We went up to Chini, where I saw many of my old friends of the year before. They pointed proudly to my sundial. They had preserved it as a monument to my memory. There were some Sahibs in the bungalow, which had been repaired. Among them was Captain M'Kenzie, a cavalry officer, and his wife. They were newly married and were passing their honeymoon on the hills, and as they were going into Tibet they joined their camp to ours.

Our route for a few marches was the same as that which Evans and I had followed the year before—by Punghi, Leepee, and Soonum. Here I found "praying wheels," or, as they ought rather to be called, "praising wheels," driven by water.* Thence we journeyed up the Spiti River to the Purung Law, which is put down as 19,000 feet.

In going over these high passes we had not the sudden change which has to be gone through in ascending a high mountain like Mont Blanc. In such a case as Mont Blanc the ascent from a low level is made in a few hours. In the Himalayas we were often for days living at a considerable altitude, and in Tibet we were seldom lower than 10,000 or 12,000 feet above the sea-level. In the case of the Parung Law, we had been ascending towards it gradually for days. Still it was a trying bit of work to get

* [Simpson wrote an interesting article on the whole subject of these praying wheels in *Good Words* for September, 1866.]

over such a great height. The snow was much less than on the Roopin. We encamped just below the snow-line. From that it was not far to the top, but it was a hard climb. Every few minutes one had to rest for want of breath. I was one of the first to reach the summit. There was a manie, or cairn of stones, with sticks projecting, on the end of which were pieces of cloth, with prayers on them in the Tibetan character. One of the bits of cloth I took as a curio. We found piles of stones on all the passes. At the Hango Pass we found a man who had sacrificed a sheep, and he was writing a prayer—probably a mantra—on a piece of cloth, to put on the manie. He explained that his brother was sick, and the performance was done to cure him. We found that most of the snow was on the other side of the pass, where it stretched over a gentle slope. Snow had fallen during the night, and no appearance of a path was visible. As I walked along, and had nearly come to the end of this slope, I suddenly fell through it into a crevice. Luckily it was only a narrow fissure and my arms caught the sides so that I was saved. On kicking away more of the thin crust I could see the dark cavern below. Icicles hanging down suggested teeth to my thoughts, and it seemed like the mouth of a dreadful beast ready to swallow whatever came within its reach. If I had sunk only a foot or two farther forward the chances are I should have slid down into that horrid hole and never been found again. Our camping-ground was only a short distance below the snow, and some of our servants suffered badly from the rarefaction of the atmosphere. I felt it only slightly, but I think Mrs. M'Kenzie stood it best of all. Some of the servants lay on the ground quite done up, with their comrades round them sympathising and attending to them.

A march or so farther we came to the Tchoomoreree Lake. As "tchoo" is Tibetan for water, I guess that we should call it the Moreree Lake. It is nearly twenty miles in length, and is said to be about 15,000 feet above the sea. We encamped at the end of it, and marched next day to the other end, where, at a place called Korzok, there is a Lama monastery. I made some sketches in the monastery.

The monks have a very long service. Tea is served out to them as a refreshment, and they offered some of it to me. It is made in a large pot like soup, with grease and vegetables. But as the monks were very civil to me, and allowed me to sketch, I thought it might seem bad manners to refuse, so I tasted some of the nasty stuff.

From Keewar, on the other side of the Parung Pass, instead of coolies we had yaks for our luggage, a yak carrying as much as three coolies. Of course there were men to attend the yaks, and I noticed that as soon as we reached our camping-ground at the end of the day's march these people started their "teapot"—a large iron vessel—and began to gamble with a kind of dice. These men were very pure Turanians, and from what I have seen since in China I am inclined to believe that the Turanian has in his nature a strong tendency to gambling.

Two marches from the Tchoomoreree is the salt lake, called by the Tibetans, from the margin of encrushed salt all round it, the Tchoo-kar, or White Lake. In its chief characteristic it resembles the Red Sea, and the cause of the saltness in both cases is no doubt the same—the want of an outlet for the water. I noticed a level line along the hills on the opposite side from the road, and I watched it as I left the lake, and found that it was level with the highest part of a valley along which I marched. When the lake touched that line, at some far distant date, it must have overflowed at that point. I found small univalve shells in the soil of this old beach. On the morning I left I saw a couple of wild horses, but they were some distance from me. So far as I could see, they had a great deal of the donkey in their appearance. The same day there came on a very heavy thunderstorm, with a good deal of rain and hail. So some moisture must fall at times; but it cannot be much, or the ground would not be dry and vegetation so scant. The country is really a mountainous desert. Villages or monasteries exist only where there is a small stream flowing down from the melted snows. It is said to be a very healthy climate, and Wilson the shikaree told me if he were ill or out of sorts a visit to it always made him well.

The next march was over the Tunglung Pass, 18,000 feet. There I found a manie and prayer flags. On the other side I descended to Ghia. My tent was pitched near a prayer-wheel driven by water, which kept up a constant clicking all night. The second march from Ghia brought me to the Indus. This was a long march, and I arrived at Marsilung.

From Leh to Srinuggar is about fifteen marches, much of the distance being a bleak, uninteresting country. The Lama monasteries interested me. There is a celebrated one, which has as its Tibetan name "Sang-gye-chi-ku-sung-thug-chi-ten," which has been translated as "The-support-of-the-meaning-of-the-Buddha's-precepts." The Lamas I found always to be good-natured, a characteristic which agrees with my impression of the Turanian character. I had no trouble with the people anywhere as I travelled along by myself, and the monks were always civil, and allowed me to sketch in their temples. The temples were dark and dingy and were very dirty. So were the Lamas. On more than one altar I noticed, placed as ornaments, bottles that had evidently been thrown away by travellers. On one altar, of which I have a sketch, were two bottles, of French make, for the name had been impressed on the glass near the neck. In another temple, one that the monks were proud of had its former contents clearly proven by a label in gold and colours, on which was figured a large tom-cat. I think the words "Old Tom," in red and gold, were quite legible upon it. In one temple I noticed an article that seemed strange for such a place, and excited some wonder in my mind as to how it got there. Over altars, or figures of gods, it is usual in these places to hang bright pieces of cloth, generally of silk. They are arranged to form a sort of canopy over the figure. Hanging among these, in the case I refer to, was a tailor's pattern card, of the kind which folds up, each page having a fragment of cloth on it. This one had "tweeds" for trousers, with the prices for a pair marked in the corner. When such a book is folded up there is a button and buttonhole to close it with. To the monks the buttonhole must have suggested that it was intended to be hung up. All it wanted was a nail or peg. So they had put it up among the bright-coloured scraps as an offering to the presiding Deva or Buddha of the temple.

At Dras I found some sculptured stones, which I sketched, and from one of these sculptures, twenty years afterwards, I found the origin of the Chinese pagoda. Chinese scholars all affirm that the design for the pagoda was brought from India at an early date, but from what particular structure it was derived was only a matter of conjecture till I deduced it from this sculpture. The stones at Dras are called Chomo by the natives, who have a tradition that they are a giant and his wife who were changed into stone.

Two marches from Dras brought me to Sonamurg, and I had then left the bleak country, and found myself in Kashmir, among luxuriant vegetation and beautiful flowers. It was something to have seen the dreary deserts of Tibet, but I have no desire to return to such a country. Still, I have often since congratulated myself that I saw the Buddhist system in that country in what I may call "working order," for it has helped me to understand what India was like in the Buddhist period, and it has enabled me to grasp the meaning of many of the Buddhist remains of India which could not have been otherwise understood. From Sonamurg it is three marches to Srinuggar, where I arrived on the last day of July.

Although Kashmir ought to be included in the Himalayas, and my tent-life was not quite finished, it may be fitting here to record what a pleasant life it is wandering about in these beautiful hills. With a small tent and a few servants, one is as free as a bird to go where one likes, and do what one likes. One day in a valley, with a clear stream and rocks and foliage of all kinds, in a day or two after you may be high up, even among the snow. You can thus choose, if you wish, any climate you care for. All that I have met, who have had experience in the hills, have expressed their delight with it. To the sportsman, the naturalist, the geologist, and I can speak for the artist, there is always something to interest. The Hindus believe it a place for the gods. You feel like the lotus-eaters—far above the world and all its strife and troubles. The life is simple and healthy, and in all my experience I know of no more pleasant kind of existence in this world than that of wandering about in the Himalayas.

CHAPTER XV

KASHMIR

I HAD a permit from the Punjab Government to enter Kashmir, but coming, as I did, into the happy valley by the "back door," no one asked me for it. I had also a letter of introduction to the Government Agent, who for this season was General van Cortlandt. He had been in Runjit Singh's service, and held in it the rank of General. As he had long been familiar with the Punjab, the Indian Government on the annexation of the country took him into their service. Under our Government he had the rank of Colonel, had been made a C.B., and was employed in the Civil Service. Two of the General's grown-up daughters had just come from England, and were with him, as well as his wife and a younger daughter, and as he was anxious that the two should keep up their drawing, he was desirous of taking me to places to sketch, so that they should come too, and get hints and encouragement. I went into one of the bungalows erected for the Sahib log, but soon found myself quite one of the General's family, and I left the bungalow, and used my tent as a bedroom in the garden in which the Agent's house stood.

The visitor to Kashmir finds on his arrival that the first thing he must do is to hire a boat. Otherwise he gets no rest, for all the boatmen wait at the door till one is selected. So, to get quit of the crowd, and find peace of body and mind, a boat with its crew has to be engaged. A boat is the cab or omnibus of Kashmir, because it can take you anywhere, and a horse cannot, owing to the river, the lakes, and the canals. Srinuggar is a mountain Venice, and you must have your gondola, which is there called a "kishti," the Hindostani for boat.

Early in the morning, as soon as you rise, the kishti wallah transfers your bed to his boat. You follow, and you are rowed up the stream a bit, where a plunge into the river is the method of performing the morning tub. One day I jumped out of my boat into the Lake of Kashmir—a rash thing to do unless one has confidence in the water, for the lake is a perfect garden of all sorts of vegetation, part on the surface and part below.

An incident took place the morning after I arrived which illustrates in a curious way Brahminical ideas about the metempsychosis. My boatman brought me some fish; he said he had been fishing for me that morning. This was repeated every day. He said always that he had been fishing for me, and that if he had been fishing for himself he would have been put in the "Jail-khana." This was explained to me by some one. When Gulab Singh died—he was the father of Runbir Singh, the Rajah at the time of my visit—the Brahmins declared that he had transmigrated into a fish, and on this account the Kashmir people were prohibited from fishing, lest they should catch the late Rajah. The Sahibs were free from this prohibition, and that is the reason my man pretended he was fishing for me. Of course his dodge was to catch enough for himself, and he brought one or two fish to me to justify his words. When I understood the case, I used to ask him if he was sure he had not caught the Rajah, when a wide grin would spread over his features. He was a Mussulman, and as the greater part of the population is the same, it is not fair that they are not allowed the benefit of this article of diet. The river and canals are swarming with fish, being so highly preserved.

The General, as an official, had a very large boat, supplied by the Rajah, with a comfortable space in it, covered with a dome-shaped canopy of red and gold. On some days the whole family went to parts of the lake where I wished to sketch. This was done in the cool of the morning; a kitchen boat would follow, and we had breakfast in some pretty spot, such as the Shalimar or Nisbat hoghs, sitting under chunar trees. There was always something to sketch in these places. In the afternoon again we would move to some other spot, and come home in the evening, while the men in the boat—I think there were forty of them—would sing "Taza-be-taza" as we glided through acres of the lake covered with the large leaves and bright flowers of the lotus.

The seeds of the lotus are not unlike green peas; they are very pleasant to eat, and are supposed to produce forgetfulness. Moore realised the beauty of the spot from the accounts of others, and it is surprising to find how accurate he has been; "Lalla Rookh" is a perfect guide-book to the Lake of Kashmir. On the occasion of a visit from two friends it was proposed to try, for my benefit, to realise the scenes described in the poem. To do this it was determined to have a nautch, and some of the most noted dancing-girls were engaged. To carry out the idea fully, the performance was to take place in the Shalimar Gardens, created by the famous Delhi emperor, Shah Jehan, and in the very building described by Moore, where Noor Mahal had sung

> "And oh! if there be an Elysium on earth
> It is this, it is this!"

The building is a class of erection common in Indian gardens—a summer-house with three doors on each of its four sides to allow the air to come in from any quarter. This building in the Shalimar is very handsome, of black marble, very beautifully carved. A small stream flowing from the hills has been led through the gardens, and the water surrounds the summer-house. Small cascades have been formed, and jets of water made to play around, giving a touch of beauty and feeling of coolness to the spot.

Our party, a very small one, crossed the lake in a boat, reading "Lalla Rookh" as we were paddled along. The programme included a dinner, to which we sat down about sunset. The fountains were playing, and a cascade had been turned on where there were small niches in the wall. Lights had been placed in these, and the water fell in front of them, producing a very beautiful effect. While we were at dinner the men had been busy lighting chirags—small earthen cups containing oil and a wick, with which illuminations are produced. They are put in rows along the edge of the water. When we moved into the verandah, with coffee and cigars, the whole place was bright with the illuminations, the fountains were murmuring, and we found the nautch-girls arrived, each with her baji-wallahs, or musicians, and were ready to begin. The first song was "Taza-be-taza"—"Now be Now"—a very beautiful song by Hafiz, and a great favourite in Kashmir. The effect was wonderful. I had been to nautches before, they are performances no one cares to see a second time. But in this case everything was different. While the dance went on our thoughts only turned to the times of Jehangir and Noor Mahal. The illusion was complete. For the moment we seemed not to belong to the nineteenth century. Had a jin or a giant appeared amongst us, or a peri from Paradise, such an appearance would not have been thought out of place.

It may be mentioned that some of the Kashmiris are so fair they have a touch of red in their cheeks. This was the case with Goolee, the principal performer of the evening. Her name means "rose" or "rosy." *

The General arranged a trip to Islamabad, near which is the old temple of Marttand. We visited Muttore, where there is a tank of holy fish. They are so plentiful that on food being thrown to them they come in such legions as to push some of their number above the water. Here and at Echibul are springs which form some of the sources of the Jhelum, the remarkable thing being the quantity of water that rises at each spring. On another trip we visited the Wuler Lake and Barramoola. On this occasion I sketched the temples at Patun. By doing this I did not get back to the boats that night, and had to sleep on a charpoy under a tree, and dine on chupatties and milk.

I bought a turquoise stone—Ferozé—for three rupees (six

* [The description of the realisation of a scene from "Lalla Rookh" was contributed by Simpson as part of an article on Indian jewellery to *The Watchmaker, Jeweller and Silversmith* of September 1, 1887.]

shillings); it was in a thin silver ring. Mrs. Van Cortlandt asked to look at it, and did not return the article again till it was very handsomely set in gold. The people of India look upon turquoise as a sort of talisman, and believe it will save its wearer from accidents.

Lord Canning commissioned me, if I went to Kashmir, to do portraits of the Maharajah, Runbir Singh, and of his son Pertab Sing. The Maharajah and his court did not come to Srinuggar that season, so it became necessary for me to go to Jummoo, which is not far from Sealkot. On September 15th, I started for Jummoo, and left the valley by the Pir Panjal Pass. My way lay through the lower hills. At Aknoor, I crossed the Chenab. At Jummoo the Rajah has a bungalow for Sahib log to put up in, and while I was there I was the guest of His Highness. A man came every morning, and my man, Jungly Khan, told him what I wanted, or rather what he wanted, for I suppose he and all my people fed at the public cost. An elephant came every day to take me anywhere I wished to go. One day I was going through the bazaar, and some one was leading a horse along the narrow thoroughfare. As soon as it saw the elephant the brute became excited, and as we neared it made a sudden movement, and jumped into a Bunnia's shop. The shop chanced to be that of a grain dealer, and I was scarcely past when I noticed that the horse had so far got the better of his fright as to be helping himself freely at the Bunnia's expense. One morning I heard much talking between my servant and some one; I inquired who it was, and was told it was the Maharajah's Khubbher ke Khagaz wallah. *Khubbher ke Khagaz* means literally "newspaper," but it turned out that this was the Court Historian, and he was procuring details about me for the Chronicles of Jummoo and Kashmir, in which I learned I was to be known to posterity as "Simpson Sahib Bahadur."

I long ago came to the conclusion that there is more resemblance than difference among the various peoples of the world, and here is what I take to be a characteristic example. In passing through the palace to the place where I had the sittings for the portraits, I had to cross an open court. On the first day I saw a boy mending a defect in the pavement with chunam or kunkur of some kind. The hole was only about six inches or a foot in size, and the boy sat there pounding the chunam slowly into it. I think I spoke to him in passing. Next day I again found him slowly beating away at the same hole. I said something about such a small hole not being yet finished, and his reply was, "Ha Sahib, Sircar ke- kam hai"—"It is Government work, sir." It struck me on hearing these words that it was not the first time I had met that boy.

Meeah Pertab Sing, the young prince, was only about seven or eight years old, but he was soon to be married to a daughter of the Chamba Rajah. While he sat to me he naturally talked. I was now able to do a little at the language, for I had been nearly two years in the country. The favourite questions with Orientals are how old are you, how rich are you, and how many children have you. Young people in India are called baba-log, or "child people," till they are married. When I told him I had no children and no wife, and added a phrase in the native idiom—"Hum abhi baba log hai" ("I am still one of the baby people"), he was surprised. I was then 38 years of age; he was scarcely eight; he was about to be married, and I was still a baby.

I was nearly a week at Jummoo. On the day I left, the Maharajàh received me in an audience of state. It was not a Durbar, for I did not present a nuzzar. When I arrived at the palace, there was a handsome carpet, with three chairs, each of them bright with gilding. Two were for the Maharajah and the prince, and the third was for me. At the Sealkot Durbar, the year before, Lord Canning had expressed to the Maharajah a wish for portraits of him and his son; these had been done by native artists, and as I was on my way to Allahabad, where I would meet the Governor-General, I was asked to be the bearer of them. They were entrusted to me at this audience. On handing them over to me, the Maharajah said, "When you deliver them, give many, many salaams from me to the Lord Sahib, and say that I and my soldiers and my country are his." On hearing these words, which had at least the sound of deep diplomatic importance,

I felt that I had the *rôle* of ambassador thrust upon me, and that too from a great king, to the head of the greatest power in the East, the Governor-General of India. In my day, as these pages relate, I have had to change my employment a number of times, but here was a new position I had never dreamt of reaching. The story told of Rubens, when he was sent to England as an ambassador from the Hague, will perhaps express the character of the situation. When he was here he painted some of the pictures in Whitehall. One day, as some of the ambassadors were passing through, one of them seeing Rubens at work, said, "Oh, see! there is Rubens the ambassador amusing himself at painting." "No," said Rubens in reply, "It is Rubens the painter amusing himself as an ambassador."

When I delivered the pictures to Lord Canning, and repeated the message from the Maharajah, I pointed out to him my claims to the position of an ambassador, and referred to Rubens. He never had heard the story, and was much amused.

At the end of this audience a tray of Kashmir articles was laid before me, and I still regret how I blundered. On the top were some of the ordinary embroidered kummer-bunds. I understood that I might select, so I took up a few of the top articles only, and carried them away in my hand. Now I believe that all that was in the tray was intended for me, and I ought, particularly in the character of ambassador with which I had just been invested, to have given a grand and ambassadorial wave of my hand, and the tray with all its contents would have been removed to the bungalow. There was at least one, if there were not two or three Kashmir shawls at the bottom, besides other things. In fact all the best articles were below, so my regret was great when I realised the mistake I had made. What I took was only worth a few rupees. What was below, for aught that I can tell, may have been worth £100.

My original intention had been to make for Multan, a place I wished to see, go down the Indus to Karachi, from that to Bombay, and then to Madras, from which I could start home at the end of the cold season. But I was obliged to alter all my plans. Letters and telegrams had come to me in Kashmir expressing the wish of Lord Canning that I should be at Allahabad early in November, as he expected to be there to hold the first investiture of the new Order of the Star of India. After all the attention and kindness I had received from Lord Canning, it would have shown but a poor acknowledgment had I refused to go. So I changed all my plans. Once at Allahabad, Calcutta would be the nearest port, and I should go from there by steamer to Madras, and end up at Bombay.

When I reached Allahabad the Governor-General's camp was there; the party had arrived the day before. Dr. Beale made me come to his tent that he might look after me, for I felt far from well. He gave me large doses of quinine, which took away the fever, but the doses were in such quantities that it made my hand shake, and when the ceremony of the investiture took place I was not fit for work. I managed, however, to get sufficient details for a picture. Lord Canning wished me to do one for him when I returned to Britain. His death made this unnecessary, but I did a picture for my own work.

It was understood at the time that the new Order of the Star of India had been suggested by Lord Canning, and this may explain his desire to have a picture of the first investiture. The object of the Order was to offer an inducement to Rajahs to exert themselves and do something to merit the honour. The tendency of our previous policy in India had been to render Rajahs and chiefs nonentities. We had an Agent, or Resident, at their courts. The Resident did everything, and the Rajah did nothing. In this condition, having no interest in what was going on, a local chief was placed in a position which tended to lead him into bad habits. The new policy was to bring out his qualities, and cause him to act for the benefit of his people—to induce him to adopt modern ideas and improvements; and the Order of the Star of India was to be a reward for those who made efforts at progress. It was thought that if the native chiefs could be led into this new line of action, it would be a great safeguard against another mutiny. The investiture and the mere fact of belonging to the Order would, it was thought, bring the chiefs into closer contact with the Government, and bind them to its interests.

The first investiture took place at Allahabad on the 1st of November, 1861. There were four persons honoured—Scindia, Patiala, the old Begum of Bhopal, and the Nawab of Rampore. Lord Canning and Sir Hugh Rose, as Commander-in-Chief, were the only persons who wore the Star and blue and white ribbon of the Order before the investiture took place.

At the ceremony there were four cushions, made in the colours of the Order. On each were the cross, collar, etc., for one of the knights. Aitchison, now Sir Charles, held the cushions up, and from them Lord Canning took the articles and placed them on the persons of the new knights. After the ceremony I received one of these cushions from Aitchison, as I said I would have to paint it in the picture for Lord Canning.

CHAPTER XVI

MADRAS

I ARRIVED at Madras on the 13th of November, 1861. The landing was done in the usual manner, in one of the Masoolah boats, which have no nails, as they would not hold long on account of the bumping on the beach. These are no doubt the kind of vessels described by Sir John de Mandeville, that had no nails, on account of the rocks of adamant, which would pull them out. The planks are sewn together with cocoanut fibre. I put up at the Victoria Hotel, but Captain Glover, who had known me in the Crimea, arranged that I should take up my quarters in the Fort with his regiment, which was, I think, the 44th. About a year or so afterwards the regiment went to New Zealand, and in an attack on a "pah," or stronghold, one-half of the officers were killed, including, I regret to say, my friend and his brother. During my short stay in Madras Glover and I became strongly attached to each other. He was very kind in his nature, and he had lately taken to literature, and published a small volume of poems. I remember how he came rushing down to the Massoolah boat, just as I was leaving, and had to wade nearly to his knees in the water to hand it to me. After my return to London we corresponded, and he kept me informed about what he was writing, which was an attempt at a novel. The last letter told me he had finished it, but was undecided about the title. What became of the MS. no one ever knew.

It was this correspondence that led me to make the acquaintance of his father, the Rev. Fred. R. A. Glover, who was then the consular chaplain at Bonn. He had learned about my correspondence with his son, and called upon me in Lincoln's Inn Fields, to inquire if I knew anything about the MS. He had himself written a book about the Coronation Stone in Westminster Abbey. His idea was that it was the actual stone mentioned in Jacob's dream, and that it came through Ireland, to Iona, to Scone, and to London, as a witness, arranged by Providence, of the Queen's descent from the family of David, King of Israel. Mr. Glover became, from his speculations on this subject, one of the leaders in the Anglo-Israel movement. When he found that I took an interest in the subject—I certainly did in the old stone—we became friends. He had been in the army before he entered the Church, so had a flavour slightly different from that of the ordinary clergyman. I never saw him after I removed to Willesden in 1881, and I think he died then or shortly after that date. He went to India when the Prince of Wales was there, and I called upon him at Calcutta. At the door of the house a native servant appeared, and I asked for Glover Sahib. The answer, which was in the affirmative, was expressed peculiarly—"Gulliver Sahib hai." Mr. Glover laughed when I told him his new name. His own derivation of his name, I remember, was from "Glaive," and not from "Glove."

To return to Madras. Captain Glover was, at the time of my visit, aide-de-camp to the Governor, Sir William Denison, to whom I was introduced. When I was at Madras the sad news came of the death of Lady Canning. While Lord Canning was at Allahabad, she had made a visit to Darjeeling, to make sketches of that place, and she had caught fever while passing near the base of the hill. She died at Barrackpore, and was buried there on the bank of the Ganges. I lost a great friend by her death.

My desire was to cross by land to Bombay. Seringapatam and the Falls of the Cauvery were places I wished to see. There were also some important temples I wished to visit, and Lord William Hay had told me not to leave India without seeing the Falls of Gairsoppa. It turned out that there was considerable difficulty in such a journey, and it would take a considerable time. Besides, I did not feel quite up to the mark after my late fever, and I feared its return. It so chanced that a Government steamer, the *Dalhousie*, was going round by Ceylon, and would call at all the ports on the Malabar coast; so I solved the problem by going in her. She was taking Government stores to the different ports, and there were some officers and officials proceeding to their stations in her.

This trip gave me a glimpse of Ceylon at Point de Galle. We stopped at Quilon, then at Cochin, where I saw a Christian church in ruins, a sight which struck me as peculiar. We made calls at Calicut, Cannanore, and Mangalore. I proposed to land at Honawer, the port for Gairsoppa, and the captain said he would try to bring out a boat. I was up early that morning to be ready, and the captain stopped the vessel, and fired a gun to wake them up, but after waiting some time it became evident that no boat was coming. There were some native craft lying in the bay, not far from the steamer, and I suggested to the captain that if he put me on board one of these, I would take my chance of getting ashore. I did not suppose that I should be in any danger, but I had not the slightest knowledge as to the character of the crews of these vessels. For aught I could tell they might be pirates, or they might be tempted by my luggage; so I told my servant to put my revolver in a handy place as a precaution. I was put into one of them, and the *Dalhousie* steamed away. The crew of the boat seemed to have just wakened up, and somehow they understood the situation, for the captain, if I might apply the title in such a case, got his "gig" manned for me. This was a tree "dug-out," not above eighteen inches wide. The "stern sheets" was a piece of wood placed solely for my accommodation, and two men were to paddle me on shore. We were a considerable distance out, and on looking to the land I could see great rollers between it and me. So large were these, that I thought it madness to try and land in such a wretched, frail craft. I could not discuss this question with my boatmen, for they spoke Canarese, one of the local lingos of that part of India. But I reasoned to myself, "These people must know what they are doing, and if they are willing to risk their lives, I may do so too. If the worst happens I can swim." Strange to say, they took me in, and not a drop of water touched me. The "captain" was only waiting for the tide to bring his ship in, which he did shortly afterwards. I saved myself a day or two by this adventure.

I found the Collector, Mr. Ratcliff, on the place where I landed, and he invited me to his house. The Falls being some distance away, a boat could not be arranged for me that day, but next evening I started. As I was to sleep in the boat, I took little with me but my sketching materials, and as I should be in the jungle, with nobody to see me, I left even my necktie behind. Early in the morning I changed from the boat into a manskeel, a kind of dooley, and arrived at the dak bungalow in the afternoon. To my surprise I found tents arriving and being put up. On asking who was coming, I was told Saunders Sahib. He was the Commissioner, or Government agent, for Mysore. I remembered meeting him nearly two years before in the Punjab, where he was then stationed, when I was with the Governor-General's camp. It turned out that he had been out here in his new district, and had come to see the Falls. Being a very kind, hospitable man, he had invited a lot of friends, so had a large party with him. When I arrived I had of course to call. He insisted that I should be one of his party, but I pointed to my whole wardrobe, which consisted of the clothes I had on. They had evening-dress dinners—some were military officers, with red coats, gold lace, etc. But Saunders would take no denial. I fell back on the absence even of such an article as a necktie, pointing out that it would be quite absurd for me to appear in such company in such a naked condition. But he covered that objection by at once turning out some of his own neckties, so I had to accept. It was a very pleasant party; they remained four or five days, and Saunders insisted that I must not leave while they were there.

In the rainy season these Falls form one mass of water, but in the dry period there are four separate and distinct falls. The latter is said to be the best time to see them, and this was the season when I was there. The mass of rock over which they pour is about 800 feet in height, so in this respect they rank among the great falls of the world. The principal fall is called the "Maharajah;" it makes a clean drop, without a break, of 828 feet. Next to that is the "Roarer," so named from the noise it makes. The next is the "Rocket," taking its name from the fact that the water comes down in sharp points, which resemble a rocket in the air. The fourth is the "Dame Blanche," so called because the water spreads itself over the rocks, producing the appearance of white lace. There is a projecting rock quite close to the top of the Maharajah, and by lying down on it you see the water rushing away from you, boiling as it falls, and producing forms suggestive of Milton's angels as they fell headlong from heaven. A stone dropped here has the curious appearance of resting in the air for a second or so before it disappears. This is owing to its moving in a straight line from the eye, so that you cannot see its motion.

At first I could do nothing but look at these wonderful falls. I never had seen anything like them. Descending from such a height, a large portion of the water becomes spray or fine mist, and when the sun shines the arc of a rainbow gleams amongst it. But as this mist moves about, acted upon by the wind or currents of air, it produces the appearance of a slight motion in the curve of colour. As the mist changes in density at each place, the colours fade slightly or brighten. This also helps to convey the idea of motion, and I remember comparing the display to the coil of the creature in Turner's "Apollo and the Python." But the coil of colour at Gairsoppa suggested a grander and more glorified monster than Turner had represented. I descended to see how near I could get to the falls at their foot. As I got near I felt sudden gusts of misty vapour, which increased as I approached, and I was soon thoroughly drenched. These gusts of watery vapour explained the coil of the wondrous serpent.

On one of the days most of the party were going out with shikare objects in view, and they pressed me very hard to go with them. But the falls were too great an attraction, and lucky, perhaps, for me, that it was so. Tiger, bison, and sambur abound in these parts. A tiger was found, and a couple of bullets struck him. He retreated, and the party followed him through the jungle by the blood they saw. This, I learned afterwards from more experienced shikaries, was the error they made. They ought to have left him and gone back next day, and they would have found him dead. This they ultimately did, and got the body next morning. But as they tracked him immediately after he was struck, and while he had life in him, as well as rage from his wounds, he sprang out. Each one scrambled up a tree as quickly as he could, but the party was taken by surprise, and a peon, a native attendant, was not quick enough. He had begun to climb, but the tiger seized his leg, and pulled him down, then caught him in the back, and gave him such a shake as a terrier gives a rat. All this was seen distinctly enough, for some were quite near the spot on their trees. But no help could be given. The peon only lived for about twenty minutes. The party were kept for three hours in the trees, and only ventured down when it began to get dark.

On returning to Honawer the difficulty presented itself as to how I was to reach Bombay. Steamers were few and far between in those days. Mr. Webster, the sub-collector, learned that a patamar was about to sail. She had a cargo of pawn leaves—leaves that are chewed with the betel nut, and as these are perishable a quick voyage was necessary. It was thought the patamar would do the journey in six days. This was much quicker than I could do it by land. The distance is about 350 miles. So I told my servant to provide food for the time estimated. Webster came on board to see me off, but when he saw the accommodation, he objected, and said I must not go. The vessel was a small one, with no house, or covered space. She was filled up with the cargo, all except a narrow space of a few feet across the middle, where my fellow had constructed a mud fire as a kitchen, and my berth was merely a mat laid on the top of the pawn, at the stern. This flat place was just about long enough for my bed. There was no room to walk; here I must merely sleep or recline till I got to Bombay. The only question was about wet weather, but that I understood was not likely to occur, so I determined to go. The object of the empty space in the middle was that, as the bottom of the boat was not at all a straight line—the keel sloped down from the stern and the bow to that space—the bilge water gathered there, and could be got at and baled out. The masts sloped forward, and she carried on each a large lateen sail. Probably the patamar is an ancient type of ship, and may be as old as the days of Manu.

There was a wind from the land which began in the evening, and we sailed with it northwards, and out to sea. The wind changed during the night or early morning, and came from the sea; then the patamar changed her tack, and came back towards the coast, where we anchored for some hours. This gave me the chance of going on shore every day, the captain taking me in his "gig," a small "dug-out." Luckily there was no rough weather, and no rain, and I saw a good deal of the coast. It was wearisome, but I passed the time pleasantly enough. The only book I had was a Bible, of which I read a large portion. As it became evident we would not reach Bombay in the six days, my man had to land and procure more supplies. But at last, on the 23rd of December, 1861, we reached our destination.

CHAPTER XVII

BOMBAY

WHEN at Allahabad in November, Sir Bartle Frere gave me a letter of introduction to his brother, W. E. Frere, at Bombay. I think he also gave me one to Dr. Bhau Dajee, a Mahratta Brahmin. This gentleman had been educated as a doctor in one of the colleges of Bombay, and spoke English perfectly. I had the advantage through him of visiting a number of houses of rich Hindus and Parsees, amongst whom he practised. In one house I was surprised and amused to see a large oil painting, about six feet in its longest dimensions, in a splendid gilt frame, of the Battle of the Alma. It was nothing more nor less than an exact copy of my lithograph published in 1854. In one Parsee family I made a number of sketches of the women and children. Dajee was a Sanscrit scholar and an archæologist, and I had the advantage of his company and verbal explanations of the Elephanta Caves, to which he took me one day.

From Bombay I went to Poonah, and from Poonah to Mahabaleshwar. There I saw the source of the Krishna, where a small stream flows into a tank from a cow's head formed of stone—another "Cow's mouth." I returned to Poonah, and went on to Ahmednugger. Here I put up with Major Edward Beale, brother of Dr. Anthony Beale. From that I went on in a bullock cart to Ellora. But I had first to go to Arungabad, and saw the wonderful old hill fort of Deogurh, with the ruins of Dowlutabad round it. One of the Delhi emperors wished to have his capital farther south, nearer the centre of India, and caused every one in Delhi to move to Dowlutabad; but on his death

SCULPTURED ELEPHANT AND PILLAR AT THE ROCK-CUT TEMPLES OF ELLORA.

Reproduced from Simpson's water-colour at South Kensington by permission of the Secretary of H.M. Board of Education.

To face p. 169.

they all went back to Delhi. There is a story that one man refused to go to Dowlutabad. According to the tale, he was chained to an elephant. When the elephant reached Dowlutabad only one bone of the man's leg was found attached to the chain. Near Dowlutabad is the Rauza, or tomb of the Emperor Arungzebe. Not far beyond are the caves of Ellora. There a tomb has been converted into a dak bungalow for the accommodation of travellers. The 3rd Dragoon Guards—the officers of the regiment—came on a visit to the caves while I was there. Among them was Van Cortlandt's eldest son, Charles, and a Dr. White, who, it turned out, had been with me in the Kertch Expedition, in 1855.

In one of the caves I found two Jogis, or Hindu ascetics. They had made a mud bench in the cave, and there the two sat, with some wood ashes of a smouldering fire between them. I sat down on the bench, and talked to them. The elder one had been ten years in the place, the other was a sort of pupil, and had been only a short time there. He lived solely on milk, and used one seer, or two pounds a day. He admitted also the use of tobacco. While we were talking a man—he seemed like a bunnia, or shopkeeper—appeared and made a salaam to the holy ascetic. The latter put his hand into a dish and gave the man a few roasted grains. These were accepted by the bunnia and carefully tied up in a part of his white cotton dress. During the transaction a few of the grains fell on the ground, and the man had scarcely left when a number of rats came out and began to eat them. The bench I sat on was so high that my feet were some inches from the floor. The rats seemed to have no fear; there they were under my feet, nibbling away. The old boyish instinct was of course roused in me at the sight of the rats. I looked about for something to throw at them, but nothing was within reach. I expected that the Jogi would fling something at them, and I looked at him with some such suggestion in my face; but he did nothing. Perceiving some meaning in my looks, he muttered something, and I muttered something in answer.

"What is it?" he said.

"Don't you see them?" was my reply.

"Yes," was all he said.

"Why don't you kill them?"

"Why should I kill them?"

Here was the whole onus of the matter between us thrown on my own shoulders, and I felt how difficult it would be, with my limited knowledge of the language, to express to this man a European's ideas about rats.

I thought to sum the whole case up in one sentence, "We people kill them." The sentence sounds much better in Hindostani, "Hum log aisa karta hai."

To which he answered, "Hum log aisa nakin karta hai."

My sentence was literally, "We people do so," his, "We people don't do so."

So far as there was any argument in either of these statements, I felt that the reply was quite as cogent as the words I had uttered, and that I was beaten by this ascetic, who sat there calm and cool, clad in little more than the wood ashes of his fire, which Jogis usually rub over the whole of their bodies. I always feel a twinkle of amusement when I look back to this conversation. At the same time it shows, not only the ideas of these particular men, but an important feature in Hindu teaching with regard to the sacredness of life.

I spent several days at Ellora, sketching the caves, and I may say my study and knowledge of the rock-cut temple architecture of India began there. From Ellora I went on to Ajunta, where the caves are all Buddhist. The sketching of these caves, as well as of temples, topes, &c., gave me a large amount of knowledge in detail of Indian architecture, and led me to study it still farther afterwards. At the time of my visit to Ajunta Major Gill was engaged in copying the paintings in the caves for the Government. The copies he made were sent home, and lent to the Crystal Palace, where they were destroyed in the fire at the north transept. The sculptures from the Peshawur district were lost at the same time. Captain Gill, the traveller, who was killed with Palmer, near Mount Sinai, was a son of Major Gill. In going from Ellora to Ajunta I passed the River Khelna near the spot where the battle of Assaye was fought.

To complete the account of the various modes of travelling of which I had experience, I ought to say something of those I had to try on this occasion. In going from Poonah to Mahabeleshwar the vehicle was a nibs—something between a small cart and a gig—an instrument of torture, I should call it. The dak gharry of the Bengal side is slow, but it is comfortable, at least in comparison with a nibs. The mail cart of the Punjab is trying, but it has, or had, speed as its recommendation. From Poonah to Ahmednugger I went in a phaeton, which means that there was a good road between the two places. At Ahmednugger I engaged two bullock-carts; one of these, when there was no dak bungalow, was my bed; the other was for Jungly Khan and an earthen cooking pot or two. We travelled at night, and put up anywhere in the morning, generally outside a village. I could sit in my bullock-cart during the day, or under the shade of some accommodating tree.

On the second morning after I had left Ajunta we put up under a large tree. On the other side of the road, or trail, only about twenty or thirty yards away, were remains of an old temple, and under a bar-ke-darrakt, or banyan-tree, sat one or two Jogis. They were nice, clean, civil fellows; so I made friends with and sketched them, and sat beside them most of the day, till we started again on our road in the evening.

I visited Nasik, which is said, as a holy place, to be the Benares of Western India. The railway was then working from the top of the Thul Ghat at Egatpoora to Chalesgaum, or Deololee. I came by rail therefore to the top of the ghat, made sketches, and then went on to the Bhore Ghat and made sketches of it. These were heavy works, and were not finished at the time of my visit. At the top of the Bhore Ghat I went on to the Karli Cave, and sketched it. I returned to Bombay on the 4th of February, and left for England by the P. and O. steamer *Jeddo* on the 12th.

At this early period of the year the crowd that migrates home from India to avoid the hot season had not set out. There were only about twenty passengers on board, and with that number a P. and O. steamer is very comfortable. One has a berth to himself, and does not require to stand in queue, like a beggar at the door of the casual ward, waiting for his bath in the morning. There is ample room to walk on the deck, and the table is not crowded at meal-time. The ship is like a private yacht.

There was no Suez Canal in those days. We landed at Suez, and went by rail direct west to Cairo. I believe the rails of this line were removed when the line to Zagazig was opened. I remember we came to a station somewhere in the desert, and all rushed out to get something to drink. We found a man in the small refreshment-room, standing with a bottle of beer in one hand and a corkscrew in the other, pronouncing in a loud voice, "Two shillings." Every one was indignant at such an exorbitant price. The best beer could be had in Bombay or Calcutta for one shilling a bottle, and, being nearer England in Egypt, we were under the impression that instead of paying more we should get it for less. None of us had any, and there was no tea, so we had to go back to our places in the train disappointed and disgusted. I remember that as the train started I said, "I see it all now; Colenso knows nothing about it." This author's work on the Pentateuch was then new, and much talked of. "He does not know the reason why the Jews left Egypt. Beer at two shillings a bottle explains it all." We were in the region of the Exodus at the moment. On cooler consideration we began to see that the price was not perhaps very exorbitant. In that out-of-the-way station there would be very few calling for beer except the overland passengers; there were only two trains a week with them; and to keep beer there for such a limited demand could not be done at the ordinary rates.

We had a day to stay at Cairo, and I managed to visit the Great Pyramid. I mounted to the top, and also saw the interior chambers and made some sketches. In those days the Cairo donkeys were not named after the most popular or notorious persons in Britain. "Yankee Doodle," "Billy Taylor," and "Billy Thompson" were common titles.

At Alexandria I sketched Pompey's Pillar, and observed on the base the name "W. Thompson," rudely painted in large white letters. I do not know what made that name popular then. There was a slang phrase current about the time, used to express doubt about any one's words or actions. It was: "It is all very fine, Mr. Thompson; but it won't do here!" This, I presume, was the origin of the "W. Thompson" on the pillar, and of "Billy Thompson" as a name for donkeys.

I came on by Malta and Gibraltar to Southampton in the P. and O. steamer *Delta*. Mr. William Day came down and met me. Prince Albert's death in the previous December caused many to wear mourning, and I recollect being struck by seeing so many people in black. To my eye, after the bright colours of India, the contrast was great, and it seemed to me that the people went about with the appearance of black beetles.

The following is a rough calculation of the space I travelled over in India, and on the journey out and home:—

		Miles.
From	England to Calcutta, *viâ* the Cape ...	8,000
,,	Calcutta to Peshawur	1,300
,,	Peshawur to Simla	600
,,	Simla to Chini and back	400
,,	Simla to Jubblepore	1,100
,,	Jubblepore through Central India and Rajpootana	1,000
,,	Agra to Mussoorie	200
,,	Mussoorie through Himalayas to Kashmir	1,500
,,	Kashmir to Calcutta...	1,150
,,	Calcutta to Madras	820
,,	Madras to Bombay	1,700
,,	Bombay to Poonah, Ellora, Ajunta, and back	800
,,	Bombay to England (overland route) ...	4,000
	Total	22,570

CHAPTER XVIII

DISASTER

64 LINCOLN'S INN FIELDS now became my permanent address and the centre of my movements for nineteen years. These premises were what is known as "chambers." I had two rooms and a very small bedroom, not larger than a berth in a P. and O. steamer. The rooms were on the top floor, with two windows in front, the two on the south side looking into the fields—a pleasant view with the dome of St. Paul's visible in the distance. My neighbour on the same landing had three windows to the front, and a much larger room at the back. His name was Thomas Woodbine Hinchliff. He was a Cambridge man, and had passed as a barrister, but was well enough off, and did not require to practice. He travelled a good deal, particularly in South America and the Alps, and had published books of his travels. As I also did a good deal of travelling while at No. 64, at times, on my return from a distant part of the world, I would find that he had gone off, or was about to start on a journey. Or it might be that when he came back he would find me going or gone. From this we called ourselves "Box and Cox." We often sat in one of our rooms smoking, discussing books, authors, botany, travels, countries, etc., etc. Often we sat till an early hour. That was nothing to him, as he never got up early; but I had breakfast at 8 a.m. every morning, in order to get to my work. As we were on the highest floor and could look down from our safe position on the deluge of life below—at least, so we figured ourselves—we called No. 64 "The Ark." He was a F.R.G.S., and one of a sacred number—there were about twelve of them—the

first members of the Alpine Club. As they had existed as devotees of the Alps before the club existed, these members were sometimes called "prehistoric." William Longman, the head then of the well-known publishing firm, was one of this sacred band. There was an asterisk put to their names in the published list. From my travels in the Himalayas, Hinchliff insisted that I must become a member of the Alpine Club. At that time none of the members had ventured so far away as the Himalayas, and as I had gone up as high as 18,000 and 19,000 feet (this last on the Parung Law, 4,000 feet higher than Mont Blanc), I was fully qualified, and was elected in 1872. I read one or two papers about the Himalayas to them, which were published in the *Proceedings*.

I had finished and sent home very few of my pictures while in India. The great mass of them had still to be done. I had only made sketches or procured the material from which to work, and most of the subjects were full of elaborate detail, and could not be knocked off in a hurry. They occupied my time for three or four years of constant work before I managed to get all finished. There were in all two hundred and fifty drawings. Some were very elaborate, owing to minute details of architecture or figures, and a number were exhibited before all were completed.

During these busy years I have little to record. On my return from India I made the acquaintance of Mr. James Fergusson, the great authority on Indian architecture. This became a very close friendship till his death in 1886. On seeing my sketches, particularly those of Kashmir architecture, of which no such complete set of drawings had before been done, he suggested that I should read a paper at the Royal Institute of British Architects. This I did in May, 1862, shortly after my return, and the paper was the first of many I read to them.

Although unknown to me at the time, it turned out that the firm of Day and Son had been drifting deeply into debt. William Day, the eldest of the three brothers, was the real manager and head of the establishment. In many ways he was a very clever man. His fault, probably, was the want of system, or method, which is necessary for the carrying on successfully of a large business. He was always full of hope; and this hope, I now believe, led him on to his destruction. He must have known of the sum the Colnaghis made out of my Crimean book, and he was, no doubt, buoyed up by the hope of making some *coup* that would retrieve his fortunes. As a last resource he converted the business into a limited company. He received shares—probably he received money as well—for his interest; but his creditors were numerous, and he had to give them what money or shares belonged to him. This was insufficient, and at last he executed a trust deed. In doing this he had to deliver up to his creditors every share he possessed. The creditors accepted this, and freed him from all his debts. But it was one of the rules of the company, that every director must hold £500 in stock. William Day had not now that qualification. It was pointed out to him, that under the circumstances, he must cease to be on the Board. He refused to go on under these conditions, threw up the whole affair, left the company, and started business in Cockspur Street, I think under the title of William Day and Son. I must explain my connection with the above events.

The company had taken over most of the works that Day and Son had in hand for publication, and amongst others they accepted my work on India. I am not quite sure of the sum it was valued at, but am under the impression it was £6,000. That was to cover the drawings and copyright. Some of the drawings had already been put on stone, and others were in hand. I had delivered the last of the drawings about the time the company was being formed, and William Day wrote me a letter saying he would transfer so many shares of the company to my name. I may explain that the artists connected with the firm drew money as they required it—it was like a bank to us. Some of us had a balance to our names, and when my Indian work was finished, I had a large balance. The place was so well established, so good and respectable, we all considered it as safe as the Bank of England. None of us knew the real state of matters till the crash came. After some months, I wrote and asked Mr. Day about the shares—I had heard nothing more about them—and he answered saying he would do everything in his power to have me paid. The real crash had not come, and I foolishly gave little attention. Now I know that it would have been useless. In the autumn I had gone to Scotland, and it was on my return to Glasgow from the Highlands, that Mr. Allan told me of Day's failure. I had never seen a statement of accounts, and it was not till I returned to London, and paid a shilling at some office of the Bankruptcy Court in Chancery Lane, that I saw the trust deed, which contained a list of creditors, and found opposite my name the sum of £2,800. All my own money had been used up in the expedition to India. Beyond my own money I had been drawing also from Day's, for I was earning nothing by other work all that time. So, when the crash came, I was really left a beggar. I had not a penny. Here was the reward of my seven years' work. It was a crushing blow, for I had been indulging in hopes. There was more than one intention in my mind as to what I would do, and the sum of money that would have been at my command would have enabled me to carry my intentions out. One of my plans was to have taken more regularly to painting for the exhibitions, but this was out of the question. I must earn money to live. And as it turned out very shortly, the 250 drawings were thrown on the market, to be sold cheap as a sort of bankrupt stock. That alone was a damper against painting. This was the big disaster of my life.

As the production of the Indian book would be a large and important piece of work, Colonel Ward, the chairman of the company, suggested that I should take some kind of charge, overlook the artists, and see that they did their work properly. When William Day left the company, John Day was the official secretary, and Joseph was manager, or superintendent, of the printing department. The directors had no knowledge of the business, and felt themselves to be helpless. This being the case, the proposal that I should look after the Indian work extended itself to the idea that I should be appointed art manager, and look after the whole of the artistic department. In my position at the time, I thought the thing worth a trial. Should the company prove a failure, a very short time would decide its fate; if a success, the position would be a fairly good one, and in a monetary sense it would be sure to improve. Besides, in the meantime I should be able to see that something like justice was done to my work. So I accepted.

John Day at last left the business, and the directors appointed me "Acting Secretary." So I had to open all the letters in the morning, and see that they were answered, etc.; and I had to write up agendas, minutes of the board meetings, and the like. I have before, in these pages, alluded to the various functions I have had to perform at different times of my life, but here was an entirely new *rôle*, that of secretary to a limited company. This was in 1867. Before the end of that year it became evident that the company could not go on, so it went into liquidation.

As nearly fifty plates of the Indian book had been completed, the liquidators of Day & Son, Limited, thought it would be best to publish them in a book with that number of illustrations. Sir John Kaye wrote the text. Most of the subjects had been poorly reproduced, for William Day, at the end of his financial struggles, had no time to attend to the details of the business. So the great work on India, on which I had bestowed so much time and labour, never came into existence, and I lost the honour and reputation which would have been due to me if such a work had been properly produced and published. This fact added to the extent of my disaster.

CHAPTER XIX

SPECIAL ARTIST

HERE again I changed my profession, though the difference lay more in the title than in the work. The real change was in the mode of publication. When I came to London in 1851 events, as well as portraits, and pictures of places, book illustrations, &c., were lithographed and published as pictures. But a change had taken place. The illustrated newspaper was taking the place of the lithograph, and the wood-engraver was supplanting the artist who drew on stone. So when I became a "special artist" for the *Illustrated London News*, I was merely following the current of the period.

In the autumn of 1866 I was in Scotland, and had gone on a visit to Duart, in Mull. While I was there a request came to me from the editor of the *Illustrated London News* to go to Dunrobin and make sketches of the Prince of Wales, who had gone on a visit to the Duke of Sutherland. This I did, and on my return to London the editor asked me to go to St. Petersburg, where the Prince of Wales was to attend the marriage of the Czarevich, afterwards Emperor Alexander III., to the Princess Dagmar, sister of the Princess of Wales. I was then negotiating with Colonel Ward and the directors of Day and Son, Limited; but nothing was settled, so I went to St. Petersburg.

After the marriage, which took place on November 9th, the Prince of Wales visited Moscow, and I had the honour of being invited to accompany him. The Emperor's special train was placed at the Prince's service. In this we had beds and food. The train left St. Petersburg in the evening. I had a compartment with one of the Mitchells—

I think it was T. Mitchell, author of "Murray's Handbook for Russia," who was Consul, or connected with our Embassy. In the morning, when we had stopped at some station, a message came that the Prince wished to see me. On my going to his carriage he introduced me to the Grand Duke of Saxe-Weimar as a friend of his brother, Prince Edward of Saxe-Weimar. He presented me with his photograph, and the Crown Prince of Denmark did the same. At Moscow we all had quarters in the Kremlin. We were only two days in Moscow, but I did a good deal in that time. I had to go about with the Prince, and make sketches of what took place. On the first night we went to the theatre, and on the last evening there was a grand banquet at the house of Prince Dolgorouki, the Governor of Moscow. I sat beside Colonel Teesdale, who was Equerry to H.R.H., and who had many friends in Moscow, where he had been a prisoner with General Williams after the Fall of Kars. It was a curious change from the conditions of his former visit.

An incident took place that evening which shows how Royal personages are often judged, or misjudged, and how little credit can be given to public report of them. In one of the rooms after dinner were some Russian gipsies, who danced and sang. Although the girls were in European costume, the dancing was so similar to the movements of an Indian nautch that I made a picture of it, which appeared in the *Illustrated*. In a corner of the illustration, but not prominent, I introduced the Prince and Prince George of Denmark. Some years afterwards, at an evening party, I met a lady who talked to me about the Prince of Wales and his behaviour, and among other things she said, "Yes, and see how he went on in Russia, among a parcel of gipsy dancing-girls." Now the only evidence that woman could have had was my sketch in the *Illustrated*, and I can give unmistakable testimony that the sketch represents the whole of the wickedness that took place. One of his suite, who had been in India, had told the Prince how like an Indian nautch the dancing was, and he came into the room to see it, a most natural thing to do. It was exactly what I had done myself, so I was as bad as the Prince.

As I was quartered in the Kremlin I was able to make sketches of the interior, and did several of the older parts with their curious style of architecture.

What beautiful plates we ate our food from in the Kremlin! They were exquisitely decorated, and each had the double-headed eagle in the centre. But on my return home I used to tell my friends that although everything was so grand it was only outward show, and that the Emperor of Russia must be hard up in two things—soap and shoe blacking. Unfortunately I had forgotten to take the first of these articles with me, and I could not manage to get a bit in this magnificent palace. My want of the language of course explains this, and I had no servant. It is certain few visitors to the Kremlin go without a servant, or a number of servants, hence no one thought of attending to me. I made a fruitless effort to get my shoes blacked. I stood at my bedroom door, holding it a little open, with my boots in my hand, so as to catch the first servant that passed. The passage was a little dark—this will explain what took place. At last some one came, and I held out the boots. He went off indignant. I got a glimpse of him as he went to a part of the passage where there was a better light, and, to my horror, it was a chamberlain in full costume of his office. For aught I know it may have been the Lord High Chamberlain. After this I succumbed to my fate, and put on my boots as they were.

On the return to St. Petersburg there was a grand performance at the Opera, to which I was taken by one of the chamberlains named Golubtzoff. He was in charge of me at the marriage and other ceremonies. On Grand State performances at the Opera tickets cannot be bought, invitations are issued by the chamberlain in the name of the Emperor. For the night the theatre is his house, the audience are his guests, and refreshments are brought round by the Imperial servants. The centre of the grand tier was occupied by the Emperor and Empress, the newly-married couple, and the Royal guests who had come to the marriage. The Crown Prince of Prussia was there, afterwards Frederick I., Emperor of Germany, as well as the Prince of Wales, the Crown Prince of Denmark, and others. The rest of the grand tier was filled with the ambassadors and their suites, and the pit with general officers. The "gods" were the students at the military schools.

At the marriage a little incident occurred—a mere trifle, but it had a peculiar interest to myself. I, of course, was in the chapel—the chapel of the Winter Palace—early. It is a small place, with no elevated seats of any kind, and I saw that as soon as it was crowded I should see nothing of the ceremony, because I could not expect to be allowed to stand in front of the many Royal and important personages attending. So I suggested to Golubtzoff that if I had a stool or something to stand upon at the back I should be all right. He gave instructions to one of the attendants to find this for me, but the man brought me an article that was not suited for the purpose. Golubtzoff had gone out of sight for the moment, and I could not speak Russian. In this fix an officer covered with decorations, who was standing near, asked in French what I required, and he conveyed my wishes to the servant. He afterwards asked if the article the man brought would suit me, to which I replied in the affirmative, and thanked him for his attention. When Golubtzoff turned up again, seeing the officer speaking to me, he asked if I knew who he was. I said "No," upon which he told me, "It is Prince Menschikoff." He was the Commander-in-chief for a time at Sebastopol, and I may say he had been at times equally attentive to me there, and when sketching too; but at that time it was shot and shell I was accommodated with.

At one of the big balls in the Winter Palace I was introduced by Ellis to Todleben, the real defender of Sebastopol. At the same ball I saw Schamyl, the celebrated Circassian chief. Knowing he was a Mohammedan I spoke to him, and said, "Salaam Alaikum." He seemed pleased at hearing these words; they could not be very familiar to him at St. Petersburg.

THE LAST OF DAY AND SONS

When I arrived in St. Petersburg, on the 2nd of November, no snow had fallen—every vehicle was on wheels. When I left on the 23rd of November the snow had been on the ground for a fortnight, and all the vehicles had shed their wheels, and become sledges. Even such small things as hand barrows were pulled over the snow on skates, which the sledge part looked like.

On my return to London the negotiations with Day and Son went on. In the beginning of 1867, as previously explained, I became "Art Manager," and eventually "Acting Secretary." This continued till February, 1868. The Abyssinian War or Expedition had begun about the end of 1867. Colonel Baigre, already mentioned, whom I met at Oodeypore, in Rajpootana, was in the Expedition, and he sent such capital sketches of the country, that the *Illustrated News* did not at first think it necessary to send out a special artist. But as the war went on the interest in it increased, and as Baigrie's sketches were only landscapes, it was felt that some one who could do figures should be sent out. They asked me if I could go, so I applied to the directors to free me from my duty in Day and Sons. This they did, and my last duty there was the writing up of the minutes of the last meeting of directors I attended in my official capacity, a minute recording the directors' high appreciation of my services to the company.

CHAPTER XX

THE ABYSSINIAN EXPEDITION

BEFORE starting on this expedition I communicated with Marlborough House, and I took with me letters of introduction from the Duke of Cambridge and Prince Edward of Saxe-Weimar. I left the Ludgate Hill Station on the 3rd of March for Marseilles, which was the port of the P. and O. steamers previous to the opening of the Brindisi route. From this I sailed in the *Pera* for Alexandria. There were very few passengers, so it was a pleasant voyage. Among those on board were the Honourable Mr. Bruce and his wife and a niece. One day the young lady was on deck sketching the servant of an Egyptian officer, who had put on some of his master's old finery. I asked if I might be allowed to sketch also, and helped to pose the figure, etc. Some years afterwards I had a letter from Miss Gordon Cumming asking if I had sailed for Alexandria in the *Pera* and had assisted a young lady in sketching. If so I was to call at an address in Mayfair, where the young lady would be pleased to see me. She was now the Honourable Mrs. Willoughby. Since that time she has become Lady Middleton, and has written two books of poetry—one "Thistledown," and a later one "Allastair Bhan Comyn"—which contain some really good stuff. She is a favourite niece of Miss Gordon Cumming.

At Alexandria, as I was not going to India, my luggage had to pass through the Custom House, which was a troublesome affair. I shall never forget one man looking down the barrel of my revolver. At last we got clear, and another man and I got the only two "honest men in Alexandria" to take our luggage to the hotel.

I went through to Suez with the Indian passengers, for I had some uncertainty as to whether I should reach Zoula, the spot where every one landed for the Abyssinian Expedition, from Suez or from Aden sooner. I thought I could discover this at Suez, but on arriving at the station there the passengers were informed that they would only be allowed fifteen minutes at the hotel. That seemed to me a *mauvais quart d'heure.* How was I to find out in fifteen minutes which plan to follow—to wait in Suez or go on with the steamer to Aden? If there were no steamers to Zoula from Suez, and I missed the one just about to sail, I should lose a week of precious time. I made for the hotel in hopes that some one there could give me the necessary information. As I pushed along, I noticed an Arab with some luggage on his back, and my eye caught the word "Abyssinia" upon it. I noticed what I took to be the owner of the property walking before the Arab. I explained who I was, and the fix I was in for the moment, so he said, "Wait here, there is a transport sailing for Zoula on Monday (this was on Saturday), and I am going with her." What a relief this was to my anxious mind! It is at such moments that the special correspondent is tried, and it is often merely a question of turning to the right or to the left. Here it was, Shall I go on or wait? But it is on such slight chances that the seeing events or missing them depends.

My new friend turned out to be Captain Arbuthnot, of Sir Robert Napier's staff. He had been to Egypt about mules, that animal having assumed a great importance in connection with the transport department in Abyssinia. Arbuthnot, though a young man, was a widower. He had been married, about a twelvemonth before we met, to a lady whose sisters were all handsome, one was Lady Dudley, another was Lady Mordaunt. All of them married well. Arbuthnot and his bride went to Switzerland on their marriage tour. There the bride was one day sketching in the Alps, when a lightning flash killed her on the spot.

Major Stansfield was in charge at Suez, so I applied to him for a passage. He was particular as to my credentials, so I showed him a letter of introduction to Sir Robert

Napier, which I think had the Duke of Cambridge's name or initials on the envelope. This satisfied him and he made an apologetic explanation. He said many had come making a request to go to Zoula, and only the other day one man had applied, stating that he had a letter from Sir Stafford Northcote, who was Secretary of State for India at the time. Major Stansfield luckily had asked to see the letter, and it turned out to be a note from Sir Stafford refusing to recommend him. With this bit of experience it was necessary to be careful.

Arbuthnot advised me to take a horse, and offered to have one brought from Cairo in time to go. The time was short, but the horse came, and we left on Monday, the 16th of March. Arbuthnot had a donkey on board, but as he was afraid he could not take it to the front I bought it from him, thinking it might be useful to carry my luggage. I christened my horse "Cheops," as he was an Egyptian; and in honour of the modern Pharaoh of Abyssinia, I gave the donkey the name of "Teodorus"—the local pronunciation of Theodore, against whom we were fighting. When the sailors on board learned the name they were delighted with it.

Our boat was the British India Steam Navigation ship *Koina*, a small steamer. We had a sailing transport in tow, which delayed our speed, and we did not reach Annesly Bay till the 25th. Zoula, our landing-place, derives its name from the ancient Adulis, the site of which was close by. Some of the Engineer Corps uncovered the remains of an old Greek church. Only the foundations were left, but I made a sketch of them. Nothing of the old city was visible above ground. I found here an old Balaklava friend, Captain Heath, R.N. He was commodore, with his flag flying on board a man-of-war in the bay. I went on board to see him, and met General Donald Stewart, who was starting for Senape next day, and kindly offered to take me with him if I could be ready. As it would be something to make a start on my long journey to the front under such auspices, I set to work at my arrangements, and managed to do this.

Servants were necessary, and I trusted to find Indians at Zoula. My Hindostani would enable me to employ them. There was a lot about to sail next day back to India, and they were mustered out for my inspection and selection. A miserable collection they seemed. It occurred to me that if I chanced to select men who had the desire to go home, I might find them unwilling servants, so I said that as it was difficult to choose, I should prefer volunteers. Two turned out of the rank, and the thing was settled.

I had almost 250 miles—that is, in straight line, not counting bends in the road—from Zoula to Magdala. Myself, horse, donkey, and two villainous-looking servants were the band setting out. I took no tents, as I learned that there were camping-grounds, or stations, at regular intervals along the whole distance, and that tents would be found at each station for travellers passing to and fro. One of my early experiences in one of these tents was in the Sooroo Pass. Repeatedly during the night I got up, walked some distance off, divested myself of my sleeping costume, and shook it in the wind, beating it against whatever was to hand. But on my return I was soon as bad as ever. The population of that tent must have been something enormous. However, I managed to derive one satisfaction out of that unhappy night. I caught one of my tormentors, and sent it home to Bonomi. He took it to the British Museum, to the natural history department, and they expressed great satisfaction at receiving it. They told Bonomi that travellers, mighty Nimrods of the chase, brought home and offered the Museum the results of their hunting, which were generally big animals, which the authorities already had, and knew all about, as there were as a rule no varieties of them; but as for the smaller creatures, such as the insect tribes, of which there are so many varieties, no one thought of sending them. So one of my "back-biters" has been reformed and converted into a teacher of science.

General Stewart took the command of the troops at Senape, so I had to go on alone. I had come five marches with him, and that was a good beginning. Between Focada and Adigerat, the third march from Senape, the road at one point goes along a narrow ridge, which forms the watershed at that place between the Mediterranean and the Red Sea. At Adigerat I waited a day to see the ceremonies of Palm Sunday. Figure subjects were wanted, and this gave me good material, for I was sending home sketches of what I came upon on the way to the front.

They told me a good story here, which is illustrative of the Abyssinians. They plait their hair in ridges from the forehead to the back. It is plaited close and tight to the skin, so that it cannot be combed or even scratched. So to make it comfortable, they put butter on it, or any kind of grease. This butter or grease gets into their dresses, and everything belonging to an Abyssinian smells of it. A man came to the doctor at Adigerat with a bad leg, and a box of ointment was given to him for it. They watched him as he left, and he had not gone far till he put his finger into the box and swept it round, thus taking the contents, and rubbed the ointment on his head.

One remarkable feature of this Expedition was that almost every Government in Europe sent officers with it to report upon its organisation. The Indian troops were no doubt an attraction for foreign Governments to learn something about. France, Austria, Prussia, and even Holland and Spain sent officers. I think two for each country were allowed to proceed. The two Spanish officers came late. One was an old General, who was anxious about comforts, and he was reported to have inquired of some one when he arrived at Zoula as to which was the best hotel in Antalo. The name of that place, for some reason or another, was in large letters on the map, so he thought it would be an important town. This was passed on as a good joke, for he might as well have expected hotels in the centre of Africa. Antalo was some distance from our camp, but I should say from its appearance that it had about a dozen houses, formed of wattle and daub, with thatched roofs. I have mentioned these foreign officers because it was at Adigerat I met the two from Austria. One was Count Kielmansegge, a naval officer. He became ill at Adigerat and could not go on.

The other was Captain Kodolitsch, a Hungarian, who had been A.D.C. to the Emperor Maximilian in Mexico and had been in all the revolutionary business which ended in the death of the Emperor. Kodolitsch and I agreed to go on together. He had a servant, a quaint fellow named "Joseph," who spoke nothing but German. Kodolitsch himself spoke good English. We got on very well all through the journey, and were of use to each other, because at some of the stations there were no European officers, only a native duffadar, with a few sowars, generally from one of the Sikh irregular corps. As Hindostani only was spoken in such cases, I had to become interpreter. On the other hand, with my two wretched Hindostani servants "Joseph" became a useful addition; he could cook and do everything.

The movement towards the interior had begun as early as January, but it was found difficult to march troops through a country that could provide no supplies, or, at any rate, very few. The sending of everything from the Red Sea became a hard task. The farther the troops went the difficulties increased. Mules had to be brought from all parts—India, Egypt, Syria, Spain, or wherever they could be found. The mule, with its pack-saddle, became an all-important subject of reports, opinions, and speculations. In fact, it became a sort of sacred animal. Had the Abyssinian Expedition occurred two or three thousand years earlier I believe the mule would have been worshipped, and myths would have arisen as to how it fed a whole army of soldiers, like the wondrous cow in Brahminic mythology.

When I arrived at the coast it was known that Sir Robert Napier was nearing Magdala, whither Theodore had moved with his prisoners, so I scarcely expected to be in time to see the fall of that place. Still we pushed on, with a faint hope that the final *coup* might be delayed. Rumours of all kinds came from the front. It was feared that a brute like Theodore might massacre all the prisoners and become a fugitive, and that it would be impossible to follow him in such a country. Some thought he would send the prisoners to us as a peace-offering. At every station we heard news of one kind or another; generally the latest news contradicted what we heard the day before, and was itself reversed next day. The nearer to the front we came, the more anxious Kodolitsch and I were to accelerate our movements. My time was not lost on the road, for I was doing figure subjects and sending them home by the mail, and that was the main thing the editor desired of me.

When an Abyssinian is baptized he receives a blue cord, which he wears round his neck. Often when we met natives they would inspect my neck to see if I had one. Not seeing it, they would point at me with their fingers and say "Hindee?" meaning to ask if I were a Hindu. On my giving a shake of the head they would say "Mussulman?" Their theory was that all Christians wore blue cords. Ultimately I procured one of these blue cords and wore it. This saved me from further trouble with the natives.

On arriving at Senape the Expedition was said to have reached "the tableland" of Abyssinia, and this tableland was much talked about at the time. The words suggested a flat country, like the top of a table, to those who were not familiar with the meaning of the geographical phrase. As the Expedition advanced, mountains were found standing upon this tableland, many of them high, peaked, and fantastic in their shapes. Two of the Naval Brigade were heard discussing this subject. One was heard to say: "I believe, Bill, they call this the tableland of Abyssinia." Then, pointing to some high peaks, he added: "Blowed, but they must have turned the table upside down, and them's the legs!"

At last, as we neared the front, the news came that Magdala had been taken, Theodore was dead, and the captives were safe and "free." Kodolitsch and I, as we guessed that Sir Robert would not wait long at Magdala, determined, as very few marches now remained, to leave our servants behind, and go off with a couple of blankets and try to reach Headquarters before the army began its return.

On the Wadela Plain we met the disbanded soldiers of

EXODUS OF KING THEODORE'S DEFEATED ARMY FROM MAGDALA.

Reproduced by kind permission from the *Illustrated London News* volume, "The Abyssinian Expedition.

To face p. 190.

Theodore. They were returning to their homes. It was a vast mass of some thousands of human beings. My first sight of them was as they came towards us, down a gentle slope. This enabled me to see the great body of the extended crowd as it moved along. At first, in the distance, it looked like a cloud shadow slowly passing. As it neared, figures could be perceived, and it became somewhat like a drove of some kind of animals. On closer inspection it turned out to be human figures of all kinds, men, women, and children, and I christened it the "Exodus" from Egypt. It was a remarkable sight. In a few minutes one was able to realise what an Abyssinian army was composed of, and what its organisation was like. Men that had been wounded in the recent fighting were being carried on rude litters.

When we reached the Headquarters it had left Magdala, and crossed the Bashilo. From the side of the deep valley of that river the hill fortress was visible, and I made sketches of it. We remained ten days before the return march began. The second division marched the morning before we did, and the released prisoners were sent on with it. I saw them start. They were a motley group, to a certain extent a miniature of the released soldiers we had seen a few days before. This was owing to the number of natives attached to them. Some had native wives; there were children and servants of all kinds, male and female. Some carried baskets, pots, pans, and luggage of every description, such as we had seen with Theodore's soldiers. They turned out to be an unruly lot, grumbling because they could not be provided with everything they wished from the commissariat. I heard one officer remark that not one of the European prisoners looked worth half a million of money. Each would cost about that sum for his release when the expenses of the war were calculated.

Theodore's Queen—or I ought to say Empress, for Theodore was Negoosa Negyst, or "King of Kings"—with her son, Dejazmatch Allamayou, was in charge of Mr. Rassam, and was to go with the first division. Her name was Tirtoo Work. That was not her title, she was Habasha Heghe, Heghe being equivalent to Empress, and Habash meaning Abyssinia. The country is known by that name in India, and I think in the East generally.

At Headquarters I found most of the foreign officers who had been sent by their governments to report on the operations. Among them was Count Seckendorff, whom I met here for the first time. He was on the suite of the Crown Princess of Prussia—our Princess Royal, afterwards the Empress Frederick. My name was not unknown to him, and as he was fond of drawing we became friends. Prince Edward had given me a letter of introduction to Lord Charles Hamilton, brother to the Duke of Hamilton, who was one of Sir Robert's A.D.C.'s. The Headquarters mess, with these foreign officers, was a wonderful babel of tongues.

Captain Speedy turned up here again. After I saw him at Peshawur he had left the service and gone to Abyssinia, remaining there about two years. Seeing, however, that nothing was to be made of Theodore or his country, he had managed somehow to leave, and had gone to New Zealand or Australia. When the war began, persons who could speak Abyssinian were scarce, and Speedy was telegraphed for, and attached to Headquarters as interpreter. H. M. Stanley was also in this expedition as correspondent of the *New York Herald*.

As the troops had advanced, luggage had been left behind, and at the front they were all existing on the scantiest of means. Tents, mess dishes, and everything that could be spared had been dropped. There was a recognised deficiency of all comforts; no beer could be had at the front, and even rum was scarce; and each tent had to hold as many at night as the space would allow. As we marched back again the things left behind were picked up.

Mr. Hormuzd Rassam, whose detention as a prisoner by Theodore, was the principal cause of the war, I began a friendship with which has continued till the present day. He had charge of the Queen and her son, Theodore's only legitimate child. One day, after we had returned a few marches, I went over to Mr. Rassam's tent and sketched the boy. He was then seven years of age. He came into the tent dressed and with a shanah over-all—that is, the white sheet with a broad red stripe near one of its edges—a necklace, and the matab, or blue cord of his baptism. The finishing touch, according to Abyssinian ideas of the toilet, had been given to him, by putting some butter or grease on his head. A small stream of it was trickling down the side of his face. A remarkable thing chanced with the reproduction of this portrait. When it appeared in the *Illustrated London News*, it was really slightly more like the boy than my picture, from which it was copied. The published likeness is thus particularly good. This, of course, was an accident, but a curious one.

The Queen was to have sat to me, but day by day the sitting was put off, as she was not well, and her death took place, so I never saw her. This occurred at Eikullet, the first camping ground north of Antalo.

There was a place called Chelicut, with an important church, that I wished to see, and on the march back from Antalo to Eikullet, I went by another road to see Chelicut on the way. An escort of two or three dragoons was sent with me in case of accidents. A large number of books had been found in Magdala. Theodore had looted churches all over the country of their books, and sent them to his stronghold, where he intended to found a church to the Holy Trinity. Sir Robert arranged to bring home a certain number of these books to place in museums, and in the libraries of the universities, and a few for presents. The books were all written on parchment, and in the old Geez character. Books of this kind are scarce in Abyssinia because they are expensive, so Sir Robert considered that it would be unfair to bring out of the country more of them than was necessary. As they were principally Bibles, gospels, psalters, and books of devotion, he was giving them, as we marched back, to the various churches we passed. So a message was sent with me—it was given to an Abyssinian servant I had picked up—to tell the priests at Chelicut to come that day to the camp and they would receive some of the books.

After I had seen the church, I was invited into a house, where one of the priests, a little man with a large turban on his head, lived. The message and my escort had impressed them with my importance. When we had sat down in the house, one of those present pointed to the little priest, and said "Episcopus," from which I learned that he was a high dignitary in the church. There is only one Abuna, or bishop, in Abyssinia—so he could not have been the "Episcopus." My servant had a bag with my sketch-books, and in it was a flask of rum, which I produced. About a glassful was poured into the drinking cup of the flask, and I offered it to this high ecclesiastic. His servants took a large white sheet and held it all round him so as to totally screen him from sight. Then I could hear the "Episcopus" gurgling the liquor in his throat while he drank, as if he thoroughly enjoyed it. This screening of a sacred or important personage while he eats or drinks is a custom of primitive races in many parts of the world. From a man I met in the church I bought a small brass cross. It had an inscription, and there was a bit of dirty cloth stuck through two holes. They attached a piece of cloth in a similar way to the large processional crosses. The origin of this I was not able to find out.

That evening at Eikullet there was a terrible storm of thunder and rain. We were at such an altitude on the table-land, the thunder did not seem to be in the clouds above us, but we were in the thunder. The crashing peals sounded as if only outside our tents. The rain poured, and in the midst of this outburst of nature news came that the Queen was dead. Messengers were sent off to Chelicut for the priests to come and perform the funeral services, and our early march in the morning was ordered to be postponed. When I got up next morning the Queen's tent had become a chapel, in which the priests, my friend the "Episcopus" among them, were chanting prayers beside the body. The Queen's servants were wailing round the tent for the loss of their mistress. Her female attendants had put on her richly-embroidered mantles, or carried in their hands, which they held aloft, some article belonging to her, such as a slipper or scarf. One had her drinking-horn. While they waited they danced about in an uncouth manner. I learned from some one who understood the language that they were calling her by all the endearing terms which could express their attachment and grief at losing her. One peculiar name by which they called her was "Supper." I suppose they meant she was their food and support. Some of them did that which is forbidden in Scripture—they scratched their foreheads with their nails till the blood came. At last a litter was prepared, and the funeral procession moved away to Chelicut. A richly-ornamented umbrella was borne before the body. The priests were around the litter chanting. One held up a large processional cross, another waved incense, and the attendants continued their strange antics. They had four or five miles to go, and I wondered whether they would be able to keep up the wail and the antics all that way. I understood that the body was to be deposited in the church of Chelicut.

It was Sir Robert Napier's intention to have made up a large party of all the foreign officers at Headquarters, and the correspondents, with whom he would have branched off somewhere about Adigerat, and paid a visit to Axum, the ancient capital of Abyssinia, where certain obelisks and other remains of antiquity still exist. In the old church at that place is preserved the real ark of the covenant which was carried off from Jerusalem by Menelik, the son of the Queen of Sheba.* But the rainy season was close at hand. In fact, one heavy fall had taken place and carried off some men in the Sooroo Pass, and the Commander-in-Chief, fearing further danger, would not risk delay. So this expedition, much to my regret, was abandoned.

At Senape, Kassai, Prince of Tigre, came to meet Sir Robert, and we waited there for a day or so while a review took place, at which Kassai was present. This was on May 24th, the Queen's birthday. Sir Robert gave a dinner

* According to this legend, Menelik was educated at Jerusalem, and when the young man was about to return to his mother country Solomon allowed a model of the Ark to be made. Some priests were to accompany Menelik to Abyssinia, and they managed to place the model in the Holy of Holies, and take away the real ark with them.

in the evening. Kassai did not attend that. One day I went to Kassai's camp and took his portrait. This, although only in pencil, Sir Robert declared was the best likeness he had ever seen. Probably this was owing to the peculiar and marked features of the man, which were easily caught. In Kassai's tent I was treated to tej, a kind of mead which the Abyssinians make. Kassai afterwards became Negoosa Negyst, or King of the kings of Ethiopia, and assumed the name of John, or Johanna.

We left Prince Kassai at Senape, but he sent some of his people with us down to Zoula to receive some old rifles. Between Zoula and Koomaylee, the entrance to the Sooroo Pass, there is a flat sandy piece of ground, extending about thirteen miles. This had been the first march to the front. On our return a rude kind of railway had been laid down. The stock for it was a contractor's material that had been brought from India. The only carriages were the waggons the contractors had used for railway making. On our arrival at the Koomaylee terminus a "special train" was arranged for Sir Robert and the Headquarters party. Planks had been laid across the waggons, and, if I recollect right, a flag—a Jack, or something of that kind—was laid on the planks Sir Robert occupied. Speedy was in the same waggon with me, and a few of Kassai's men were in the next "carriage." They did not have seats, but squatted down on the floor. Some of these people had to walk, and when we passed them they tried by hard running to keep up with us, but were soon left behind, much to the amusement of their friends in the waggon. I noticed that they were conversing among themselves very earnestly, and I asked Speedy to inquire what their thoughts were. They said they were considering "whether Solomon in all his glory had ever conceived such a wonderful method of travelling as this." They had no doubt been thinking of Solomon's wonderful throne, on which the genii carried him through the air.

One day on the march some one came into our tent, and the question arose as to whether or not we should get a medal for the war. I suggested that the first thing to be done was to design a medal. This led me to try one or two ideas on paper. I knew that every one was against the "half-crown" design which had been rigidly adhered to in all war medals. So I made a sketch. Almost every detail of the design was derived from Abyssinian sources. The general design was an Abyssinian cross—of bronze, I suggested—with the Queen's head of silver in the centre. The ribbon had a red stripe horizontally. This was taken from the shama, a large sheet with a red stripe near one of its edges, a dress of honour—in fact, a sort of court dress in Abyssinia. Every one in the Expedition was familiar with it, and recognised its appropriateness. To the clasp, with the word "Magdala" on it, I added small pendants, characteristic of Abyssinian jewellery.

It soon was known that a design had been made. It was even rumoured that it was settled all were to receive medals. Our tent became thronged with those that wanted to see the design. Even men I did not know came up to me on the march and asked as a favour to see it. Sir Robert heard of it, and I had to take it to him. He was delighted with it, and suggested some small alterations. These I made, and then did a very careful drawing, which he took home, and submitted to the Government when the question of a medal came up for consideration. I believe he tried hard to make them adopt a design like mine. He sent for me in London, and I twice over made alterations in the details, which he hoped would make it acceptable. But he failed. This was explained to me by the suggestion that the high officials who have the settling of these matters all wear orders or crosses on their breasts, and any mere war medal beyond the traditional half-crown pattern they think might be mistaken for one of those higher orders of decoration. Hence their rigid adherence to the old type.

I learned afterwards that the Princess Louise made the design which was actually adopted. She was limited to the half-crown shape, but there are still traces of my design in the medal. The Queen's head is within a contracted circle, and what formed the cross in my sketch became a zig-zag line or scallop, with the letters of the word "Abyssinia" between the points. In one of the designs I introduced a crown above the medal. As there is some difficulty in producing ribbons with cross stripes, the red band was put perpendicularly instead of horizontally as I had it.

It had at first been arranged to send Theodore's Queen and her son to India, but upon her death it was determined to bring Alúmaya to England. The boy was placed in charge of Captain Speedy, and at Zoula the two joined our mess. This was a great change for the little fellow, as a European table and all its details were new to him. His fingers had been his knife and fork previously. He chanced to sit beside me on the first morning at breakfast, and I remember how I gave him his first lesson in manipulating bread and marmalade. He had not the faintest notion what to do with these articles when placed upon his plate. At last he was sent on board the *Feroze*, an Indian steamer that was to take Sir Robert Napier and the Headquarters party to Suez. I was one of those invited to go with this party. Sir Robert was about the last man to leave, and this involved a delay of about a week at Zoula. It was now June, and the heat was great. Nearly all day, across the sandy plain between the bay and the hills, blew a fierce, hot blast, full of sand and dust. With the perspiration on the skin from the heat, the sand and dust stuck and gathered, till one had a thick coating all over. Externally at least one felt that man was only dust. The wind went down before the evening, and a dip in the bay became a necessity and a relief.

I left Zoula for the front on the 27th of March and reached Headquarters on the 20th of April; started on the return march on the 22nd of April; arrived at Zoula on the 2nd of June; left Zoula in the *Feroze* on the 12th June; arrived at Suez on the 18th of June.

A curious theory regarding Theodore occurred to me, which I have not seen suggested by any writer about the war. He was a wonderful man—another Napoleon, whether as great one cannot say. He had a more limited field of action than Napoleon; but he was able, had great mental power, ability, and ambition, and was at the same time bad and brutal. The cruelties related of him are terrible. Like Napoleon, he rose from almost nothing to be an Emperor. He had conquered the whole of Abyssinia; but an ambitious man is never satisfied, he always wishes to extend his power. Now the Abyssinians have a prophecy that they will one day conquer Jerusalem, and that this will be achieved by them under a King named Theodore. This man, whose first name was Kassa, no doubt knew of that prophecy, and most probably adopted the name Theodore when he became Negoosa Negyst, with a view to fulfilling it. He likened himself to David, who from a shepherd boy became a monarch. If his previous history was like David's why not complete the whole likeness? David conquered Jerusalem, might not he do the same? He could raise an army, but he had no artillery, and without artillery he felt himself powerless for such an undertaking. The first question Theodore asked when any European arrived was, "Can you make guns?" If they said "No," he demanded, "Will you try to make guns?" If they refused to try, he kept them as prisoners in the hope that they would try. He did manage to have a big mortar made, and I think something in the shape of a gun or two had been attempted. This intense desire for artillery tells in distinct language that he wished to extend his conquests beyond the boundaries of Abyssinia. Here, it seems to me, is the key to this man's conduct. It explains why he kept Europeans. Even if they could not make guns, he may have thought he could turn them to account in some way or another. This is only a guess on my part, but I believe it a suggestion which makes the whole of this man's conduct capable of being understood.

As an illustration of Theodore's cruelty, I shall relate an incident. One morning on the march back an Abyssinian with a strange dress spoke to me. From my ignorance of the language I could not understand what he said, but by a lucky chance an interpreter turned up, who questioned him and got his history. Towards the end of the King's career the Abyssinians were falling away from him. His exactions for his army had become severely oppressive, and he was hated. Even his soldiers had begun to desert him. This man had been a soldier and had deserted. Theodore placed a number of the wives and children of deserters, this man's wife among the number, in a house, and set fire to it. All perished. This was to frighten those who had not yet deserted, for although a soldier could slip away by himself, he could not take his wife and children with him. This man, when he heard what had been done, had renounced the world and "taken the cowl," and was now on his way to Jerusalem to visit the tomb of his Lord. His reason for speaking to me when we met was to inquire how he could manage to get there. The story here told is quite in keeping with others I have heard of Theodore. At the same time the Abyssinians in general have a character for barbarity. They cut off the ears, noses, and other parts of the bodies of their prisoners as trophies of their valour.

I had some experiences of Theodore's son Alumaya on the way home worth recounting. A few Abyssinian servants were brought to attend upon him. Among others was a priest named Alika Zenub, who was to be his tutor. One night on the Red Sea, before we reached Suez—we all slept on deck on account of the heat—a considerable noise was heard among Alumaya's party. Speedy went to them, and brought the boy away. It would seem they had tried to frighten him, for what purpose I did not quite comprehend. He slept beside Speedy that night, and next morning would not look at one of his people. Speedy asked him what was to be done with his servants. He gave a significant jerk with his hand to the gunwale of the vessel, and said, "Throw them into the sea." When these words were reported every one made the comment, "A chip of the old block." I believe the servants, including Alika Zenub, were all sent back to their own country from Suez.

I went on shore with Speedy and Alumaya at Suez. We soon had a crowd at our heels when it was known that we had the son of Theodore with us. Speedy's object was to buy some clothes for himself and for Alumaya, so we entered a shop; but the difficulty, in a place like Suez, was to find garments for two such extreme customers. Speedy was 6 feet 6 inches, and the boy was only seven years. Speedy did find a pair of trousers that he could wear, but they suggested to my eye that he had grown a little out of them. Alumaya was more easily rigged out, and in that shop I saw him for the first time in elastic-side boots. A curious change for a young savage. From Alexandria the *Urgent*, a Government troopship, took us to Malta. On board this ship Sir Robert had a ball made, and tried to get Alumaya to play with him. If Sir Robert threw the ball, the youngster scarcely tried to catch it, and Sir Robert had to go and pick it up himself. Speedy asked him why he did not run for the ball. His answer was, "Am I not a king's son, why should I go and fetch it?" At Malta we had evidence that he was very sharp. Lord Clarence Paget was then Commander-in-Chief in the Mediterranean, and Speedy was asked to take Alumaya to Lord Clarence's house, as his wife and children would like to see him. As Lord Clarence was an old Black Sea friend, I went with Speedy. The children brought in all their toys, and even offered them to Alumaya, but he sat calm and sedate, not unlike the figures of Buddha. He appeared to take no notice of anything. Among the toys was one of a cat that played on a harp. The children thought it would interest, but he only gazed at it with an expression of supreme indifference. Kassa, Speedy's servant, an Abyssinian, was in the next room waiting, so I took the cat and harp to show it to him. He became wild with excitement, and said to Speedy in Abyssinian, "How in the name of the Father, Son, and Holy Ghost, can you people teach cats to do such things?" The contrast between Kassa and Alumaya was most striking. Here comes the sharpness of the boy. When we left, Speedy asked him if he was not surprised at the cat, and he said No, he saw it went with a screw, because he had given a slight wave of the hand, and the cat did not wink, so he knew it was not real. These illustrations of his conduct, which came under my eyes, may indicate his character and capabilities.

The Queen, I understood, took charge of the boy, and confirmed Speedy as his Comptroller. They lived for some years at Freshwater, Isle of Wight. Speedy got an appointment in India, somewhere in Oudhe, and took Alumaya there. On his return the Queen presented a gold watch to Speedy as a mark of her appreciation of his services, and the boy was placed under a tutor. He died at Leeds of consumption, and was buried, I think, in St. George's Chapel, Windsor, in October, 1879. His age at his death would be seventeen or eighteen at the most.

From Malta we came to Marseilles in H.M. dispatch steamer *Valetta*, and arrived at Dover on the 2nd of July, at 4 a.m., where, at that early hour, an address was made by the Mayor to Sir Robert. At Herne Hill Station I bade Sir Robert goodbye, and was back at 64, Lincoln's Inn Fields, by 7 a.m. Thus ended my Abyssinian journey.*

* [The *Illustrated London News* published a folio volume on *The Abyssinian Expedition*, containing the drawings of Simpson, Baigrie, and others, with letterpress by Mr. Roger Acton. Simpson himself in October, 1868, contributed to *Good Words* an article entitled "An Artist's Jottings in Abyssinia"; and he read a valuable paper on "The Church Architecture of Abyssinia" before the Royal Institute of British Architects in June, 1869.]

CHAPTER XXI

THE NEW ROUTE TO INDIA

THE Prince and Princess of Wales had arranged to visit Egypt during the cool season of 1868-69. And the *Illustrated London News* thought it would be a good move to send me to illustrate the new route to India, and pick up at the same time as much as I could connected with the royal visit to Egypt, Constantinople, etc. The new route to India was to be *viâ* the Mont Cenis Tunnel, Brindisi, and the Suez Canal. Before the Mont Cenis route was opened, the P. and O. port, by which the mails and passengers in a hurry went to the East, was Marseilles. I accepted this commission and left London on the 22nd of December, 1868.

On Christmas Eve I arrived at St. Michel. This was the terminus of the French railway, and the starting-point of what was known as the Fell line, a narrow-gauge railway, with a central rail, by means of which the ascent and descent of steep inclines could be accomplished, and sharp curves passed with safety. It was a British undertaking, and the managers lived at St. Michel. I spent Christmas Day with them, made sketches, and the day after started to cross Mont Cenis with the head manager, Passmore I think was his name. We stayed at Modane on the way, the entrance to the tunnel on the French side. I only made sketches of the entrance, as my plan was to go in from the Italian end. This I did from Susa, going up the Dora Valley to Bardonnêche, where my letter at once secured me admission to the workings. I was taken into the tunnel in a waggon drawn by a horse, and had some miles to go, though there was still a mile or so of rock to pierce before those working from each end could meet. Thence I went by Turin and Allessandria to Bologna, where I stopped for twenty-four hours, and saw the sights of that place—the cathedral, the falling tower, and the group of seven churches in Santa Stefano, etc.

Brindisi I found to be a nice, old, dirty town with a large store of archæology in it. There are the remains of a round church of St. John. In the old cathedral I made the acquaintance of Archdeacon Tarantini, who was devoted to antiquities. There is the Casa Virgile, and the pair of columns that mark the end of the Appian Way.

From Brindisi I passed over to Alexandria. M. Lesseps was in Cairo, and my letter of introduction to him was sent on. The answer to it contained an invitation to a ball or fête in Cairo on the birthday of the Khedive, Ismail Pasha. A splendid new palace had been built at Gezireh, and the fête included the "house-warming." It was a very grand affair. M. Lesseps arranged to take a large party, to which I was invited, over the Canal. The party included the Duke of Sutherland and his son, the Marquis of Stafford, Professor Owen, Dr. W. H. Russell, of the *Times*, Mr. John Fowler, C.I., Major Allison, and Count Waldstein, a Hungarian. There were also some French. M. Lesseps "personally conducted" us over the Canal from one end to the other, and we had his chief engineer and other officials to explain everything as we went along. M. Lesseps knew that Russell was to write letters to the *Times*, that John Fowler was a celebrated engineer who would give practical opinions on the technical details, and that I would illustrate the whole.

The history of the British views regarding the Canal had been peculiar. Lord Palmerston was in power at the time the enterprise was begun, and he now gets the credit of misrepresenting everything about the undertaking. It had been the traditional policy of British statesmen to oppose French influence in Egypt. So, of course, the Canal was pooh-poohed. Not a share was sold in Britain. "Pam" affirmed that the sand of the desert would fill up the Canal as fast as it was made. This was believed, and no one thought that the scheme could ever be practical. There was great surprise therefore when letters from Russell and Fowler, as well as my pictures, announced that the Canal was a success, that it was nearly completed, that the sand of the desert was a myth, and that the work when finished would be of the greatest advantage to Britain. From this explanation, it will be seen that, so far as Britain was concerned, our visit had almost a historical importance.

Our first day's journey was to Ismailia, then the head-quarters of the Canal Company's people. M. Lesseps had a châlet there, and when living at that place it was his custom to go down to Lake Timsah every morning, and jump into it. This exactly suited my taste, so I went with him on the morning we were at Ismailia, and had a dip. Our second day brought us to Port Said. We went in a small steamer of M. Lesseps called *Mathilde*. We stopped at "Al-Kantura" (an Arabic word meaning bridge), where the road from Egypt to Palestine passed—a road as old as the days of Abraham. The curious thing is that at this point the Canal Company had to respect this ancient "right of way," and place a barge there capable of conveying across not only people, but also horses, camels, and donkeys. We stayed a night at Port Said. There were two ships at the place, one Russian and one British, both dressed out with flags in honour of our visit. M. Lesseps was so pleased with the mark of respect, that he invited the captains of both to dinner. They did not accept, but excuses accompanied the non-acceptance. People are often perplexed, when they wish to avoid a dinner, to find a proper excuse. Here were two entirely new and original models. One of the invited guests, we were told, had already dined, the other was drunk. Which was drunk and which had dined we never knew, and we all acknowledged that it would be a very fine point to determine *à priori* between the chances in such a case as to the particular one that was drunk, when the individuals were a Russian and a Briton.

We came back to Ismailia, and proceeded to Suez, visiting

the ground which is now "the Bitter Lakes." At the time of our visit, workmen were busy making arrangements for filling the space then empty. We saw lines of camels and men passing over the ground, which was all dry, and formed part of the desert. The depression was scarcely visible to the eye. When, at a later date, I attended the opening ceremonies of the Canal, what a change had taken place! A lake between 20 and 30 miles in extent had come into existence, and I saw vessels "hull-down" upon it in the far distance. It suggested that the *Jins* had been at work—the genii were the *corps du genie*?

We passed on to the Sweet Water Canal, which was in reality the remains of the ancient Canal of the Pharaohs. The Canal Company had merely cleaned it out, and repaired it in some places, and by its means Nile water was passed on to Suez. This was the first part of the undertaking, for without an ample supply of fresh water nothing could have been done in the desert.

I understood it as accepted that the Bitter Lakes had at one time been the end of the Red Sea. The part of the Canal between that and Suez was dug out by what the French called the *proces sec,* instead of by dredgers. In cutting through the ground, a thick coating of salt was found near the surface, showing what had been the level of the sea when it extended over that space.

We were from Monday till Friday going over the Canal, and we returned from Suez to Cairo, all of us very much pleased with the expedition.

During these few days, I was brought a good deal into contact with Professor Owen, and I was delighted with his conversation. I heard him tell his two ghost stories. One of them I wrote out in a rough way from recollection for the *Daily News,* where it appeared a day or so after his death, in December, 1892. It will bear reproduction here. In his early days, when he held the post of surgeon to the prison at Lancaster, a negro died in the gaol, and a post-mortem examination was necessary, as well as an inquest. After the inquest, the young surgeon saw the body put into the coffin, and the lid screwed down, to be ready for the funeral next day. Owen had already been attracted to the study of comparative anatomy, and negroes' heads were not plentiful; so he made up his mind that this one should not be lost to the cause of science. In the evening he returned to the prison with a black bag containing a brick. From his official position he had no difficulty in getting admittance to the mortuary. There the coffin lid was quickly unscrewed, and screwed down again. During this process the brick and the negro's head changed places.

The ground outside the principal entrance to the gaol had a considerable descent, and, the time being winter, with snow and frost, Owen had scarcely passed out when he slipped and fell all his length. The bag went from his hand, and the head tumbled out, and rolled down the paved way. He jumped up, caught the bag, and, following the head, clutched it just as it finished its career in a small shop where tobacco was sold. Pushing it into the bag again, he vanished out of the shop with all the speed he was capable of. Next morning, when Owen was going to his usual duties at the prison, he was called in by the woman at the shop where the accident had occurred on the previous evening. She wished him to see her husband, who was very ill. He had had, she said, a fright the night before that caused him to look wild and dazed-like. The man, it turned out, was a retired sea-captain, who had been in many adventures among the West India Islands, when many deeds were done that did not require to be accounted for. Among these had been the killing of a negro in which he had a hand, and the transaction had left a touch of trouble on his conscience. After giving these details the old captain told of the horrible event which had taken place the night before. He was sitting in his shop, all was quiet, and it so chanced that he had been thinking of the negro, when suddenly he saw the man's very head roll into the shop in front of the counter, followed by the devil, all in black, with a black bag in his hand. The devil snatched up the head, and both disappeared through the earth like a flash of lightning. The description was perhaps not quite complimentary to the young anatomist, but it was satisfactory so far that it showed that his identity had not been recognised.

I waited in Cairo till the Prince and Princess of Wales arrived, and went up the Nile. One day later I called on Mr. Rogers, the Consul at Cairo. The British post had come in, and the letters for the Prince's party were being arranged for forwarding. The clerk who was doing this came in to Mr. Rogers with a letter, the address of which he could not find on the list. It was

BARON RENFREW,
Care of Colonel Stanton,
Cairo,
Egypt.

The letter was from the Queen to the Prince of Wales, one of whose hereditary titles is Baron Renfrew.

Caves under Jerusalem, explored by Captain, afterwards Sir Charles, Warren.
Reproduced from Simpson's water-colour by kind permission of the Palestine Exploration Fund.

To face p. 209.

CHAPTER XXII

JERUSALEM

MY acquaintance with Mr. Fergusson, as well as with the Rev. George Sandie, who had written a book about Jerusalem, for which I had done some illustrations, had led me to read up questions about the topography and archæology of the Holy City. This brought me into contact with the Palestine Exploration Fund when it was founded. The Fund was anxious to have illustrations in the *Illustrated London News*, but their explorers at Jerusalem only sent home plans and sections, and the editor wanted pictures. So, when I started on the new route to India, I suggested that when I was in Egypt, if time permitted, I might go up to Jerusalem, and do something with Captain Warren's diggings. Mr. Jackson, the editor, consented. I communicated this to Mr. Walter Besant, then Secretary of the Palestine Exploration Fund, and unknown to fame as a writer of novels, and he sent word to Warren * to expect me. Having seen and illustrated the ceremonies of the arrival of the Prince and Princess of Wales at Cairo, I found myself, luckily, with time to go to Jerusalem.

At Suez I met two Americans, named O'Brien and Flanner. The first of these had made his "pile" in America, but had been born in Ireland. They were also bound for Jerusalem, so we made a *parti du voyage*. At Port Said we found a steamer for Jaffa.

On board was a large party of American clergymen.

* [Captain Warren, to come before the public at a later day as Major-General Sir Charles Warren, commander of the Bechuanaland and other African expeditions, and one of the chief officers engaged in the last Boer War.]

When we landed we were surrounded by a howling crowd of Arabs, greedy for backsheesh. One reverend gentleman remarked to another, "I suppose we are at last in the Holy Land." "Yes," said his friend, with a glance at the yelling mob, "I would scarcely have thought it." In the hotel a dragoman presented his card to me. The original list of languages he spoke had contained nearly all the tongues of Europe, including English. Since the American War, however, the people of the United States had come over in such numbers that the man had added "American" to his list.

Arrangements were at last made for the whole party, and we started on horse-back, with one cart. This last-mentioned conveyance proved of use to me, for on the way to Ramleh I got a kick on the shin from a horse, which disabled me for several days, and forced me to do the rest of the journey to Jerusalem in the cart.

My first venture out in the Holy City was with O'Brien and Flanner, who came in and said they had engaged a dragoman, and insisted I should come, and they would walk slowly on my account. The dragoman took us to the houses of Dives, and the Prodigal Son's father, and then to the American Church, and showed us "the stones that cried out." I asked how it was that the stones cried, and he turned upon me as if I had been an ignorant boy at a Sunday school, and asked if I did not know that the Scripture says that the stones would cry out. "These," he said, "are the stones," and he pointed to a number of stones in the wall of the church, with slight hollows in their surfaces. Such are some of the "lions" the dragomans show to visitors. Still I was a puzzle to this learned authority, for I knew where most of the places were, and where we were going, and what we should find when we went round the next corner. So he insisted that I must have been in Jerusalem before to know every spot so well.

I was soon able to look up Captain Warren, and he took me to his diggings. First he took me down the shaft at the south-west corner of the Haram. This was about 75 feet in depth, and at the bottom I saw the foundation stones of wall and the characters upon them in red colour, supposed at the time to be Phœnician.

Another day he took me down below Robinson's Arch, where I saw and sketched the fallen vousoirs of the arch. Below that again I descended into a cistern with a conduit, the bottom of which was about 80 feet beneath the present surface. At the Golden Gateway he had made a shaft and a tunnel. This was intended to see how the approach to the Golden Gateway had originally been planned, but the looseness of the soil made the tunnel so dangerous he had to stop and fill it up. These excavations are now all closed, and are not likely to be opened again. So it was a rare chance to have such glimpses of underground Jerusalem. Wilson's Arch and the Masonic Hall were other underground spots through which we scrambled, and of which I was able to make sketches. John Macgregor—" Rob Roy "—had been to the source of the Jordan in his canoe, and returned to Jerusalem while I was there. His brother, who was in the 97th Regiment, I knew in the Crimea. I spent a very interesting day with him and Warren in the Haram. Warren went down into all sorts of queer holes, while Macgregor and I kept the sheik of the Haram engaged. I think it was on that day that Warren took me down to the Bahr-el-Khebeer, or Great Sea, a hollow, or excavation, in the rock under the temple area. He burned magnesium wire to light it up sufficiently for me to sketch it. Except a small sketch I saw in some one's rooms in Oxford in 1863, I have seen no other drawings of this wonderful reservoir, and I think mine is the only one that has ever been published. It occurred to me at the time that as I was procuring quite new and original materials regarding Jerusalem, I would utilise my leisure wholly at that place, and make sufficient sketches for an exhibition. This I did, but it was not till 1872 that I managed to have forty drawings ready, which were exhibited in Pall Mall. Lord Bute bought some of these drawings, including the largest in the exhibition, that of the Sakrah, or Sacred Rock, on which the temple is supposed to have stood. Mr. Walter Morrison bought most of the subjects representing the underground explorations of Captain Warren, and afterwards presented them to the Palestine Exploration Fund, in whose possession they now are. These drawings possess a special value. Owing to the filling up of the shafts and galleries, these places are not likely to be drawn again.

This task I had proposed for myself kept me in Jerusalem for the couple of weeks I had to spare. Dr. Russell, of the *Times*, turned up at Jerusalem, and we spent a day together, going to Bethlehem.

Another notable person, much talked about at the time, whom I met in Jerusalem, was the Marquis of Bute. A night or two after my arrival, a large party came to dinner at the hotel. There were three gentlemen and two ladies. The rule was that new arrivals sat at the end of the table, and moved up as others departed. I had been the previous arrival, so one of the newcomers found his seat next me. I am under the impression that we had all heard Lord Bute was coming, and that he had his doctor with him, because I remember coming to the conclusion that night that the gentleman sitting beside me was the doctor. It turned out, however, to be the Marquis. Our positions being fixed, we sat together at table all the time I was there. His Lordship had just joined the Catholic Church. The ceremony took place, I think, in some church in Italy. Bute had his yacht there, and he came direct in the yacht to Joppa. One of the three gentlemen was, from his costume, evidently an ecclesiastic, and he turned out to be Monsignore Capel. He got the credit of having converted Lord Bute, but this, I believe, was a misconception. The other gentleman was the doctor. The ladies were Lady Loudon, a cousin of the Marquis and an elderly lady, Miss Eden. Lord Bute was made a Knight of the Holy Sepulchre when in Jerusalem.

Lady Loudon—the title is now Loudon and Hastings—was a descendant of the Lord Loudon referred to in Tannahill's song, "Loudon's Bonnie Woods and Braes." The "laddie" and the "lassie" of the song were Lord Bute's grandfather and grandmother. He told me a story,

THE SACRED ROCK AT JERUSALEM, SITE OF THE ANCIENT TEMPLE OF THE JEWS.

From the water-colour by Simpson, at Mount Stuart House, Bute. Reproduced by kind permission of the Marchioness of Bute.

To *face p.* 213.

which I have never seen in print, about Tannahill and his grandmother. Some one thought to do the poet a good turn by introducing him to Lady Loudon, and as the song was so popular, this mutual friend assumed that it would be agreeable to the lady. In this he was unfortunately mistaken. She did not like the song because her husband was called a "laddie," and she herself was a "lassie." The interview was stiff and most uncomfortable to both parties. At the end of it Lady Loudon, thinking that as Tannahill was a poor man—he was a Paisley weaver—she should offer him something, took out her purse and presented him with a sovereign. This touched the poet to the quick, and as he was leaving Lady Loudon's presence, he tipped the flunkey before her eyes with the coin he had just received. Bute told the story with a touch of relish at the manner in which his grandmother had blundered, and her discomfiture by Tannahill. I wished to make a sketch of his Lordship's investiture as a Knight of the Holy Sepulchre, but he asked me not to do it. He said there had been lately so much about him in the papers. He did not object, however, to my sending home sketches of the sword, spur, and cross used, which were said to have been those of Godfrey of Bouillon. This I did, and some one wrote pointing out that the spur could not be Godfrey's, as it had a *roulette*—spurs had only a spike in his time.

I wished to make sketches of the Sacred Rock, under the Dome of the Rock, and Mr. Moore, our consul, made arrangements for me. He gave orders that I was to be allowed to do as I pleased, and my pleasure was to get the place all to myself that morning. This desire I practically realised. A man attended upon me, but while I sketched he fell sound asleep. This temple struck me more than any I have seen. Santa Sophia at Constantinople, and St. Marks at Venice, although in some respects finer, have not the solemn effect that belongs to the Dome of the Rock. The great Sacred Rock, which covers nearly the whole space under the dome, contributes largely to the influence of the place. On this morning, as I sat sketching, there was a perfect silence. Only a clock could be heard ticking, and a cat could be seen at times.

It was the knowledge I acquired during that visit to Jerusalem which led chiefly, about 1878, to my appointment as a member of the Executive Committee of the Palestine Exploration Fund. My sketches in the *Illustrated London News* were a large advertisement for the association at the time, and most of the illustrations which appeared were afterwards utilised in the works published by the Fund.

I travelled back to Jaffa alone with a dragoman. On the way we saw a long procession on horseback approaching. There were some forty or fifty persons, and I mentally ejaculated "Cook's Circus!" I was nearer the truth than I supposed. It turned out to be, not Cook's Circus, but Cook's tourists, the first party that enterprising provider had sent, "personally conducted," to Jerusalem.

At Jaffa I found the *Scamandre*, a Messagerie steamer. She moved slowly along the Syrian coast, stopping each day at a port, putting out and taking in cargo. So we were able to land and see the places. We stopped at Beyrout, Tripolis, Latakieh, the ancient Laodicea, Alexandretta, or Iskenderoom, Mersina, near the ancient Pompeyopolis, Rhodes, and Smyrna. Captain Gaudion, of the *Scamandre*, had a great liking for "escargo" snails, and they were on the breakfast table every morning. There was a young American on board, and he followed my example, and liked them. There was another American, a tall man, thin in figure, always dressed in black cloth, which meant a surtout and a slouch hat. This at that time was the typical costume of a well-to-do man from the Far West, who was got up in what he considered the right style. No inducement would make this person touch a snail. Even the successful effort of his compatriot had no effect in leading him to try. There was a clergyman from Australia on board, and we four went ashore every day to see the places we stopped at. The first day, after walking about, wanting a rest, I proposed going into a coffee-shop. It was a native Turkish one, and not inviting, I must say. The clergyman objected, but at last was prevailed upon to come in. Whilst sitting there I found that a man sitting beside us was a Haji, that is, he had made the pilgrimage to Mecca. So I pretended also to be a Haji. I talked to the man about the water of the Zem-well at the Kaabah, which every one drinks; of the Black Stone that is kissed; the *Tawaf*, or circumambulation of the Kaabah; and the throwing of stones at the Shaitan—Satan—at Arafut. In fact, I described everything that a Haji does at Mecca so correctly that I passed for a very good one. On landing afterwards, more than once the clergyman was eager to go into a coffee-shop, and pointed to me as a Haji. We landed at Mersina, and were able to visit Pompeyopolis.

At Smyrna I had to change steamers, and in the *Saintonge* I went to Constantinople, where I put up in the Hotel de Byzance. At Constantinople I found Mr. Alexander Shanks and his uncle Tom. Alexander was then head of the Sultan's engineer department in the navy, and was afterwards made a Bey. He was originally an apprentice with me in Allan and Ferguson's, but went to Napier's in Glasgow, as their mechanical draughtsman, and from that to Constantinople. On this occasion my friend Shanks sent an Effendi with me to visit Santa Sophia, and I did so under very different circumstances from those of my first visit in 1855.

CHAPTER XXIII

THE CRIMEA REVISITED

THE route from Constantinople to the Crimea was at that time by one steamer to Odessa, then by another to Sebastopol, where I arrived on the 21st of April.

There was one hotel, Vetzel's, where I put up. The proprietor was of German origin. He had been in Sebastopol all through the siege, and told me much that was curious. We on the outside knew little or nothing at the time as to what was going on in the town. Vetzel spoke a little English, just enough to make himself intelligible. If I recollect right he told me he had been the manager of the principal military club in Sebastopol. After the first bombardment this building had been converted into a place for operations on the wounded. Fort Nicholas became an hospital, where all hopeful cases were sent. The unhopeful cases were sent to another establishment. The men soon found this out, and understood their fate from the particular hospital to which they were taken. This had a depressing effect on the less hopeful cases, and is said to have killed many by its mere influence. There were 10,000 military prisoners in Sebastopol when the siege commenced. Admiral Korniloff set them free, and put them into the works, and Vetzel said they proved the best soldiers in the place. These men and the sailors were never changed in the batteries, but the soldiers were changed every day, or at least at regular intervals.

One of Vetzel's most interesting narratives was the history of the man who gave the name to the Malakoff Tower. Malakoff had been a purser in the Russian navy at Sebastopol, and part of his duties was the supplying of provisions and liquor to the ship he belonged to. In supplying the liquor he had discovered a method of cheating the excise, and pocketing the proceeds. He was court-martialled, and found guilty of cheating and swindling, as well as of drunkenness, so he was dismissed from the service. Although now an outcast, it was necessary for him to live, and in his case it was important that he should be able to "drink." To accomplish these ends he determined to start a grog-shop. The schemes by which he could swindle the excise he could still practice, and he was thus able to undersell the other grog shops. This made his establishment better frequented than others, for the Russian when he indulges has a methodical manner of going to work. He does not resort to drinking with the same motives as a Western European. The latter likes to sit down with a friend for a friendly chat; and may at times, if the chat is continued, perhaps absorb a little too much. The Ruski knows how much it requires to make him drunk, and he acts accordingly. If he can accomplish this for a less sum in one shop than in another, he goes to that shop. Malakoff presented this particular form of attraction to the Russian soldiers and sailors, and was patronised accordingly. The place selected for starting his shanty—I think Vetzel said it was only a wooden erection—was the hill which was afterwards known by his name. Previously it had only been a bare, stony height outside the town, its reputation an ignominious one—it was the burial-place of suicides. The Karabelnaia, where the sailors of the fleet lived, was close to the spot, and the grog shop became a resort of these men, and was noted for many irregularities as a consequence of the business carried on. In due time the height became known as the "Malakoff Hill," from the name of this drunken, swindling and disgraced purser, and at last it became the proud title conferred on General Pelissier, as Duc de Malakoff. The Russian officers who chanced to know this bit of history, must have grinned very broadly when the honour to the French Commander-in-Chief was announced.

My first surprise on seeing Sebastopol, after thirteen years, was that of finding it still a city in ruins. A house here and there only had been repaired or rebuilt. The great barracks, which we, during the siege, called the "White Buildings," were still in the shattered state in which they were left at the end of the struggle. In front of them, looking towards the great harbour, a monument had been erected since the war to Admiral Lazareff. The inscription on it was 1866, so it had only stood there for two years. It was a colossal black figure, and had a rather ghastly effect standing up against the ruins of the white barracks, close behind. Lazareff was the creator of Sebastopol and the Black Sea fleet, hence the honour intended to his memory by the statue. But it was striking to see the figure of this man standing amid the ruins of the town he had produced.

I ought to mention the splendid memorial church which had been built over the graves of four admirals. Lazareff, already mentioned, died in Vienna in 1851, but his body was brought to Sebastopol in great state in a man-of-war, and admirals bore the coffin to the top of the hill, near the Temple of the Winds, as it was called. The war came on and prevented the erection of the church at that time. The siege gave Lazareff companions in his vault. Admiral Korniloff was killed in the Malakof on October 17, 1854. Admiral Estonian was shot through the head in May, 1855. And when Admiral Nachimoff was killed in August of that year, an addition to the vault had to be made. These are the four admirals over whose tomb a very fine church, dedicated to St. Vladimir, has been raised on the highest point of Sebastopol. Vetzel told me that Nachimoff was a very patriotic man, and that, had he lived to see the fall of Sebastopol, he would in all probability have killed himself of horror and despair at the event.

On the day of my arrival in the town I walked over the fatal ground to our most advanced sap, and then into the quarries, where three of our burial-places lay, all enclosed. Another small enclosure behind these again must have been close to the spot we knew as "Egerton's Pit."

Next morning some soldiers were drilling somewhere in the Karabelnaia, and the drill included musket firing. These sounds, so familiar in my first visit, recalled the old times. This morning I went in the direction of Quarantine Bay, to see the remains of ancient Kherson. There are numerous rock-cut tombs, and the remains of the ancient church of St. Vladimir. A new church has been built, and the old church left inside. The altar of this old church still remains, formed of stone.

From Inkerman I had often looked across the valley to the perpendicular cliff, honeycombed with caves, on the other side of the Tchernaya, and wished to visit the place; but "our friends the enemy" occupied the place. At the time of this second visit everything was different, and I was able to walk without danger over to this most interesting spot.

It has been described as a "city of caverns." A young monk, named Feodor, took me through the caves and churches or chapels, excavated in the rock. We had only one or two words of Russian between us, but I understood from him that the caves were all tombs, except one or two larger excavations, which were chapels. The principal chapel had become ruinous in front, and had been built up. It had been lately painted and decorated; the iconastis seemed quite new. The altar I understood was of solid rock. St. Clement is supposed to have been the founder. Its name accordingly was *Sobore Swetie Clement*—*sobore* meaning "church" and *swetie* being the Russian equivalent of "saint." According to the Latin Church, St. Clement followed St. Peter as Bishop of Rome, but was persecuted and sent to work in the quarries at Inkerman; so in this history the Latin and Greek Churches agree. Feodor informed me, so far as I could make him out, that St. Clement came there in 93 A.D., and was buried in the church. Feodore pointed below the altar on the south side as the spot. The church had a wooden floor, a peculiar feature in a rock-cut church. On the top of the stairs, outside of the church, there are tombs, "grabnitza," Feodor called them, and in one is a coffin, with a black pall. In another within a glass frame or window are seen some skulls. We came back to one of the houses below. There was a samovar, it was hot, and we had some tea.

Feodor did the honours of the table, pouring out the tea, etc., with all the grace and kindness of a well-bred lady.

One morning I started early for Balaklava. I went by the head of the harbour, mounted to our most advanced work on the Left Attack, and saw the pit, partly a cave in the rock, in which I had spent a day sketching Sebastopol. I crossed our trenches, walked up to Cathcart's Hill, and then to the sailor's camp, and on to Headquarters. At the col or neck, where the road from Balaklava left the plain for the plateau extending towards Sebastopol, I came upon traces of our railway, and looked down on the celebrated ground of the Balaklava charges. I found the plain dotted over with cultivation, vineyards had been extended from Kadikoi, and a long line of dark fence stood where the thin red line received the Russian cavalry. As I walked down to Kadikoi I could see the old lines held by Sir Colin's division.

Here again after thirteen years was Balaklava—so quiet and still—once more here was peace! What a contrast to my first experience! Instead of the closely-jammed crowd of transports, there were only a few small fishing-boats. The water was calm and blue. As I neared the town not a soul was to be seen—the place had gone to sleep. I was tired and thirsty, and entered the first house that seemed to promise rest and refreshment. The man, like the place, was asleep. He got up, and turned out to be a Greek who could speak Italian; so he understood the word "vino," and produced the article. I asked "Questo vino?" and he answered, "Balaklava." It was white Crimean wine.

A man chanced to come in, and I asked if he were a Tartar, but the answer was no—"Kareme," he said. From this I guessed he belonged to the Jews of the Crimea, who are known as the Kareme, or Karaim Jews. They repudiate the Talmud, and adhere strictly to the Pentateuch. They live at Tchoufont-kaleh and Bakchi-serai. I wanted to know if he understood Hebrew, as I tried him with *Barashit bara Elohim*, the three first words of Genesis. He knew the words. I then wrote the word "Jerusalem" in Hebrew and he read it at once. His designation was Yakob Karakush, Karaim, Bakchiserai. His dress was of the Tartar type, but was good, and he seemed well to do.

I had a letter of introduction to Colonel Braker, the gentleman who lived at Lord Raglan's old headquarters. I called, found Madame Braker at home, and saw over the old place. Madame Braker informed me that before the Crimean War the house belonged to her husband's family, and they only left it when our army arrived at the place. Most of the furniture had been left, but was of course gone when they returned after the war. The rooms at the time of my visit were well furnished, and very pleasant with flowers, plants, etc., contrasting to my eye with the old, bare, military barrack look the place had when it was the British Headquarters. Mrs. Braker used what had been Lord Raglan's bedroom as a sitting-room, and on the wall was a marble slab with the following inscription:—

In this room
died
F. M. Lord Raglan, G.C.B.,
Commander-in-Chief
of the British Army in the Crimea,
on the 28th June, 1855.

Below was another slab with the same inscription in Russian. The Brakers kept flowers growing beside the inscriptions; and in a photograph, a copy of which they gave me for Lady Estcourt, there are two cypress-trees which they kept in the house during the winter. On the panel of the door between this and the larger room, in which Lord Raglan and his suite had their mess, was an inscription as follows:—

F. M.
Lord Raglan
Genl.
Sir J. Simpson
Genl.
Sir W. Codrington.

The only other inscription was that of "Captn. Ponsonby," on what had been his room.

Lord Raglan's body was embalmed before it was sent home to England, and where the heart, etc., had been buried in the garden, was a stone with an inscription:—

To
the memory of
Field Marshal
LORD RAGLAN, G.C.B.,
Commander-in-Chief of the
British Army
in the
Crimea
died
28th June, 1855.

There is a well at its head, and a willow-tree. The apple and other fruit-trees were all in full blossom round the spot.

Lady Estcourt had given me permission to spend any money I thought necessary for the repair, or putting into good order, of her husband's grave. But I found it all right, and requiring nothing. It was at the northern end of the garden. I picked a flower or two from it to send home to Lady Estcourt.

From Headquarters I returned to Cathcart's Hill and passed over to a burial ground near the "Picquet House." There I found the graves of Colonel Handcock and Major Welsford. The grave of Hedley Vicars was beside them, with a very small stone; but the inscription was quite legible. I also found the grave of John M'Gregor's (Rob Roy's) brother, and discovering that he belonged to the 97th, a recollection came back to my mind of his death, which was in the attack on the Redan, when Handcock and Welsford fell.

On my return to Odessa, I saw our consul, George H. Stevens, and he told me a good deal about the graves in the Crimea. He told me there were in all 89 burial places, spread over a space of 80 square miles, which made it a difficult undertaking to concentrate all the remains in one spot. He had an idea of buying the Headquarters, and gathering what was left of the bodies into it. He gave me details about Granville Murray, who had been his predecessor in Odessa—how money had been sent by our Government to put the graves in order, and Murray had applied it to his own purposes. Granville Murray was a very able man, and a clever writer.

At Odessa I found a steamer for Galatz. Thence I took another up the Danube, passing the "Iron Gates," and at Bazias got a train to Vienna. Thence I came by rail to the Rhine, and *viâ* Cologne and Brussels to London.

CHAPTER XXIV

THE OPENING OF THE SUEZ CANAL

ON the 13th of August I signed an agreement with Mr. T. Parry that I was to be retained permanently on the staff of the *Illustrated London News*. Mr. Parry was a contractor, an old friend of Mr. Herbert Ingram, the founder of the paper. He succeeded him as M.P. for Boston, and managed the paper at that time in the interest of Mrs. Ingram. I was to receive a retaining fee, and my services were to be paid for in addition.

The Suez Canal being nearly completed, its opening in November, 1869, had been announced. It was also known that a great Council of the Roman Catholic Church was to begin in December at Rome. So it was arranged that I should attend both of these events. Owing to my personal acquaintance with M. Lesseps, the invitation to the opening ceremonies of the Canal came to the office in my name. It was arranged that I should start a few weeks in advance, and make a tour through Brittany in order to make sketches including the old so-called Druidical remains.

I left Waterloo on the 15th of October, sailed from Southampton to St. Malo, and went thence by train *viâ* Rennes and Redan to Auray. On the way I got a glimpse of the ancient city of Vannes, saw its cathedral, and spent a short time in its Museum of Antiquities.

Next morning I started from Auray, on foot, alone, with my plaid, a tooth brush, a comb, and a piece of soap, on a visit to Loch Mariaker and the Druidic stones at Carnac. At the former place I paid a visit to the interesting tumulus known as the Mane-er-H'rouich, or "Mountain of the Fairies," of which the key is kept at the village school.

The schoolmaster was rather a wild-looking fellow, with long hair and large staring eyes. I got into conversation with him about the old sculptured stones, of which there are many at the place. One large dolmen is known as the Table of Cæsar, and one of the stones which support it is covered with curious "pot-hooks."

Early next morning I set off for Carnac. The church there is dedicated to Ste. Cornelie, who is known as the "Sainte Patrone des Bestiaux." If a horse or cow is ill, it is brought to the church, and a prayer or service from the priest is a certain cure. I spent the day inspecting and sketching the wonderful alignments of stones at that place. The stones are in three groups, said to be about three miles in length. Some say that originally the lines extended to St. Barbe and Erdeven, and even farther to the west, and thus were ten or twelve miles long. The theories as to the purpose of these lines of stones as propounded by different writers have been very various. According to one, they represent the trail of a serpent. Of course there is an idea that the place was in some sense a temple, and that its serpentine form is in connection with that purpose. Some explain the lines as a processional route of the Druids. Others give them an astronomical signification. Others again see in them the plan of an army in three divisions on the march. A racecourse has been suggested. Ninepins has been another guess. A popular notion is that there is an evil spirit held down under each stone. This helps to confirm the theory that the ground is only a vast burial-place. The numbers of tumuli everywhere favour this view. As yet, however, no satisfactory solution has appeared. The Stones of Carnac are still an unsolved riddle.

In the evening I passed on to St. Barbe and slept there. Next day I went on by Erdeven and returned to Auray. There I visited the shrine of Ste. Anne d'Auray. It is described as the Mecca of Brittany, and is an old and celebrated place of pilgrimage. I went from Auray to Quimper, then to Brest, and from Morlaix I passed to St. Pol de Leon, and on to Nantes, thus making a tour round the whole of Brittany.

From Nantes I went to Bordeaux and Nismes, getting a glimpse of the Pyrenees, and the mediæval town of Carcassone. At Nismes I visited the amphitheatre, and the Maison Carrée. I reached Marseilles on the 5th of November.

When I left London the P. and O. Co. had arranged that the "invités" to the ceremonies of the Suez Canal opening were to be taken in the *Poonah*, which was commanded by my old friend, Captain Methven. But to do due honour to the occasion, the company put on a special vessel. This was the *Delta*, and we were much more comfortable than in the regular ship, which is generally crammed on the outward voyage at this season of the year.

Among the invités were Lord Dudley, Lord Houghton, the Hon. Mr. Lyttleton, Mr. Vivian, Sir Edward Russell, Sir Seymour Blane, an old Indian friend, Sir Fred. Arrow, of Trinity House, Mr. Hawkshaw, C.E., and Mr. Bateman, C.E.; Messrs. Thornton, Melville, and L'Estrange, deputies from the P. and O. Co.; Mr. Pender, afterwards Sir John Pender, and Mr. Ramsay, of Islay; the Hon. Mr. Bruce, Mr. Gregory, Captain Chapman, special for the *Shipping Gazette*, Mr. Hall, correspondent of the *New York Times*, and Mr. Green, of Green's Indian Line. I think Mr. Lloyd and Mr. Wright, from Birmingham, were on board, because they were with us on the Canal, as was Mr. Elliot, son of Elliot of the Telegraphs.

At Alexandria the P. and O. Co.'s people invited us all to go through the Canal in the *Delta*, but we were the guests of the Khedive, and most of us came to the conclusion that we should go in one of his ships. So we moved on board a large yacht called *El-Musr*. We regretted the change afterwards. This yacht was so large the authorities did not allow her to go through the Canal. So we had to change again at Port Said.

Among the great personages who came to the ceremony were the Empress Eugenie, the Emperor of Austria, and the Crown Prince of Prussia, afterwards the Emperor Frederick. The Crown Prince of Denmark was also there, and one of the royal family of Italy.

BALL AT ISMAILIA

On the 16th of November the ceremony of blessing the Canal took place at Port Said. This was a kind of Pan-religious function, as there were Latin, Greek, and Mohammedan priests officiating. Some of our party were put on board the *Garbiah*, an Egyptian vessel, and "grub" was scarce on board. We started through the Canal on the 17th, and as it was necessary to catch the weekly mail from Egypt, I remember I had to sit on a pile of luggage getting my sketches ready to post at Ismailia. When we arrived there on the 18th, Shepherd, who represented a Bombay paper, and I went ashore to post letters, and when we came back our ship was gone. At least, the passengers had all been removed, and our luggage with them, where, no one could tell. It took Shepherd and me seven hours to find our baggage. At last, after a most exhausting, I might say despairing hunt, we discovered our traps on board an Egyptian corvette called the *Senaar*, and Shepherd and I managed to dress and go to the Great Ball that night for a short time.

At supper the imperial and royal personages were screened off in one corner of the great building erected for the ball. There were palms, ferns, and flowers. Through these, however, I managed to get a glimpse of the Empress Eugenie and the Crown Prince of Prussia sitting at the feast, and what I saw that night often came back to my recollection during the Franco-German War. The group at Ismailia that night did not suggest the relative positions which the next twelve months were to bring about.

There were no provisions on board the *Senaar*, our new ship, and our party were nearly starved next day. We sent a begging deputation on board the nearest ship to ours as we passed through the Canal, and were so fortunate as to obtain enough to serve till we reached Suez.

The accommodation at Suez was limited for such a crowd. I had a bed in the hotel, and when I came into the *salle à manger* in the morning, I found that there were still earlier birds than myself. Although nothing was on the table but a white cloth, every seat round it had been secured. Those sitting round it had a pleased and satisfied expression on their countenances. They felt secure, and sure of their share in the "worms." But there is often much between the cup and the lip. More birds came down, but there were no seats, so we could only wander about, and at last some of us wandered into the kitchen. There we found the viands, and so far as my knowledge goes, none of these ever reached the table. So the old proverb did not hold good that morning. An hour or so later I saw Lord Dudley, in a frock-coat and a chimney-pot hat, with a loaf under his arm, struggling to get into a third-class carriage, where I presume he partook of breakfast, and it must have been a frugal meal. It occurred to me that if this grand ceremony had lasted for another day or so, the far-west custom of using a revolver when you wished for mustard would have become the rule. The truth is there were far too many people, and it became a struggle for existence. At Cairo the condition of things improved, but even there it was difficult at first to find beds. I went out one day and saw the Emperor of Austria lugged to the top of the Great Pyramid by two Arabs as if he had been only an overland passenger. I left Cairo on the 25th of November, and reached Rome on the 1st of December.

THE PYRAMIDS OF GHIZEH.

Reproduced from Simpson's water-colour by kind permission of Baillie William Bilsland, Glasgow.

To face p. 228.

CHAPTER XXV

THE VATICAN COUNCIL

AT Rome I put up at the Hotel d'Angleterre, in the Via Bocca di Leone, near to the Piazza di Spagna. Next morning I went to St. Peter's to sketch the screen that had been put up to separate the north transept, and form it into the Council Chamber. The screen was merely wood, but its architectural character was in keeping with the church, and it was painted like marble, and quite in tone with the marble walls around it.

All around the chamber, as high up as the architrave, were painted portraits of the popes who had held councils, and at the north end, over the Pope's seat, was a picture of the Pentecost, which the Church considers to be the first Council. The Holy Ghost came down at that time, and it is believed that the same Spirit comes and guides all councils of the Church. I saw a picture published in Rome at the time of the Council, in which the meeting was represented, and a dove shown with its bill close to the ear of His Holiness, as if in the act of inspiring him.

When I parted from Lord Bute at Jerusalem, he said he hoped we should meet in London. I never called on him there, but learning that he had come to Rome—he had taken the Palazzo Savarelli, the former residence, if I mistake not, of one of the Stuart family, probably the Cardinal, and Bute is a branch of the Stuarts—I called and said I had never visited him in England, but now when I wanted something, I came. What I wanted was an introduction to the Catholic Church authorities, and he gave me one to Monsignore Stonor, who was then the Monsignore for the English-speaking nations. Monsignore Patterson, afterwards a bishop or the head of a Roman Catholic College in the north of England, was living with Stonor, and was of considerable assistance to me from his knowledge of everything connected with the Church. Monsignore Capel was also in Rome, and he was of use to me.

The Council was opened on the 8th of December. An English clergyman in the hotel arranged to go with me, and we rose as early as 4.30 a.m. and reached St. Peter's at 5.30. It was still dark at that hour, a slight rain had been falling, and around the outer door of the church was what at first appeared to be a crop of gigantic mushrooms. These turned out to be the umbrellas of about a dozen people who were earlier birds than ourselves. Here we had to stand for nearly an hour. While doing so we heard a crackling sound, and a thud on the ground, followed by an exclamation and the remark in a strong American accent, "I guess the confounded thing has gone to smash." The lady had brought a stool on which she had been sitting, but its strength had not been equal to the weight upon it. When the outer doors opened, I stepped forward, and found myself exactly at the middle of the inner central door. There we had to wait again till about seven o'clock, when these doors opened, and from my position I entered at the apex of the crowd. Being thus the first person to enter that morning, I have at times laid claim to the distinction of being the individual who opened the Council. I once made this claim in the presence of a Roman Catholic, who looked glum at the implied disrespect towards his Holiness the Pope. As soon as I discovered the situation, I hastened to add that there was only one other person who had a claim that could possibly compete with mine. That other person, I explained, was the man on the inside who opened the door. This so changed the whole complexion of the case that even my Roman Catholic friend smiled.

On no other occasion has St. Peter's looked to me so grand as during the few moments while I ran at the head of that crowd. Only the first grey light of the dawn had begun to appear, but it was enough to show faintly the lines of the great church. This it did so softly, that the place seemed larger and grander than in full daylight. I could not resist gazing at the beautiful effect though my mind was full of a serious point of practical importance. There was the whole of the church before me, all clear and open, to select any position I chose. Which would be the best spot? What would be the chances of seeing the ceremony? I learned that not a soul could enter the Council Chamber but those officially connected with it. My friend and I were soon opposite the door of the chamber, and I suggested that we should stand with our backs to the high altar, which was in a line with the door, and from which we could see straight to the Pope's throne. We also found that by standing on a projecting base moulding of the altar, we were raised a foot or two above the heads of the crowd, which was an immense advantage. My friend remarked that even if he had come in a balloon, he could not have chanced on a better place.

We remained there some time, and I was able to make notes; but about eight o'clock a large number of Pontifical Zouaves entered the church, and marched right up the centre. It was some time before we quite understood what they were doing. It turned out that they were forming a path in the crowd for the bishops to enter the Council. This indicated a great blunder on the part of those who made the arrangements. Soldiers ought to have been placed on the line of this way before the crowd entered in the morning, or it might have been marked out by a line of fence so that as the people came in they might have taken up their places on each side. When the soldiers came in, the church was crowded with a dense mass of people, and the only thing the Zouaves could do was to cut their way through. This they did by turning the butt ends of their muskets down, and using them as rammers to beat the toes of those standing nearest to them. Slowly they forced themselves forward by this brutal means. The crowd was closely packed before, but this made matters much worse. On the space between the chamber door and the altar, the people had already become so dense that it was almost impossible to force a way. Some of the soldiers ordered us, the few who had the advantage of the base of the altar, to step down, so we lost our good position, and were forced into this mass of human flesh. I had put on evening dress, as I had heard that in that costume one had a better chance of a good position in ceremonies at St. Peter's; but as it was raining in the morning I had put on a great coat, and I had a billy-cock hat. As I required both my hands, I had placed my hat between my legs, and at last I found myself with my two hands held up about the level of my forehead, and in them were a sketch-book, a pencil, my binoculars, and my pocket handkerchief. We were so jammed that there was no space to move my hands down to my pockets, either to replace an article, or to get anything out, and I stood in this position making notes, swayed about by the crowd. The heat became great, and I had constantly to use the handkerchief for the perspiration on my face. We heard groans, sobs, and wild cries at times from different parts of the crowd. I believe that people fainted in some places, and I read afterwards that a baby was born in the press, and that the Pope was to be its godfather.

I stood making rough sketches, if such a word can be used for the lines I was able to draw, while the Bishops entered, and at last I saw the whole conclave gathered and the proceedings of the Council begun. This took an hour or two. When things had reached this stage, I felt quite exhausted, and I thought I had seen enough for my purpose. It might have been somewhere between ten and eleven o'clock, when I determined to try and find my way out. It took me an hour or more to find my way out of that crowd. When I found myself in the open air, the first thing I discovered was that my hat would not go on my head. It had been squeezed into something like a "cocked hat." The next discovery was that I could scarcely walk. I was quite done up. I went into a wine shop, and had a rest while I drank some wine. This revived me and I was able to walk back to the hotel. Before going in, I called on the Haghes, just to let them see, as a matter of curiosity, the state I was in, and they often talked of it afterwards. The perspiration had gone through all my clothes; even my dress suit was wet. At the hotel I changed my suit, and had something to eat, and I was able to go back to St. Peter's again, where I heard the 700 or 800 Bishops singing a Te Deum at the close of their first day's proceedings. These old men had good voices, the volume of sound rolled from the Council Chamber with grand effect, and filled the whole church.

The large sketch which I did of the opening ceremony was drawn on wood, when it came home, by John Gilbert, and I believe it was the last thing he did on wood for the *Illustrated London News.* It appeared as a "two-pager," the term used in the office for a subject filling two pages. There is one curious but important inaccuracy in it. Each Bishop as he walked up the nave of the church, knelt at the confessional of St. Peter, which is before the high altar, and prayed for a moment or two. This I introduced into my sketch, and the Bishop in the picture, I represented with his mitre on his head. In the crowd, I could not see the Bishops when on their knees, and as they passed into the Chamber afterwards they had their mitres on. When the paper with the illustration came out, it was pointed out to me that I had made a blunder, and it was explained to me that the Blessed Sacrament was exhibited at the time on the high altar, that it was to it they knelt and prayed, and that the rule of the Church was that a Bishop, or any one, would uncover his head at that time. After this I submitted all my sketches to Monsignore Stonor before sending them home. Monsignore Patterson also saw most of them, and I believe that all my sketches of the Council, with the exception given above, will be found to be accurate. When I did a large "two-pager" of the Grand Mass in St. Peter's on Christmas morning, it of course was submitted, and Monsignore Patterson kindly wrote out the descriptive text which appeared with it. This contribution of his is interesting, because he describes what is known as the "deglutitionary" part of the rite, which only takes place when the Pope celebrates.

One morning I was invited to breakfast at Lord Bute's, and among the Church dignitaries present was Monsignore Patterson. I had read somewhere a statement of Dean Stanley's that the Pope did not require to be a priest, so

I asked Monsignore Patterson, who was sitting opposite me, if this was the case. He very kindly undertook to explain the whole matter to me, to this effect: "If Dean Stanley affirms that the Pope need not be a priest, he is not stating what is correct. The mistake he makes probably results in this way. Supposing his Holiness were to die, which God forbid, there is no reason why you," meaning myself, "might not be elected to succeed him. It is usual," he said, "to select the occupant of the Papal throne from among the Cardinals; but the field of selection is not limited to Cardinals. They might elect a bishop, or even an ordinary priest; but they are not limited even to the priesthood. They may elect a layman, and there are lay cardinals." If I recollect right, I think he said that lay cardinals have been elected. "But supposing you were elected, before you could sit in the Papal chair you would have to be ordained priest, and elevated to the rank of bishop. The Pope must be a priest."

In describing the Inkerman caves, I mentioned that the chapels in them were dedicated to St. Clement, who generally in the list of Popes is placed as the immediate successor of St. Peter. At Rome there is a church between the Coliseum and St. John Lateran dedicated to him. At the time of my visit it was a place of great attraction, from the fact that an older church had been found under the present one. As I naturally was anxious to make sketches for the *Illustrated London News*, Monsignore Capel gave me a letter of introduction, and it turned out to be the church of the Irish Dominicans, its Prior being the bearer of a good sounding Hibernian name, Father Mulooly. Some of the brothers were present, and I was introduced to them. Among the names I heard that of Costello. Now my old friend Dr. Costello, with whom I was so long associated in Balaklava, was a Catholic, so I had at once the intention, after the introductions were over, to ask if there was any connection implied by the name. But I found I was anticipated. Father Costello had moved round the group, and when I had been introduced to the others he was at my elbow to ask if I were his brother's friend. This naturally made me at home among my new friends, and I was invited every day to dine with them. They dined about midday, and it did not suit me to eat, but I attended and drank a glass of wine, and talked with them. "Silence" is not the rule of the Dominicans, and these men, although most of them a long time out of Ireland, retained an accent with a good deal of the brogue in it. They were naturally much interested in what I had to tell them about the caves in the Crimea, and their connection with St. Clement. I sent home for the copies of the *Illustrated London News* containing the illustrations of the caves, and presented them to Father Mulooly, who presented me with his book describing the discoveries he had made in his own church.

Among the bishops attending the Council were many Orientals, and among them were representatives of sects which the Western Church had at various times received into communion, although their rites were somewhat different. I suppose it was for the information of the Council that a number of those Oriental rites were celebrated in the Church of St. Andrea della Vale. I was only able to attend a few of the celebrations, but was interested in the details. The circumambulation of the altar was a feature of some of them, and in the Coptic Mass it was performed with the left shoulder to the altar. As a pradakshiva it was the wrong hand to the centre. The going round the altar is a peculiar feature of the Greek or Oriental rites. It is done in the Russian and Abyssinian Churches. Another feature of these rites was that in some a cloth or canopy was held by the attendant over the priest and the sacred elements at the supreme moment. According to a guess of mine regarding the symbolism of this, it represents the firmament, or dome of heaven, that was placed above when the great act of Creation began. It is possibly another form of the Veil as well, for the great dome separated the visible from the invisible. The blue, starry peplos, or robe of the Virgin, becomes an evidence in favour of this. The canopy in the Jewish ceremony of marriage would in my idea be only another form of the dome. The robing of the priests at the altar was another form peculiar to the Oriental rites. This is not, however, a rule belonging exclusively to the Eastern Church, for when I attended High Mass in St. Peter's on Christmas morning his Holiness was robed for the ceremony at a throne behind the altar.

The mass performed on that morning, 1869, was in one respect, perhaps, unique. All the bishops and dignitaries who represented the Church at the Council—somewhere over seven hundred—were present, and there never had been, I understood, such a collection of bishops at a Council before. This was owing to the spread of Catholicism, more particularly into the new worlds of America and Australia, which has largely increased the number of episcopal seats. There must also be added the facilities of travelling which now exist, and which enabled so many to attend. Cardinal Antonelli and Archbishop Manning were the Deacons of the Mass on that day. The bishops occupied, and seemed to fill, the space between the high altar and St. Peter's chair. I got a very good position for my purpose just under the altar on the south side, so I saw everything done in the ceremony particularly well.

On January 1, 1870, one of the people in the hotel told me there was to be a function that day at the church of S. Paolo alle tre Fontane. It was the "profession" or reception of a member into the order of St. Benedict. The neophyte was a young American. I could not find out his name, except that his new designation was to be "Jacobus." It is a rule belonging to most of the Church's initiatory rites that as the person becomes a new individual he receives a new name. This is the case with nuns, sisters of mercy, &c. At baptism a new name is given in addition to the family name. When the Pope assumes, or is initiated into, the chair of St. Peter he takes a new name. We saw in St. Paul's the novice laid down in a simulated death, a black pall put over his body, and candles lighted at his head and feet. He remained in that position while the abbot celebrated mass. Then one of the deacons of the mass came to where the neophyte lay, with a

High Mass in St. Peter's, Rome, Christmas, 1869.

To face p. 236.

paper in his hand, from which he repeated in Latin the words, "Oh thou that sleepest, arise to everlasting life." The young man rose, went to the altar, and received the sacrament. If my memory serves me I think he received a cowl. He then kissed the brethren, and took his place amongst them. He had become a "brother." This ceremony was not quite unknown previously to students of Masonry, but from the illustration and description which I sent of it to the *Illustrated London News* I daresay it is now more widely familiar.

During the twelve days from Christmas to Epiphany I was a constant visitor to the Ara Cœli Church, on the Capitol, to see the curious cult of the Sacred Bambino, who is the principal doctor in Rome. I was on the top of the long flight of stairs when he was brought out on the last day to bless the people. I saw him taken away one evening in a box. The box was covered with red velvet, and had "I.H.S." on the lid. This was put into a carriage, and the Bambino went to visit some patient. As the box was carried through the church, and at the door, every one went down on his knees.

January 19th is St. Antony's Day, so I went to that saint's church to see the blessing of the animals. Rich people send their carriage horses, poor people their donkeys, pigs, goats, cats, &c. A priest comes to the door of the church and says a prayer; an attendant stands by with a large can of holy water; and the priest with a large brush, something like a broom, sprinkles—I might use the Scottish word "jaups"—the water on the beasts. I was close at hand at one of the performances and received a large share of the water. St. Antony is the patron saint of swineherds, and is connected with Egypt. His cross is a letter T, probably derived from the *crux ansata* ☥, which the Egyptian deities carry in their hands, and with which they confer everlasting life.

Joseph Bonomi gave me two letters of introduction; one was to a cousin of his, Monsignore Bonomi. It may be mentioned that priests who receive appointments on the Pope's suite receive the title of "Monsignore." Unfortunately Monsignore Bonomi could speak neither English nor French, so we had to smile at each other. But a thought struck him, he went out of the room, returned with a number of copies of the *Illustrated London News* and turned up the illustrations of the Council that had appeared. We smiled again, and although, under such circumstances, the interview was short, it was pleasant.

The other letter was to Joseph Severn, then British Consul at Rome. I was particularly desirous of meeting this man, on account of his intimate connection with John Keats. So when Severn asked what he could do for a "brother brush," as he expressed it, I asked if he would take me to Keats's grave. This he kindly did. The little stone was there, just as it had been first put up. Severn designed the old Greek harp, which is the only effort at art or ornament upon it.

Another interesting man I met in Rome was the son of Mrs. Hemans, the poet. He was well acquainted with mediæval Rome and its archæology, and gave me information on some curious points I wished to know. I heard him give a most interesting lecture to the British Archæological Society on the Coliseum. I joined this Society for the time I was in Rome, and read a paper on the Suez Canal.

At the time of my arrival at the hotel I learned that there was a great millionaire in it. Such a great man, I supposed, had his meals in his own rooms, and would not be visible among the crowd at the ordinary table. His yacht, in which he had come, lay at Ostia. I noticed a little old man going about, and as he had a gold-lace band round his cap, which gave him a naval look, I took him for the captain of the yacht, and supposed he had come in attendance upon the great man. It chanced that he generally came down to breakfast about the time that I did, and we soon became friends. He was a Scotsman, and I found that he was particularly fond of a good story or a joke of any kind. One morning he asked if I had ever been in Glasgow. I saw that he had noticed my accent and guessed the place of my nativity; so I put on a thoughtful expression and seemed as if I were looking back through the past to discover any memory of a visit to that place. At last I said, "Yes, I believe I once visited Glasgow many, many years ago, when I was very young." He followed my idea perfectly, and quite understood from my words that by that visit I meant my birth. He never forgot it, for often afterwards, when inviting me to come and see him, he always added, "next time you visit Glasgow." This, of course, turned out to be the rich man himself—James Young—said at the time to be the richest man in Scotland. He made his money from paraffin oil, by means of a process of his own invention. There was a kind of coal, or rather shale; he managed to extract an oil from it, and "Young's paraffin oil" has long been famous.

After I knew who he was, and that he was a chemist, I was telling him one morning that while very young I used to attend lectures on chemistry in the Mechanics' Institution and the Andersonian University, in Glasgow, and among the lecturers I heard Professor Thomas Graham. On my mention of this name, he turned quickly round and said, "If you have heard Graham, you must have seen me, for I was the wee laddie that held the candle," meaning by this that he was Graham's assistant. I said I did not remember him—at that time my attention was directed more to the experiments than to the laddie that held the candle. Young had been a cabinet-maker, and in that capacity he did jobs in the Andersonian. This led ultimately to a permanent position as assistant. In this capacity he picked up a knowledge of chemistry, which at last enabled him to make the discovery which resulted in his great wealth. Graham was a great chemist, very advanced in his ideas. He was appointed Master of the Mint, and died in London. Young erected his statue in George Square, Glasgow, and published for private circulation some of his writings. Young was a great friend of David Livingstone, and it was more in imitation of him, I understood, than as the proprietor of a yacht, that he wore the gold band on his cap.

Young had some of his daughters with him, and he was going on in his yacht to Palestine, so I gave him a letter of introduction to Captain Warren, at Jerusalem. As he intended, further, to visit Constantinople, I gave him a letter to Skender Bey, saying as the latter was in the engineering department of the Sultan, and was in one way an official in the Naval Service, he might be of use in securing a safe berth for the yacht. Young was tickled when I accompanied this information with the extra explanation that "Skender Bey" was a "Sandie Shanks frae the Gorbals."

Before I left London Mr. Bonomi asked me to look out for the forgeries on the obelisk of the Lateran. I did so—saw them quite distinctly, made sketches of them all, and sent them to Bonomi. I forget the exact date of these hieroglyphic forgeries, but, roughly speaking, they are as old, if not older, than the time of Moses.

CHAPTER XXVI

THE FRANCO-GERMAN WAR

WAR between France and Germany was declared on the 15th of July, and I left for Paris on the 20th. My ignorance of German determined me for the French side. I put up at the Hotel de la Grande Bretagne in the Rue Caumartin, a good central position, and I stayed there for some days, finding good subjects from incidents on the streets.

On the 25th I started for the front, going by Nancy to Metz. It was difficult to get quarters in the latter place; the hotels were full of military officers. At last I got a bedroom in a private house belonging to a German, and I got food in the Hotel de Metz, which all the British correspondents frequented for their meals. Sydney Hall turned up here at the beginning of his career as a special artist to the *Graphic*. G. A. Sala was the life of the party. There were about a dozen of us, but generally two or three were in custody as spies, and a considerable portion of our time was occupied in running about among the military authorities to get them released. Spy-fever among the French became the most serious obstacle in carrying out our work. A sketch-book was a most dangerous article to be found in your possession. In spite of the difficulty I managed to send home a number of sketches of Metz. I was particularly fortunate in a trip I made to Forbach, which was the advanced position of the French army. Mr. Hall, a young Irish gentleman, went with me. We started early by rail, and breakfasted at the buffet of the railway station. I managed, from quiet corners, while my friend kept watch, to make a few sketches, which I worked up and sent off next day. That was Monday, and on Saturday the great fight took place. By that time the editor had my sketches in hand. At Forbach the idea occurred to me of sketching on a book of cigarette papers. One could do a good deal on a book of that kind, and in the event of being apprehended, could make a cigarette of the sketch and smoke it before the eyes of one's accusers.

On Saturday, 6th of August, the Battle of Forbach took place. We had news of the fighting the same night, and the next morning Mayhew, who was special for the *Standard*, his son, who was helping him, and I went early to the railway station expecting to see the wounded coming in. On our way we met a Mr. R. M. Stuart. He had been correspondent for the *Daily News* in Florence, the paper had ordered him from that place to Metz, and he had just arrived. When he understood where we were going he joined us. At the station there were no signs of the wounded. By this time we knew that the Prussians were the victors, and it dawned on us that as they would hold the ground after the fighting, the wounded would be in their hands. This explained why none came into Metz.

We noticed a handsome new carriage in front of the station, and learned that it had come for the use of the Emperor as he advanced with his army to Berlin. It had some exceptional arrangements, amongst which were pockets, like portfolios, for maps. This was too tempting a subject, and I was making a slight sketch of it, in a very small note-book, when some soldiers surrounded me, and told me I was a prisoner. My companions were also apprehended. We were then marched into the town, all four of us, two soldiers guarding each. We formed quite a little procession, and as we went along the crowd that followed increased. "Espions," "Espions Prussians!" were words we heard as we passed along. These phrases were varied with many uncomplimentary terms, and we heard one man say, "Spy was written in every line of our villainous countenances." Closed fists were shaken at us, but luckily the presence of the soldiers prevented actual violence. By the time we reached the police station, in the open "place" south of the Cathedral, the crowd had increased to a large multitude, from which we were glad to escape within doors. The first thing we asked for was paper, pens, and ink, and we were amused at our captors declaring this demand very suspicious. Mayhew wrote a note to the Quartier-General, where we were known, and we got one of the soldiers to take it, promising him a *pour-boire* if he brought an answer. While we were waiting my sketch-book was carefully inspected, and the most absurd conclusions were come to regarding its contents. People from the crowd came in and volunteered information. One man pointed to Mayhew and said that Monsieur came every evening to a certain café. To give effect to his denunciation, he wagged his forefinger violently up and down within an inch or so of Mayhew's nose. The finger became more violent when he came to the last part of his accusation, which was that "he sat every night on the same seat." This dreadful conduct Mayhew admitted he had been guilty of. Another individual came in. He was editor or printer of the local newspaper, an officer of pompiers, and a chevalier of the Legion of Honour. He accused young Mayhew of coming to his office to buy copies of the paper. "Yesterday," he said, pointing to Mayhew, and wagging his forefinger close to his face, "he came and bought a paper, and another Monsieur came with him, and bought a paper, and"—here was the awful part of the charge—"that Monsieur asked how much the postage of the paper would be to London." Our messenger came back presently, and had a smile on his face when he told the officials that we were known at Headquarters, and were not to be detained. The officer of pompiers apologised nicely on hearing this. He had not a card upon him, but he wrote out his name and honorary title on a bit of paper for me. The authorities advised us to leave Metz, because the people had become so excited owing to the defeat that it was dangerous, and they could not promise us protection from the mob. Even French correspondents were being maltreated on the streets.

I left that night for Nancy, where I found Sala and other correspondents; Mayhew and his son followed next day.

We had in the hotel an artillery officer and a naval officer, the latter was on his way to join a gunboat on the Rhine. Of course he never reached the Rhine, unless he did so as a prisoner of war. At dinner we naturally recounted our experiences at Metz, and the artillery officer, a jolly kind of man, sympathised with us, but the naval officer, who was already far gone with an attack of spy-fever, saw the matter in a different light. He said if he caught a spy there would be very short work with him. We said, "Quite right; only be quite sure that the person is a spy before you dispose of him." By way of reply he gave a shake of the head which showed that shooting would be his line of treatment. After dinner he went out, and presently came back again—chased by the mob as a spy! After that we had the laugh against him.

We found Nancy too hot for us, and all returned to Paris. Here I remained till after Sedan. Some of the correspondents ventured to Rheims, where there was a camp, but had to return by the next train. In fact it was dangerous for a stranger to leave the boulevardes. If one did so, and opened his mouth, his words at once told he was a foreigner, and suspicious looks were the least result to be looked for. My friend Morin told me he had been mobbed and made prisoner when sketching. He also told me of a friend who had been fishing somewhere, not far from Paris; his hook caught in some weeds and, to save his line, he waded into the water to undo the hook. Some one had been watching him and had come to the conclusion he was sounding the depth of the stream, and he was at once apprehended. By great care I escaped all further trouble of this sort. I never produced a sketch-book, but used my eyes. One day I saw a small gunboat, which had been newly made at St. Cloud. I looked at it, took a stroll, and in my head drew the lines. Then I returned to get more details, strolled again, filling them in, and did this till I felt certain I could draw every detail from memory. The actual sketch I drew when I got back to the hotel. By this process I was able to send lots of incidents which made good material for the paper. Parry wrote me to wait events, so I filled up my time in this way.

REPUBLIC PROCLAIMED

The news of the battle of Sedan and the taking of the French Emperor oozed out on Saturday, September 3rd. The people in Paris became wild with excitement, and there were processions along the Boulevards of men calling out "La déchéance!" It might be about nine o'clock when I found G. A. Sala in the middle of a group discussing the question as to what would take place—whether a Republic would be declared or not. I got him to come with me to the Grande Café near the Opera. In this place we sat and discussed art, including the career of Haydon, whose life Sala had written many years before. Occasionally we would rush to the doors as some excited band passed, calling out, "La déchéance!" and "Vive la Republique!" I expected every moment to see a charge of cavalry, or a mitrailleuse come into action, and I was rather surprised that there was no movement by the authorities. Next day revealed the utter collapse of the Government.

On that day, the celebrated 4th of September, I was on the Place de la Concorde all forenoon, and saw the fraternisation of the troops of the line and the National Guards. I learned there that the Empress had fled, and that a Republic had been proclaimed. I saw written in chalk on the Tuileries "*Maison à louer*," and as I came along the boulevarde, saw the shopkeepers removing from their signs all reference to their claims of patronage by the Emperor or Empress. I was standing in the Rue St. Honore, as some of the troops marched past, when an old woman at my side on the pavement, said, in a rather loud voice, "A wheen damned fules!" The words and accent were in such pure Scottish, I turned and asked who she was. She was a native of Dunbarton, and had come over with her husband, who was a workman on the railways. She had seen four revolutions, and evidently did not approve of them.

Certain friends were bound for Namur in Belgium, and as I reasoned that the sooner I was out of Paris the better, I left next day with them. My intention was to go to Sedan; they came on with me and saw some of the horrors of the battlefield. The dead had all been buried, but horses wounded in the fighting were still to be seen, and the ground was covered with muskets, knapsacks, helmets, and all the details of soldiers' belongings. We found letters and photographs. Some of the letters had been written to send to friends, but had not been posted. My friends took these and posted them in Belgium. I could have carried off any quantity of relics, but as I was not about to return they might have proved "white elephants." I did bring off a broken sword and a Prussian eagle, which I took off the helmet it belonged to. The globe on the claw of the bird is slightly bent back at its extreme edge by the bullet which must have killed the man. I saw the hole in the helmet and a hole in the back of it, where the ball passed out.

One day I went to Donchery, where King William, the Crown Prince, Bismarck, and Moltke took up their position on the last day of the fighting. There was a château at the place. The family were away, but the man in charge allowed me to sketch from one of the windows from which there was a capital view of the whole ground of the battle. I had only a sketch-book with me, and seeing in the room some rolls of wallpaper, I cut off a piece, and sketched on the back of it. This man had seen the fighting from this spot. I put in the smoke of the battle to indicate the position of the Germans and the French from what he told me. The sketch, which I did in colour, was folded and sent home through the post. It was copied into the *Illustrated London News*, and when I afterwards received it, it was rather the worse of the wear. I had it mounted on a board and mended the defects. When placed in some particular lights, the pattern of the paper on the other side is slightly visible. I visited every part of the three days' fighting—from Mouson, where the fighting began, to Donchery. I remained a couple of weeks, and found very good material for the *Illustrated London News*.

There were no newspapers in Sedan, so I knew nothing of what was going on. When I left I made for Luxembourg, to get news of the outer world. There I met Henry Kingsley, brother of Charles Kingsley, the well-known

The Battle of Sedan, from the Chateau of Donchery.

Reproduced from the original at Dalmeny by kind permission of the Earl of Rosebery. This picture was done a few days after the battle on the back of a piece of wall paper, the design of which may be noticed here and there. The accuracy of the details was afterwards verified by one of the German military attachés in London who had been present at the battle.

To face p. 246.

author. He had come out on the war-path as a correspondent. From the news I picked up I started for Strasburg—rather, I ought to say, as the siege was going on, the outside of Strasburg. At Schillingheim, a village on the outskirts, I at last found a room and a bed in the house of a farrier. The German soldiers were billeted in every house, and the officers were in the hotels. There were so many of them that beds were scarce, and "*Rempli des militaires*" became a sentence I hated to hear. The bed in my new quarters had a bolster, but no blankets. Luckily I had a plaid. There was one chair, but nothing to wash in. The woman brought in an old pan with some water in which I did something to my face and hands. This had to be carried off again for the use of the soldiers billeted in the house. The nights were horrible, something past description. All the fleas of Strasburg had come out, it seemed, to this village, and my conviction was that most of them were in my room. Food could always be procured, however; I had whatever I required in the "Cheval Blanc."

Von Werder, who was in command before Strasburg, had his headquarters at Mundalsheim, a village about four or five miles away. I started for that on my first morning. I saw some of the Staff, but they spoke as if a passport for the trenches was out of the question. I was almost giving up hopes, when by a chance I mentioned Sebastopol. I was able to show my passport to the Crimea from our Foreign Office, and an officer, Lepel was his name, at once took an interest in me. The result was a passport for the trenches before Strasburg.

Luckily I did not require to remain long in my wretched quarters. It was not on quite my first visit to the trenches, but it was when I first ventured into the advanced works, that Strasburg threw up the sponge. I chanced to be in an advanced work, where the Germans were sapping up to two bastions. I had made some sketches and was about to return, when a white flag appeared on one of the bastions. The first idea was that it was a "flag of truce," but it was immediately followed by a white flag on the spire of the cathedral. The siege was over, and I was able to walk back across the works.

Next morning I had a hard day's labour before me. I was up with the first streak of light, and did a sketch of the event of the day before. This I had to take to Mundalsheim to the post. I calculated that if sent off that day it would reach Mr. Jackson, the editor, in time for the "next Saturday," which it did. I walked back from Mundalsheim as fast as I could, and saw the French prisoners come out. Then I went into Strasburg. I went round part of the fortifications on that day, and I could see from the state of the batteries, that the defence had not been properly conducted. Guns had been dismounted, and not replaced; the parapets had not been repaired, etc. My old experience at Sebastopol told me that things had not been right in Strasburg. I learned afterwards from Sir Charles Wilson, R.E., that there were, when the siege began, only one regiment of the line in the place, and a few scattered fragments of MacMahon's troops that found their way there after the Battle of Woerth. Four engineer officers only were in the town, and they were soon killed or disabled. The defence had for some time towards the end been carried on by volunteers furnished by Strasburg itself. This supplied a striking illustration of the military capacity of Napoleon le Petite.

After nine or ten days in Strasburg, I left for Savergne, and visited Phalsburg, which was besieged, or at least blockaded, by the Germans. From Savergne I went to Weissenburg and Woerth, going over the ground of these battlefields. I then turned towards Saarbrucken. Metz was still holding out under Bazaine, and Saarbrucken was the point of approach. Here I found Nicholas Wood, acting as "special" for the *Scotsman*. I had known him in the Crimea, where he did good work either for the *Standard* or the *Morning Herald*. It was at this place I first met Archibald Forbes. Maclean of Lochbuie, in Mull, was also here, acting for the *Times*. It became known that Metz could not hold out much longer, and most of us went to Remilly to await its fall. This occurred on the 21st of October. On the 29th I saw the French army march out as prisoners of war. I went into Metz on an ambulance waggon that evening. In the courtyard of one hotel I saw a horse trying to eat his manger, which told how hungry the poor brute must have been. Afterwards, when I went about the town, I noticed that, as high as a horse could reach, the bark on the tree trunks had all been eaten away. I remember trying some of the hotels for a bed; but the French officers had not left, and the hotels were full of them.

Next morning I breakfasted in an hotel full of French officers, and we had only horse to eat, badly cooked, and with very bad bread. "Revenons à nos moutons" I thought was a saying that at least would express what these Frenchmen wished, but it was a day or two before the saying could become practical. I was sitting in the crowded *salle á manger* at an extemporised table close to the door, and doing my best to eat a very bad breakfast, when a very bald head was projected close to mine, and its owner expressed in French an inquiry as to whether a bed could be found in the hotel. On looking at the face, I recognised Laurence Oliphant. The answer I gave was in English: "Do you recollect breakfasting with me in Circassia on roasted eggs?" He said, "My name is Oliphant; who are you?" I told him, and said, "You had better sit down and have some breakfast; beds are scarce." He was acting for the *Times*. At that time Oliphant was under the spell of Harris. He was at times in America, working in the community near Buffalo, but when there was anything exciting going on in Europe he came over and did duty as "special" for the *Times*. After breakfast, as he had never been in Metz before, I went out to show him the principal places. I remember in the market-place how the women expressed themselves against Bazaine. I believe they would have torn him to pieces. The name stank in the town, not one had a good word for him.

I have never seen what I should consider a full explanation of Bazaine's conduct in Metz, but I formed a theory for myself. It was well known that communications were going on, during the siege, between Bazaine, Bismarck, and the Emperor Napoleon. It was also known at the time that the question arose, who, in the event of a peace being arranged, was to take Napoleon back to Paris? It would not do for the Germans to undertake this. So Bazaine's army would have the duty to perform. The Garde Imperial was part of that army. Here was Bismarck's clever bait, and it humbugged the scoundrel Bazaine. If he took the Emperor back to Paris, he would be a very mighty man. With this in view he must not spoil his force by making sorties. Bismarck kept this carrot dangling before the eyes of Bazaine, while the cavalry horses were being eaten up. The German strategist was, no doubt, accurately informed about the horses, and when he knew that the French had neither artillery nor cavalry, and that Bazaine and his army were harmless, he broke off negotiations. Nothing was left but capitulation. If Bazaine had made sorties in force in the earlier part of the siege, he would have added very considerably to the task of the Germans. This is exactly what Bismarck managed by his cunning to prevent.

I visited the various battlefields round Metz—Gravelotte, Mars le Tour, Rezonville, St. Privat, etc. I slept one night at Rezonville. The man to whom the auberge belonged had gone into Metz with his young daughter for safety when the Germans arrived, and the two could not get out again during the siege. The wife had to take charge of the establishment, and she had a number of soldiers billeted on her. Her pig, poultry, and live stock were all eaten up. Even the furniture had been burned; and the house was a wreck. The man knew nothing of the fighting, and as he could not show me the ground, madame offered to do so. The daughter came with us. The ground was still covered with all the litter that is left on a battlefield. The quantity and variety of brushes which soldiers require was a surprise. The girl began gathering them, and brought home her apron full. One could tell where French and German soldiers had stood from the papers in which the packets of cartridges had been wrapped. Then there were mounds, on which stood pieces of wood with a label affixed, telling that perhaps ten or a dozen Germans or French had been buried at the spot. These mounds were plentiful, they told how murderous the fighting had been.

On returning to Metz I found myself very ill. For weeks past I had not been well. It was a dreadful kind of life I had been obliged to put up with. It was then November, and as winter advanced, things would become worse. So I determined to return home. I returned by Saarbrucken and Luxembourg, to Namur, where I found my portmanteau. I had been for weeks knocking about with merely a plaid, and a small knapsack with my sketching materials. From Namur I came to Brussels, and got back to 64, Lincoln's Inn Fields, on Wednesday November 16, 1870, having been nearly four months away.

CHAPTER XXVII

THE COMMUNE IN PARIS

THE peace was followed by the Commune. Hostilities between the Communards and Versailles began in March, and as the winter was past, I, in April, undertook to start for the scene of the struggle. Mr. William Ingram—now, when I write, Sir William J. Ingram, Bart.—went with me. We started on the 11th of April. At St. Dennis, which was held by the Germans, we left the train, and, being in light marching order, started on foot for Versailles. On the way we could hear the heavy guns firing, which recalled Sebastopol to my memory.

Next morning we went off early and walked to Fort Valerien, which was held by the Versaillais. They were exchanging compliments by means of their heavy guns with the Communards. The latter had guns on the high ground to the west, from which they sent shells. Some of these came pretty near to us, as I sat and sketched. Most of the shells fell short, and dropped into the village of Suresnes, on the Seine, below Valerien. From seeing these shells drop on the village I had doubts about venturing down to it; but it was our only chance of getting breakfast, and we began to feel, after our long and early walk, that something substantial would be acceptable. I had another object in descending to the village. I had hopes of interesting "incidents." This hope was not disappointed, for we had just entered the village when a shell arrived. It went through a garret window, and burst inside. I with others ran up the stair. The door was burst open, and at first we could see nothing for the smoke and dust. When it cleared a little we found a man with his wife and child in a frightened condition, but fortunately unhurt. This was an "incident" quite after the editor's heart, and it will be found in the *Illustrated London News* for 29th of April, 1871, honoured with a position on the front page.

Mr. Ingram remained with me till the 22nd of April. We made an excursion almost every day to the advanced posts held by the Versailles troops, and generally found subjects of interest. Often we had adventures, as well as risks. I shall recount one of these, as it caused me to change my plans. We had gone one day to St. Cloud, when a man spoke to us, and said we must come with him. This we did. I noticed curiously how the man trembled as he went along. We followed him to a house, and it turned out that he had an attack of spy-fever, my old enemy. At the house were military, and we were presented to an officer, who took notes of what the informant said. We had to sit down till a report was made. This was sent off to some one, and our trembling friend retired. I then began talking to the officer, who was one of the Corps du Génie, or Engineers. He had been at the siege of Sebastopol, and he soon saw from my knowledge of that place that I was not likely to be a spy. He apologised for detaining us, but said that certain formalities must be gone through. Coffee and cigarettes were produced, and at last we were allowed to go; but he said we must have passports. I had tried before to procure a passport at Versailles, and I now made another attempt with a letter from our Embassy. But after three or four days' attendance at a sort of circumlocution office, or offices, for there were many of them, the final answer was a refusal. This put a complete stoppage to my work, for I could not run the chance of being "run in" again as a prisoner at St. Cloud.

Among those I met at Versailles was Captain, now Major, Kodolitsch, my old Abyssinian friend. He was military attaché to the Austrian Embassy, and had, in his particular duties, to make visits to Paris for the information of his ambassador. He advised me to go into Paris, and told me not to believe what I read in the Versailles papers. Lies and misrepresentations, he said, were published about everything. On the 27th of April I at last acted on his advice, and went into Paris. I had to go round by St. Dennis, and arrived at the Gare du Nord. Having only a knapsack, I escaped the Douane officers. I pitched the knapsack into a voiture, telling the man to drive me to the Rue Caumartin. "But, perhaps," I said, "I will not find a bed." "Oh," he replied, "you are mocking me." He said to his knowledge all the hotels in Paris were empty. I said, "Perhaps the hotel is *demenagé*, but go, and we will see." As I had guessed, the hotel was out of order, but they got me a room. There was no cuisine, so I had to find meals out of doors.

My first move was to go to our Embassy. It was in charge of Mr. Malet, whom I had met before. Lord Lyons, our Ambassador, son of my old friend, Admiral Lyons, was in Versailles. Mr. Malet gave me a written document to show, if necessary, that I was a British subject. He also gave me a letter to Paschal Grousset, who might be called the minister for foreign affairs. On presenting the letter to Paschal Grousset, he gave me a passport at once. The interview did not last five minutes, and was quite a contrast to my experience of the Versailles authorities.

Paris was empty. That is, there were no visitors. I have often said that I liked Paris at that time better than on any of my other visits. One could walk along the boulevards without being jostled by the crowds, and in a café I had all the *garçons* to attend upon me, for as a rule I was the only customer. Generally I walked about during the day, going often to the outposts, where I seldom failed to find "incidents." I went early to bed, and got up by times, when I did a sketch of any subject I had seen the day before. This I would finish by breakfast. The only post from Paris to Britain at that time was through the Embassy, and Malet enclosed my sketch. The rule was to send the letters to Versailles, from which they were posted home, but Malet often sent dispatches direct to London. From the Embassy I went to some restaurant for breakfast. After that I started for a long walk, on the look-out for subjects, returning in time for dinner, and then to bed.

My adventures during the few weeks I was in Paris at this eventful time would make a volume. Some of them illustrate the curious condition in which the capital of France was at that date.

One favourite walk was through the Champs Elysées and on to the Arc de Triomph. Fort Valerien directed most of its guns towards that point, and as I neared it figures on the road got scarce. Only a boy or two ever ventured to the arch, and these came to capture the fragments of shell, which they sold in the boulevards. One day I went down as far as Port Maillot, where there were batteries, which faced down the straight line of road to Courbevoie. Two Communard soldiers wanted to know who I was, so I put my hand in my pocket for my passport, but I had forgotten it. I told them to take me to their chief, which they did. He was in a house on the right of the battery. The colonel was absent, so I saw Major Lefevre, who could speak English. He was a cabinet-maker, and had been fourteen years in London working at his trade. When the war with Germany began, he, being in a volunteer corps in London, at once went to Paris as a volunteer in defence of his country. He had gone through the defence of Paris, and when the peace came he got into the Commune movement, and could not now get out of it. His wife was in Pimlico, and he asked me if I could send a letter to her. Then he said he would be obliged if I would write the letter, as he had no time nor proper place to write. The place he was in had been smashed with shells. I did write, and had a letter from his wife. He gave me a passport for Port Maillot, and I went up next day and made some sketches. Afterwards, when the Versailles troops came into Paris, he managed to transform himself, and escaped capture for some months. At last, however, he was denounced, and taken to Satory, and I think he got a year's imprisonment.

Another day I went as far as the Point du Jour. This is where the old fortifications of Paris came to the river at the point nearest to St. Cloud. Here were two cannonieres, or gunboats, which lay under the arches of the railway bridge. I made the acquaintance of the officer in command, whose name was Girard. There had been a tea-garden at this place. The sign was still up, and it mentioned wedding parties. "Parties des Noces" could be attended to. But the place was a complete wreck. I suppose it had suffered during the siege by the Germans, and now, on account of the gunboats, it was continually under fire from the batteries at Meudon. The proprietor had dug a cave in the earth, into which he had retired with his family and as many of his bottles as the place could hold, and he supplied Girard and his sailors with food. After I had finished a sketch, Girard and I chanced to be standing in one of the works, when we saw a shell coming direct towards us. We had just time to crouch under the parapet, when it struck the earth outside and exploded, almost burying both of us with the mass of stuff it dislodged. I saw at a later day that Girard had been tried and sentenced to death. He had held the rank of officer in the French Marine, so I suppose his fate was certain.

During the Commune I saw a good deal of a very old man, Jean Frederick, Count de Waldeck. I met him first in London at my friend Witt's, Prince's Gate, and he came to my rooms to see my Indian sketches. There were doubts about his great age, but he was said, or believed himself, to have been born at Prague in 1766. So, in 1871, he was 105 years of age. It would be hard to say what this man had not been in his day. In 1793 he was manager of the Old Porte Saint Martin Theatre. He had commanded a privateer in the Bay of Bengal in the time of the first Napoleon, and as a captain in the 4th Hussars had been wounded at Austerlitz. He was painter, sculptor, archæologist, and traveller. He had been some years in Central America, and had drawn and studied the ancient remains in that region. The Lord Buchan of the date of his birth had been his godfather, Lord Buchan being at the time, if I recollect right, connected with our Embassy at Vienna. When a young man De Waldeck had visited Lord Buchan

THE COMMUNE IN PARIS: THE PONT DU JOUR BARRICADED.

To face p. 256.

in Scotland, and when there had produced a statue of Wallace, which still stands near Dryburgh Abbey on the Border. There, too, he had picked up some broad Scotch. He had lived in London, and Mr. Haghe recollected when he had a shop in Charing Cross Market, a place that existed when I came to the city. He dealt in old prints, his great qualification being his power of delicately touching up or mending old engravings, and making them as good as new. His writing was small, minute, and perfect. I have yet some of his letters. He had married at eighty-four. It was not his first marriage. The lady was English. By her he had a son, who was in the Commune forces, and the old man was very anxious about this Benjamin of his old age. The last time I called, Waldeck and his wife were planning to get out of Paris with their son. The old man died in 1875, and I wrote a notice of him which was published in the *Morning Post.** This brought me into contact with another son, living in London. I managed to send letters for Madame de Waldeck to her friends in England, and took to her the letters in reply.

I had been for some time watching the operations at the column in the Place Vendôme, and on Tuesday, the 16th of May, I saw it fall. The Commune have been blamed for a wholesale destruction of public monuments. This accusation has been made in its broadest sense, as a charge of ruffianism, and without regard to distinctive qualification. The column in the Place Vendôme was the only monument they pulled down, and a reason was given for the deed. The column was a monument of Napoleon; it represented the glories of that aggressor's dynasty, and it was antagonistic to the nationalities of Europe. I do not justify the pulling down of the monument; I am only pointing out the unfair character of charges against the Commune. I think that a public monument, once up, should not be destroyed. Those who follow at a later date may not approve of the object, or the motives, of those who erected it, but it should be left, though it may remain only a monument of the folly of those who erected it.

* [May 3, 1875.]

Next day, the 17th of May, occurred the great explosion at the Champ de Mars, where the Communards manufactured their cartridges. I chanced to be in the hotel at the time. Wondering what the sound could be, I rushed out, and when near the Madeleine I could see, towering in the sky above the houses away towards the south-west, a great pillar of smoke. It suggested the pillar of smoke in the pictures of the Tabernacle. The great mass was dark in colour, but a white portion projected at the top, which twisted and curled and seemed to be shooting up still higher.. I went walking, or running, as fast as I could, and I managed to reach the ground before a cordon was formed round it. There was not much to see, the explosion had been so terrible. Not a scrap of the buildings in which it occurred had been left. Blackened fragments of human remains lay scattered about. These fragments were all so small, and they were so black and burnt, they were more like bits of peat than anything else. It was hard to believe they were bits of men and women.

The Versaillais managed to enter through the defences at the Port Auteuil on Sunday, the 21st of May. Few people in Paris knew of this till next morning. It so chanced that I slept that morning till about seven o'clock, when I was wakened by the *garçon* coming in with some coffee. He said hurriedly, "Les Versaillais sont dans les Champs Elysées. Entendez, Monsieur." I could hear the rattle of musketry. I dressed and made for the boulevard. Not a soul was to be seen. The sharp noise of the firing came from my right, so I turned towards the Madeleine. I supposed that the shots were coming up the Rue Royale, so I walked over to the corner, where there is a well-known *café,* intending to look down the street. But before I reached the corner I found myself in the line of fire, which was coming down one of the streets on my right. The bullets were striking the walls round me. On returning from this hot corner I was met by a soldier of the Commune, who ordered me to go up the street where the fighting was and work at the barricade. I was discussing the propriety of this with the man when one of the chiefs of the Commune appeared, wearing a tri-colour scarf round his waist. On my explaining to him who I was, he told the soldier to let me go, and I walked with my new friend back towards the Opera. Before we got there I saw Dr. Austin, the *Times* correspondent, coming towards us. It was a curious feeling which the surroundings produced in me. Here was the boulevard, which one supposes to be always full of people, with not a soul but ourselves visible. My friend here left us, and Austin and I turned down towards the Tuileries. In this direction we found a very few people moving about. The soldiers were making barricades, and our great difficulty was to avoid being pressed into this work, for they forced all to do so. We found ourselves at one time standing at the end of one of the streets leading into the Rue de Rivoli, opposite the Tuileries. We were looking towards the Champs Elysées, where we heard firing going on. While we stood there a rifle bullet passed between us. We certainly could not at the moment have been more than twelve or eighteen inches apart. The bullet struck the wall behind us, and in lifting it up I noticed a small, circular bit of cloth, about the size of a shilling, on the ground. It looked so like the cloth of Austin's coat that he searched and found the hole. It was in the skirt of his coat, towards the front, and proved that the bullet must have passed close to his thigh. We could do little that day. The fighting was going on close to us on three sides, and the danger of being pressed into the service of barricade-making caused us correspondents to remain in close quarters.

On the Monday Colonel the Hon. John Stanley turned up. We met first in the Governor-General's camp in India, where he was an A.D.C. to Lord Canning, and he seemed very pleased to see me again. He was living in the Hotel Mirabeau, in the Rue de la Paix, a short street running from the Opera to the Place Vendôme. Some time after breakfast on the Tuesday he invited me to his room, and I went. It so chanced that after I was in Stanley's rooms, which were on the third or fourth floor, the Versailles soldiers appeared at the Opera House. They occupied the windows of the houses on the eastern side, and from them began firing down the Rue de la Paix, where there was a barricade at the Place Vendôme. This shut me up in the hotel, for it would have been madness to go into the street with bullets flying up and down. At one time I could see that the Reds had left the Place Vendôme, but after a short time a few of them came back and continued the defence. One of the Versailles soldiers mounted to the roof of the Opera House, and ascended to the topmost pinnacle, on which stands a figure of Apollo holding up a harp. The red flag of the Commune was attached to this, and the soldier removed it. Although I watched all the afternoon, neither side took the slightest notice of me. When it grew dark, after dinner, I lay down with my clothes on, and fell asleep. About four next morning I was wakened by people in the streets clapping their hands, and on looking out I found that the Versailles troops had occupied the Place Vendôme.

The week's fighting between the Versailles troops and those of the Commune began on Sunday, the 21st of May, and the last shots were fired on the Sunday after. The struggle began at the Porte Auteuil, on the south-west of Paris, and ended on the north-east, somewhere in the region of La Roquette and Père la Chaise. From this it will be understood that the line of fighting—a very irregular "line"—moved day by day from west to east. On Tuesday morning the end of the boulevard, the Opera House, and the Rue de la Paix were occupied by the Reds. On Wednesday morning the Versailles troops had advanced as far as the Rue Poissonnière. On leaving the Hôtel Mirabeau I found Austin, and we went off eastward and soon reached the Faubourg Poissonnière. The Versailles troops had just arrived, or were arriving, as we reached the principal street. At the end of the streets beyond were barricades, on which we could see the red flag. At the end of one of these streets the Versailles soldiers began to place barrels, or whatever they could lay their hands on, to make cover from which they could fire at the barricade at the other extremity. While we were looking at these movements some of the soldiers appeared with a Communard prisoner, and the officers present ordered him to be placed in the middle of the street in the direct line of the fire of his own party. There the poor devil stood, but luckily nothing struck him. This was the first indication I had seen of the bloodthirsty tactics of the side which made such high pretensions to law and order. Leaving this we went to the next street, where the Versailles soldiers had occupied the windows. Some of them had even found a way to the roofs of the houses, from which they fired up the street. Here some prisoners were caught. One of them was a woman with the red cross on her arm, showing that she belonged to the ambulance department of the Commune. A brutal, fat officer tore it off, and she would be sent away to Satory classed as "a Petroleuse." I mention these facts to show the feelings that prevailed at the time.

After breakfast at the "Chatham," on Thursday, Austin and I went off. I remember others started with us. I think at first we numbered five or six correspondents. As we neared the line of action, our party, like an iceberg moving south, melted away. Austin alone stuck to me. We found ourselves in the Quartier du Temple. Some people took us into a public building to look at the dead body of a young boy. He had been shot, and they showed us the hole made in his breast by the bullet. On leaving this I remember advancing to a barricade that had just been left by the Communards. I have always claimed that I took that barricade, because I was the first man in it. Of course I was heavily armed with a sketch-book, a pencil, and a penknife.*

* [Austin notices this incident in his letter to the *Times*. "I need say nothing about what I saw until I found myself in the Rue Vieille du Temple, between the regulars and the Reds. We had already been among the former, and were anxious to see something of the latter, but I confess I should hardly have ventured near them if my companion, Mr. Simpson, an old campaigner, who sketches as coolly under fire as in his own room, had not fairly dragged me on. I had lost him for a moment in a desperate rush I had made out of the clutches of a colonel who was ordering all passers-by to be pressed into the service as amateur firemen, as a new fire had just commenced. When I returned to look

After this we moved to our left, which brought us nearer to the line of the boulevard. There we found a very pleasant Versailles officer, and a few men who had just commenced firing up a street. At the far end there was no barricade, only two men, one at each corner, held the street. Shortly the soldiers said that one of the men was shot, and the other had gone, so the officer determined to advance, and we went with him. When we reached the spot we found the man that had been shot, lying on the pavement, I may say dead, for there was only a slight quiver about the mouth. The bullet had carried off a piece of his skull, about a couple of inches in size, and from the wound the blood flowed and ran along the pavement. This blood at once recalled to me the blood as it is represented in Regnault's picture of sudden justice. He shows the dark blood which has flowed first in the largest mass, while over it runs what seems to be the lighter arterial blood, of a brighter red—the one on the top of the other, and apparently not mixing with it. From this the soldiers advanced a little farther east, where a street turned to the left and crossed the line of the boulevard. A little beyond the boulevard there was a barricade, from which a heavy fire was opened by the Reds. I remember the hard, sharp crack of the missiles as they struck the wall of the houses on our right hand. The Versailles soldiers fired under the protection of the corner of the street. After some time one of the men, close to where we stood, had chanced to put his foot too far out, and a mitrailleuse ball struck him on the ankle. The smash of the bones was so great that I noticed his foot dangled down as if only held by a shred. Austin and I helped to carry him to the rear.

On Friday, 26th of May, Oliphant turned up at the "Chatham" at breakfast time. Since we left each other at Metz, he had been back to America, but the events of the

after my friend, I was not a little alarmed to see him far away at the other end of the Rue Vieille du Temple, in the enemy's line, on the other side of the barricade. The red flag was still floating over it, at the end of a bayonet, but its defenders had retreated—fortunately for the invader, or it might have gone hard with him."]

Commune had attracted him to the war-path again. The fighting in the streets had stopped the usual communications with the world outside Paris, and I had not sent off any of my sketches. It may have been on Tuesday or Friday, Austin told me that he was sending a man with his letters, who would make an effort to pass through. It was very doubtful if he would succeed, but if I had anything ready, and cared to send it with this man I could do so. Austin said he was spending a good deal of money in the attempt. I had three sketches, and I risked them, but they never reached the Strand. In all my long connection with the *Illustrated London News*, these were the only sketches I have lost in transit, and as I have had to use the post from all parts of the world, the fact speaks for the good working of the postal arrangements in other countries, as well as in our own.

On Saturday, 27th of May, after breakfast, Captain Hartopp, of the 10th Hussars, appeared. He had come into Paris some days before with two friends, one an officer of the 42nd Regiment, and the other a son of Lord Minto. They managed to enter the city by means of dispatches which they brought from Lord Lyons to Mr. Malet. Their object in coming, as declared by Hartopp, was to see the fun, and they told an amusing story at their own expense. After delivering the dispatches at the Embassy they started for the scene of action. There was at the moment a large fire going on where the Rue St. Honore crosses the Rue Royale. The fire brigade of Paris carries on its operations by pressing passers-by into the work. At this particular time soldiers with their muskets were placed as sentries in an extended line some distance from the fire. The three British subjects had scarcely left the Embassy when one of these sentries said to them, "Passez par ici, messieurs." Thinking there was some danger in the direction in which they were going, they obeyed, and they found other sentries on this new path who kindly repeated the "par ici." They had no notion of the object of the advice till they found themselves in the net, and ordered to be part of a chain of many, handing buckets of water to extinguish the fire. They were kept at this, I think, for seventeen hours. They were quite close to their Embassy, but there was in such a case no appeal. If they had refused they would have been shot. After escaping from this, they had made efforts to get to the front to see the fighting, but had failed in each attempt. As a last resource Hartopp came seeking me. The great struggle was still going on at the place known as the Chateau d'Eau, which might be said to be the last battlefield of the Commune.

We worked round to where Austin and I had been on the Thursday evening. The barricade that had been firing at us then had been taken, and we advanced into it. The officers were at first doubtful about us, but they softened and allowed us to see everything. There were dead bodies still lying about the barricade, for the Reds still held the street beyond. A wine shop at the eastern corner was occupied by the Versailles troops, and we went upstairs to the first floor, from the windows of which the men were firing. One man had been killed and his body was under the table in the centre of the room. Below, in some rooms behind, was an extemporised hospital, where Versailles soldiers and Reds were both being attended to. The main part of the shop presented a wonderful appearance of disorder. The shop in the opposite corner was a barber's, and it also was in a dilapidated condition. The officers expected an order to advance, and they spoke as if they wished us to remain and see it; but it was drawing towards darkness, so we returned.

On Sunday, May 28th, after breakfast, I went off alone in the hope of penetrating to the eastern end of the city, but failed. People had begun to go about again, and this prevented one from passing into the line of action. But by that time the fighting was about ended. While I was walking along the boulevard towards the Place de la Bastille I heard a musket ball singing through the air. It must have come from the Reds, for the Versailles fire would be in the opposite direction, and that bullet must have been about the last that was fired. I passed the Mazas Prison, and it so chanced that a kind of omnibus came out, into which I got a glimpse. It was filled with dead bodies—poor devils who had, I suppose, been shot as Communards.

This finished the week's fighting. On the Monday morning I accompanied Kodolitsch, Colonel Connolly, military attaché to our Embassy, M. Hubner, and a Count, whose name is not in my notes, in a drive to the Battes des Chammont, Père la Chaise, and the Prison of La Roquette. These places included the region where the defence of the Reds ended and where a cruel shooting of prisoners had been done by the Versailles troops. In La Roquette, to which our party were admitted, we saw a piled-up heap of dead bodies. The bullet marks were visible on the wall where they had stood to be shot. It was told us of one man that the bullets had missed or he had not been fatally struck. He pretended to be dead, and, after lying in the heap all night, had crawled out, saying, "God has saved me; you will save me?" But the words fell on deaf ears; he was one of that ghastly heap at the time of our visit. I had not time then to make some sketches that I wanted, but one of the officers said if I came in the afternoon I could do so. As we drove back we passed the Place Voltaire, where there is a statue of Voltaire; a bullet had gone right through the bronze, making a very absurd hole. There must have been some shooting of prisoners here, for the ground was littered with muskets, caps, cartouche boxes, &c., and one part of the pavement was a sheet of blood. This was not like a battlefield, where the blood is absorbed in the earth and does not appear to the eye.

In the afternoon I was hurrying on my way to La Roquette. Unfortunately, I was late, and as I sped along I did not keep my eyes on the alert. Owing to this I came upon a sentry, who suggested that I was to "passe par ici." There was no doubt as to what that meant. Some place was burning, and I should find myself *en chaine* and handing buckets all night. So I refused. He raised his musket and said "Je vous fusillerai." The end of the barrel was not a yard from my head. I told him I was British, and I drew from my pocket my letter from Mr. Malet and held it up at the point of his gun, saying, "Lisez." He said, "Je ne peus pas lire." Then I demanded that he should take me to his chief. To do this would be to leave his post. By this time the musket had ceased to be pointed at my head. I insisted on the fact that I was not a Frenchman; I was a stranger, and had nothing to do with matters going on. So at last he let me off, using a phrase about me that I cannot repeat here. It was not complimentary to my courage. When I left, a gentleman who had been watching the incident came up and advised me to be off as quickly as I could. "Promenez, monsieur," were his last words. His tone as well as his words indicated the danger I had been in. This episode made me too late, and I could not find my friend at La Roquette, so I missed the sketches I hoped for. This was bad enough, but not so bad as if I had had a bullet through my head.

I remained in Paris till the 10th of June, and was back in Lincoln's Inn Fields on the morning of the 11th.

History, so far as popular accounts of the Commune in Paris may be called history, has so misrepresented everything, that I should like to add a few words on that subject. I have no intention of defending the Commune. It was a blunder and a crime, and the guilty deserved punishment. But that is a very different thing from the cruel massacre of prisoners shot in thousands in cold blood. I do not know how many were shot; I have heard estimates that ranged from ten thousand to twenty thousand, and even as high as thirty thousand. It was war—civil war. The troops of the Commune were a regular army, and all prisoners ought to have been treated as prisoners of war. The Versailles party claimed to be the party of law and order, but the shooting of prisoners of war is contrary to all law. To justify these acts the most gross lies were published. Documents were forged, or papers that had no existence were said to have been found. The intention of burning Paris was ascribed to the Reds. They were accused of preparing places for burning, and setting them on fire when they retreated. I was during all the Monday and the forenoon of the Tuesday among the Communards, and saw no such preparations. They had ample time to gather materials and set on fire all the houses between the Madeleine and the Grand Opera, but there were no preparations and there were no fires. I can speak positively of that particular part of the city, since I was in it on these two days. There was a great fire in the Rue Royale where it crosses the Rue St. Honoré, but a barricade had been there, and something like two days' fighting at it. The fighting would account for the fire. Along the boulevard there was not a single house burned as far as the Porte St. Martin and the Porte St. Dennis. Close on the east of these some houses were burned, but a barricade was there, at which there had been a long and hard struggle. The real fact was that all the fires took place close to barricades where there had been long and heavy fighting. The only exceptions were two or three public buildings, such as the Tuileries, the Ministry of Finance, etc. Both of the buildings mentioned were under fire from the Versailles troops for nearly two days. I saw the mark of shells on the face of the Tuileries next the Jardin des Tuileries, and the shells would account for the fire. That some excited Communard may have set fire to some of these public buildings is probable enough, but there is no evidence on the subject except the assertions of the Versailles partisans. The accounts of the Petroleuses are equally untrue; in fact, nothing could have been more wicked, for it caused a few poor, helpless creatures to be shot. It was said they were in regiments and drilled. If so, they must have burnt a large number of houses. They did nothing of the kind. No house burned by them could be pointed out. Where there had been hard fighting at barricades it did not require women with petrol to do the damage. Every woman taken prisoner was called a "Petroleuse," and it was said there were two thousand of them at Satory. It was some time before any of them were brought to trial, and then only one or two appeared in court. The evidence against them was ridiculous, and the trial was abandoned. This shows how unsubstantial the statement was that two thousand Petroleuses had been caught. The people of Paris believed all this bosh, and a photographer tried to earn an "honest penny" by its means. He published portraits of the Petroleuses. For his purpose he utilised some old negatives of female faces that chanced to be unprepossessing, but at last he was prosecuted by a citizen for using in this way the portrait of his mother-in-law or some other near relative.

One great accusation brought against the Communards was the shooting of the Archbishop of Paris. This event is always related without any explanation. Here are the facts of the case as I understand them. Early in the struggle between the party of the Commune and the Versailles people prisoners taken by the latter were shot. The Commune authorities, learning this, seized the Archbishop and five or six others as hostages, and sent word to Versailles that if any more prisoners were shot these hostages would suffer a similar fate. The shooting of prisoners was thus stopped at the time. But it began again with the prisoners taken in the fighting after the Versaillais entered Paris. While the fighting was going on communication between the two sides was difficult, but about the middle of the week the Commune authorities learned of the wholesale shooting of prisoners, and in their rage they ordered the hostages to be shot. If this be true—and it is the story as I heard it—the Versailles party were the real murderers of the Archbishop.

The story of the Commune has been to me a lesson as to how history may at times be written. When one side has the means of telling the tale, and the other has not, anything may be said.

CHAPTER XXVIII

WITH THE PRINCE OF WALES IN INDIA

IN 1871 I went to Edinburgh to attend the centenary celebrations in honour of Sir Walter Scott. I afterwards went on to Inverary to attend the home-coming of the Marquis of Lorne and the Princess Louise. Mr. Young of Kelly was there, and he kindly arranged that I should be his guest on board his yacht. A daughter of Dr. Livingstone, the African traveller, was on board. There was a grand ball at the castle, and the Duke of Argyll asked that I should be presented to him. In September I went to the opening of the Mont Cenis tunnel. After the opening we all went on to Turin, and there the concluding part of the ceremonies took place.

It was announced that the young Emperor of China was to be married in October of the following year. The *Illustrated London News* thought it would be a good subject for the paper. The temptation to add China to the Eastern countries I had seen was great, and I accepted the invitation to go. I also arranged with Mr. Robinson of the *Daily News* to send him letters, so that I started as a "double-barrelled" correspondent. By hard work I managed to send a large number of letters to the paper. These letters led, on my return, to the idea of publishing a book. I did it as a bit of variety, for I had to rewrite everything, and I had no hopes of a return for the work. I did receive a few pounds, but it was nothing for the labour I was put to. My illustrations for the *Illustrated London News* were reproduced in the volume. The book, which was entitled "Meeting the Sun," brought me into contact with the Rev. G. W. Cox, better known as "Aryan" Cox, and later as the Rev. Sir

G. W. Cox, Bart. He was then reader to the Messrs. Longman, and had to correct my proofs. On this trip I made a new arrangement with the *Illustrated London News*, by which I received back all my sketches. These, with others, I exhibited after my return in Mr. Thompson's gallery in Piccadilly, under the title of "All Round the World." A full account of my journey is given in "Meeting the Sun," so I need say no more of it here.

I left London to follow the tour of the Prince of Wales in India on September 28, 1875, and arrived in Bombay on October 30th. It would be wearisome to detail what took place in each locality as we went along. I have often described the Prince's tour in India as four months of Lord Mayor's Show. It was a hard struggle for us correspondents to follow the party and do our work. Great crowds came to each place visited by the Prince, and the few hotels were crammed before our arrival, so it was often difficult to find a lodging. We had also to run after the local authorities to get the necessary cards of admission, then to dress for the ceremony, and get ready again to start on the journey to the next place. Often no time was left to work up the sketches. I was one of the very few admitted into the terai, where the Prince spent a few weeks tiger shooting.* These few weeks, far from the madding crowd, made the only pleasant time I had during the four months. I had a tent to myself, and an elephant to take me about.

Among other incidents I went to the ball given in the palace of the Fort at Delhi. There I saw the son of the Queen of Britain dancing in the Dewan Khas, the private hall of audience of the Emperors of India. To realise the significance of the incident one ought to imagine the

* [Two reproductions are inserted here of the picture made by Simpson of an incident which created some sensation at the time, the attack of a tiger on the elephant of the Prince. One of these, reproduced from the Royal collection at Sandringham, by gracious permission of the King, shows the original sketch made by the artist. The other, inserted by kind permission of Sir William Ingram, Bart., shows the same picture re-drawn in the office of the *Illustrated London News* for production in that paper. The two together afford an interesting example of the way in which such work was treated.]

ATTACK OF A TIGER ON THE ELEPHANT OF THE PRINCE OF WALES.

From Simpson's original sketch in the Royal collection at Sandringham. Reproduced by gracious permission of His Majesty the King.

This original drawing, with its reproduction as a line drawing, also here given, affords a good example of the way in which such work was treated.

To face p. 271.

The Prince of Wales's Elephant attacked by a Tiger.

Drawn from a sketch by Crimean Simpson. Reproduced by kind permission of Sir William Ingram, Bart.

To face p. 271.

conquest of Britain by the Great Mughal, and the son of that potentate visiting London, and holding a Durbar in Buckingham Palace. That would be the counterpart of what took place at Delhi on January 12, 1876. It was in the Dewan Khas that the last King of Delhi underwent his trial after the Mutiny. He escaped hanging, but was transported for life to the Andamans. I have a sketch, done by Wagentrieber at the time, of the old Emperor as he appeared at his trial. He is represented sitting on an old charpoy, or bedstead. This hall was considered a triumph of architectural art—all marble and precious stones. Somewhere on its walls was a Persian inscription of the well-known words, "If there is a heaven on earth, it is this, it is this!" Imagine that old man, last of a long line of great emperors, sitting on a dirty old bedstead, in the principal hall of his own palace, and reading these words while being tried for his life.

I left as soon as I had seen the Prince dancing. There was an immense crowd of people, and I was glad to get away. There had been great difficulty in getting a gharry, or carriage, on going to this fête, and when I left, shortly after midnight, I saw it was hopeless to call for one. So I determined to walk. Lord Napier's camp was on the other side of the Ridge, but I knew from former visits every foot of the way, and I think it was a moonlight night. I went up the Chandney Chowk to the Lahore gate, from which I got to the Ridge, and walked along that historic piece of ground. This brought me close to the camp. It was a long walk, and a curious one under the circumstances. Of course I was in evening dress. So far as I remember I did not meet a soul on the way.

Before I started from London on this occasion Count Seckendorff wrote asking me to secure a passage for him along with my own on the P. and O. He suggested I should come by way of Berlin, and we could go on together. This arrangement led to a request by the Crown Princess that I should bring to Berlin some of my sketch-books of India, that she might see something of the country her brother was about to visit. I took over my small sketch-books, and I had to carry them down to Potsdam, where the Crown Prince and Princess were living. The Princess said she could not look over so many books at that time, but if I would leave them they should be safely returned to London. I was afterwards invited to a drive. There were the Crown Prince and Princess, Count Seckendorff, and some of the children. We went first to Sans Souci, then to the home farm of the Princess, where we had tea, the Princess herself making it. The Princess presented me with a gold pencil-case as a souvenir, and made the request that should anything happen to Count Seckendorff—should he become ill—I should do what I could for him. The Crown Prince left us, and Prince William, now the Emperor William, came in. He was 16 or 17 years of age, and he drove me to the station on my return to Berlin. I kept him laughing nearly all the way by relating my experiences at Metz, when I was called "un espion Prussien," etc.

Seckendorff and I had the same cabin on board the *Sumatra*, and with us was Count Goblet D'Alviella, a Belgian, who was going to India as correspondent of the *Independence Belge*. He has since become an authority on archæology, and delivered one of the courses of Hibbert Lectures. The stewards on board the steamer were rather bothered with D'Alviella's foreign name, but they found a way of getting over the difficulty by calling him "Mr. Devil."

I opened with Mr. Thompson in Piccadilly an exhibition of two hundred sketches made on this tour. They were all sent to Windsor for the Queen's inspection, and Her Majesty bought four. The Prince and Princess of Wales visited the gallery, and His Royal Highness bought fifteen. These included some of the principal events of his tour, and are now at Sandringham. On Lord Northbrook's return from India—he was Viceroy during the Prince's visit—he came by appointment, and selected a considerable number of the drawings.

The Prince of Wales holding the Investiture of the Order of the Star of India at Calcutta, Jan. 1, 1875.
Reproduced by kind permission of the Earl of Northbrook.

To face p. 272.

CHAPTER XXIX

MYCENÆ, TROY, AND EPHESUS

ON the 2nd of February, 1877, I left London for Athens, on my way to visit Mycenæ, Troy, and Ephesus. The fame of Dr. Schliemann's explorations at Mycenæ, where he declared he had found the tomb of Agamemnon, led to this expedition. It was arranged that I should go afterwards to the Troad, and illustrate Schliemann's previous explorations at Hissarlik. Further, the Temple of Diana at Ephesus, discovered a little before that time by Mr. Wood, was to be included in the tour. Dr. John S. Phené desired to accompany me, and it was arranged that he should also go. As the King of Greece is brother to the Princess of Wales, I wrote, before leaving London, to Marlborough House, and had a reply telling me to call at the Palace when I reached Athens, and see M. Rodostamos, Maréchal de la Cour. Mr. Knollys had written to him expressing the desire of the Prince of Wales that I might receive every facility for visiting and making sketches of Mycenæ. On calling at the Palace I was told to come another day, when M. Rodostamos presented me to the King, and I received letters to remove all obstacles to my purpose.

A day or two after our arrival in Athens, Lord Bute and his secretary, Mr. Sneyde, turned up at the hotel. His lordship had never been to Athens, and had come on from Nice for a short visit. We were all invited to dinner one evening by our Minister, the Hon. William Stuart, C.B. There was a very striking eclipse of the moon that night, which we all saw at the Legation. After dinner, when the moon was quite clear, it being a beautiful night, instead of walking back direct to the hotel, we, *i.e.*, Bute,

T

Sneyde, Phené, and myself, passed to the west of the Akropolis, and finally went round it. When on the south side, we heard an owl hooting high up on the wall above the Theatre of Dionysius—appropriate for Athenæ.

At last we got away for Mycenæ. We were in charge of a dragoman, Dionysius Dragonus, who was to find us carriage, lodging, and food during the whole of our trip. From the Piræus we went by steamer to Kalamaki, and across the Isthmus of Corinth rode on pack-horses with a bit of rope for bridle. I was much struck with the resemblance of these horses to those in the sculptures of the Parthenon. They were small brutes, and had all the character of those represented in the marbles. It was something to have ridden a descendant of the horses which had been models to Phidias. At Corinth we were quartered with the local Æsculapius, whose wife, like Penelope, had a loom in the house at which she wrought—a custom which has continued from Homer's time. We climbed the Acro-Corinthus. From this height one can see almost the whole of Greece, but the grand view is of course that looking across the Gulf of Corinth to Parnassus and Helicon beyond. Next day it snowed, but on the day following we reached Mycenæ *viâ* Cleone. We remained a couple of days, then left for Argos, Tyrins, and Nauplia, where we found a steamer which took us back to the Piræus.

To reach the Troad it is necessary to land at the Dardanelles. We had a dragoman, Nicola Yanmaki, who had been Schliemann's foreman during the explorations at Hissarlik; we had also a Bashi-bazouk as escort. We arrived at Khalifatli, the nearest village to Hissarlik, on the evening before Easter Sunday. The Greeks keep a very rigid Lent, and make up for it by feasting and dancing when it ends. We were wakened at midnight to see the beginning of the Easter celebrations. There was a service in the church porch, and a figure of Judas Iscariot was burned while guns were fired. After a day's sketching we moved up the Scamander to Bunar-bashi—" head fountain," and the ancient walled city of Gergis, or Balidagh, supposed by some to be the site of Troy. This was Chevalier's Troy.

The Lion Gate of Mycenæ

Chevalier might be called "Schliemann the First," or Schliemann "Chevalier the Second." In one of the villages the proprietor of the café beckoned me. He was very mysterious in his movements. In an inner part of the café he led me to a box, and after looking in every direction to see that no one observed, he opened the lid just high enough for me to see an owl-headed vase, similar to those Schliemann found in his explorations. He held up all the figures of his right hand, and pronounced, I think, the word "lira." My Turkish was not sufficient to discuss the latest quotations for archæological curios, so I closed with the man, and became proprietor of what I believe is the only specimen of this peculiar kind of vase not in the Schliemann collection.

We were five days on this trip. On my return to the Dardanelles we found a steamer for Smyrna. Thence there is a railway to the neighbourhood of Ephesus, or rather the swamp where Ephesus once stood, and I saw all that remains of the temple of the great Diana. From Smyrna we also made a trip along the other railway line, by the Hermus River, as far as Philadelphia. We returned to Sardis, and visited the extensive group of tumuli near that place. Of these tumuli one is said to be the tomb of Alyattes, of which the construction is described by Herodotus. We also made a halt at Magnesia, to visit the so-called rock-sculpture of Niobe. Dr. A. S. Murray had asked me to try and see this figure, and my conclusion was that it represented a male and not a female.*

When I set out on this expedition I was naturally impressed by the great interest Dr. Schliemann's discoveries had excited. In Athens I saw the explorer; but one cannot discover all the character of a man in a short interview. At Mycenæ I noticed the character of one wall which had been described as the remains of a Cyclopean palace of vast dimensions, and was surprised. At Hissarlik I put the question, "How did Dr. Schliemann know it was the palace of Priam he had found?" If any one will read the first book about the excavations at Hissarlik, he will see there is

* [Simpson communicated his opinion in a letter to *The Academy*, May 14, 1881.]

no evidence, unless it be that Schliemann found in the palace Priam's plate-chest. But how did he know it was Priam's plate-chest ?—because he found it in Priam's palace. The matter is not expressed in this particular form in the book, but that is what the proof amounts to. Putting this point aside, the palace itself, or that to which Schliemann gave the name, was of itself sufficient to give the whole affair the character of a farce. Priam had a very large family—fifty sons and their wives, twelve daughters and their husbands. According to Homer there was accommodation for these people in the palace, which had polished porticoes, and was very beautiful. The structure Schliemann declared to be the palace contained only three small rooms, which could not have contained Priam and his family unless they had been packed like sardines in a box. The whole building was not above twenty or thirty feet in its longest dimension. It had no doors or windows. The well-polished porticoes of Homer's description suggest marble or at least stone as the building material; but Schliemann's palace was built of mud. I made the remark that if I had been told it was the palace of Priam's pig I could have believed it. Schliemann knew that the literal or historical character of Homer was a strong article of faith in this country, and that to find Troy was to produce a crowning evidence that the story of the Iliad was not a myth. His announcements carried away Mr. Gladstone and many others, who became advocates of the great explorer. I had the honour to be the only person who ventured to doubt Schliemann's conclusions in print in England at the time. On my return home I wrote an article which appeared in *Fraser's Magazine* in July, 1877, and I wrote a second article, on Mycenæ, which appeared in December of the same year. Schliemann replied to my Troy article in a letter to the *Times* of August 16, 1877, and I replied in a letter on the 24th. Later on he invited me to dinner; I had another engagement. Then he sent me the later editions of his Troy books, and he even wrote me saying there was no difference of opinions between us. But—as soon as he returned to Hissarlik he removed the "palace."

CHAPTER XXX

THE AFGHAN WAR

ON the 15th of October, 1878, I left for my third visit to India, in expectation of war breaking out with Shere Ali in Afghanistan. I went on this occasion by the new and now the regular route, *viâ* Paris, Mont Cenis tunnel, and Brindisi. Here I went on board the steamer the evening before she sailed, and when I got up in the morning found I had a companion in my berth. This was Major Lance, and he told me he had come by rail with Lady Browne, General Sir Samuel Browne's wife, and that she had a message for me from Sir Dighton Probyn. The message was, that letters of introduction, written by request of H.R.H. the Prince of Wales, would be forwarded to me. In fact, the letters were on board, and I received them from the postal official in charge.

An ultimatum had been sent to Shere Ali that if he did not communicate in some way or another by the 20th of November our troops would cross the frontier, and march on Cabul. Three columns were preparing to move—one by Shikarpoor, towards Kandahar, under General Sir Donald Stewart, my old friend of the Sooroo Pass in Abyssinia. Another under the command of General Roberts, now Lord Roberts—he was Captain Roberts, R.A., V.C., and Quartermaster in Lord Canning's camp when I first knew him—was to advance by the Peiwar Kotal. The third was to advance through the Khyber under the command of General Sir Samuel Browne. This was the column I elected to go with, as it had the political agent, Major Cavagnari, with it.

At last, on the 20th of November, we were all at Jamrud, ready for the first move. This began very early next morning. I determined to go on foot, so as not to be bothered with a horse. I started with the early dawn, and as I reached the entrance I was quite alone. Troops had already gone in, and others were following, but I was in a gap of the movement, and apparently as solitary a figure as if there were not a soul within a hundred miles of me. I pushed on and reached the Shagai heights in time to see the first shot fired. At this point we were in sight of Ali Musjid, or the fort of that name. Our artillery came up and opened fire, the infantry advanced, and the fighting went on all day. When darkness came on we had just to lie down and find a bed on the ground. Archibald Forbes, Phil Robinson, and myself, found quarters in a hollow or valley where we were safe from the fire of the enemy. Part of our general's tactics was to send part of his forces by a road over the hills on our right so that they should enter the Khyber in rear of Ali Musjid. The Afghans discovered this stratagem, and evacuated the fort during the night. Next morning we entered, finding none in it but the dead and wounded. I climbed up and entered the fort with Sir Samuel. Afterwards, when I learned the peculiar character of Buddhist masonry, I realised how old some parts of the wall must have been. My impression now is that the fort was an old Buddhist monastery. Mr. Beglar, of the Archæological Survey Department, made some explorations, and found remains of stupas, which fact supports this supposition. The Musjid or Mashad of Ali is a small tomb-like structure on the banks of the stream, below the almost perpendicular cliff on which the fort stands. We stayed all day and night, and I was able to finish sketches and catch the mail. Next day we advanced through the pass, and I stopped to make sketches of the Ishpola Tope. When darkness fell, I found myself struggling through a gorge where some of the troops were bivouacking for the night. At last I heard a voice calling out "Simpson." It was Bartram of the Engineers, and he told me the headquarters were on in advance, and I had better stay with them. I had something to eat, and slept in a dooley. Next morning I rode on to the headquarters at Lundi Khana. I did this ride of some miles all alone, unconscious of the danger I was running, for it turned out that if the Afghans caught a solitary person no mercy was shown, the body was always found crimped all over with their long sharp knives. We advanced to Dakka that day, and stayed there for about a fortnight.

Macpherson's Brigade had been sent on to Basawal, and I went on in advance to it. The 10th Hussars were at that place, and they put me up. Here I soon became familiar with a character well known in camp. I had not been long in the large mess tent till a voice, it was that of one of the officers, called out "Beaconsfield! Lord Beaconsfield!" It did not lessen the surprise which this call made on my mind when I heard a voice outside say "Hai Sahib," which meant that Lord Beaconsfield was in attendance. D'Israeli was known to be profound in something that was known as an "Asiatic Mystery"; here was a mysterious something of that kind. What could it mean? How was this to be explained? Had Lord Beaconsfield an astral body? and could he, like a Maha-Atma, be in Downing Street and in Afghanistan at the same time? These were the strange questions that shot through my mind, when the officer said, "Brandy pawni lao." "Lya Sahib," was the answer. When an Indian servant is told to bring anything, he does not say he will bring it, nor does he use phrases like a French *garçon*. He says it is brought. *Lya*, pronounced *leea*, is the past of bring. Scarcely a minute elapsed before "Lord Beaconsfield" appeared with the brandy pawnee. This person turned out to be a khitmagar, or table servant, but his likeness to Lord Beaconsfield was very striking. He was servant to Lord Ogilvy, and the officers had taught him to repeat one of Beaconsfield's speeches. It was the speech about Gladstone, in which the sentence "inebriated by the exuberance of his own verbosity" occurs, and he had often to repeat this for the amusement of visitors at the camp fire. I asked the quite unnecessary question of this man if Lord Beaconsfield was his name. He said "Nahin Sahib. Sahib log aisa bolta hai" (The Sahibs speak like this.) His name was

Futteh Khan, a name as common as John Smith in another part of the world.

On the 18th of December a general advance was made, and the whole column reached Jellalabad on the 20th. The death of Shere Ali stopped a further advance. The Government waited to see who would succeed to the Ameership, and whether the successor would come to terms. Owing to this we remained in camp at Jellalabad till the 12th of April, when we advanced to Gundamuck. Yakoob Khan, the new Amir, came to that place on the 8th of May, a peace was arranged and signed, and the troops returned in the beginning of June. I left with the Goorkhas on the 2nd, and reached Peshawur on the 12th.

Archibald Forbes having left, I took his work in hand, and telegraphed and wrote letters to the *Daily News*. This gave me plenty of work, but I also managed to give some attention to the Buddhist remains, of which there are many in the Jellalabad Valley. These consisted of topes, mounds, and caves. I made sketches of most of them, including the details of the architectural features. Our knowledge of the architecture of India was limited to the mouth of the Khyber Pass. Masson had made drawings of the topes and caves of Afghanistan, but they were so small that no idea of the architecture could be formed from them. Masson was not an artist, and he knew but little about Indian architecture. So I was entering upon a new and all but untrodden field for an architectural archæologist, and was anxious to sketch whatever I might chance to see in the way of remains of an architectural character.

About a mile south of our camp there was a well-marked group of mounds, and among them a high heap I took for the remains of a tope. The name, *Ahin Posh*, or "iron-clad," was attached to this place. Sir Samuel Browne promised me a working party to excavate it as soon as he could get the camp into order for the winter. It turned out that Lord Lytton had written to Cavagnari saying that excavations should be made, if such work could be done. Major Cavagnari, hearing that I wished to excavate, offered to provide a working party of Afghans, and we found a man in

Signing of the Treaty of Gundamuck by Yacoub Khan.

The figure on Yacoub's right, with glasses, is that of Sir Louis Cavagnari, afterwards assassinated at Cabul. Reproduced by kind permission of the Earl of Northbrook.

the Guides, who could speak Puchtoo. As he had been in the Sappers, he could act as foreman. I started one party to excavate on the outside of the mound, to lay bare the architecture, if any existed. In this I was successful; I was able to make a plan of the stupa, and on my return home it enabled me to make a restoration of the monument. Another party began a tunnel into the centre. This was a long job, for the base of the tope was about 100 feet square, and this meant 50 feet of a passage, which had to be made by extracting the boulders with which the structure had been erected. At last they reached the centre, and luck favoured me. The position, so far as height is concerned, of the cell in such monuments is quite uncertain; but it so chanced that I went in with the tunnel exactly on a level with the cell. It was a Saturday evening when Bartram, who had been to the tope, told me the men had come to a large flat stone or slate. Next morning I went over early to be there before the men began. Two sergeants of the Sappers, as it was a Sunday morning, had come over for a walk, and I asked them to lend me a hand. I felt that they would be more useful than the natives, as I could direct more exactly in English than in Hindostanee. They would also be witnesses as to what might be found. We removed one slab, which was of slate embedded in mud. A second lay below it. This was also carefully taken up, so as not to let any of the dust or fragments of hardened mud fall into the cell, which was now uncovered. There was enough light by the tunnel to do all this, but it was too dark to see the cavity or what was in it. I had anticipated this, and brought a candle in my pocket, which we lighted. The cell was very small, being only about 15 inches square, very neatly formed with small fragments of slate. There was a small heap of a brown-looking stuff. By supposing that the contents of a coffee pot had been emptied, an idea of this will be formed. Something lay on the top of this heap, which I at last lifted. It turned out to be a gold relic holder. One of the Sappers pointed to another object, which turned out to be a gold coin. I began to collect the dust into a piece of the *Saturday Review*. On taking up the first handful another glittering object was seen; this was another coin. One of the Sappers pointed to another, part of which projected out of the dust. As I removed the brown stuff coin after coin appeared, till I had eighteen of them in my hands. Two more were found in the gold relic holder, making twenty in all. The brown stuff, I assumed, was the ashes of some holy man, in whose honour the tope had been erected.

It was a very strange experience that morning—three of us sitting or reclining, as space permitted, round that small hole, bringing to light objects that had lain there for perhaps fifteen centuries. There was a touch of the Arabian Nights about it. To myself there was at the same time the satisfaction of success in the work I had been superintending. It was a success beyond my expectations. I took all the coins, the relic-holder, and the ashes, to show to Sir Samuel Browne, and delivered them over to Cavagnari, who sent them to Lord Lytton at Calcutta. A paper was read on the coins to the Bengal branch of the Royal Association Society by Dr. Hoernle. Seventeen of them were of the Indo-Scythian period, and three were Roman. These were of the reigns of Trajan, Domitian and Hadrian. Hadrian died A.D. 137, so the tope could not be earlier than that date, but it might be a century or two later. My notion is that at the consecration ceremony of the tope, when the ashes were deposited, those present walked past, and each dropped in a coin. Had some one collected the coins from those present, that person would have laid them down in the cell in a heap together. The coins must have been dropped, for they had sunk through the ashes, and they lay anyhow, one here and another there. The relic-holder had been laid on the top of the ashes, but not in a methodical manner, just as if some one had laid it down in passing. The news of the find spread among the people of the locality, and some weeks afterwards a chief who had come to see Major Cavagnari, asked if it were true that a gold chest full of gold coins had been found. Evidently the story had not lost in the telling. My own object in the exploration was to find details of the architecture, and in this also I was successful.

Some explorations were also carried on at a place called

Gunda Chismeh. This was a smaller tope than the other, but I found nothing in it. Colonel Jenkyns of the Guides, having plenty of men at his disposal, asked if I could point out a tope for him to try his hand at. We had to leave for Gundamuck before the centre of the tumulus he attacked was reached, but here again I got some details of structure that were interesting. The spot where this tope stood was to the west of Jellalabad, where the Surkhab joins the Kabul river, and I have since identified the spot as the site of the ancient Nagarahara, the capital of the Jellalabad valley in the Buddhist period. This tope was as large as the Ahin Posh, and I believe older. In all probability it was the one described by Hionen Tshang that contained a tooth of Buddha.

I had one interesting adventure, which was almost a serious one, in an excursion I made one day for archæological purposes. Lieutenant Adye of the Goorkhas liked to go with me on these trips, and this day, 26th January, 1879, Rose of the 10th came with us. We took a guard of a few of the Goorkhas. General Macpherson, to whose brigade the regiment belonged, gave an order that a guard was to be given me when I left the camp to sketch. I had not asked for this, but the Mohammedans of Afghanistan are apt to be dangerous in times of excitement, and the Brigadier issued this order on my account. I had been in the habit of going into the town and sketching, and going about in what he considered a reckless manner, and he considered that a guard was necessary for my safety. It may be explained that a Ghazee is a man who has devoted his life for the benefit of the faith; if he is killed he goes straight to the bliss of heaven. To become a Ghazee he has only to say, "In the name of God I am a Ghazee!" An excitable man, on seeing a giaour or infidel, may, when only a yard or two away, pronounce these words. An Afghan carries a long sharp knife; this comes out in an instant, and the victim has no chance. When our troops first occupied Peshawur, Ghazees were in the habit of coming from the hills simply to kill in this way the first European they met. Shooting or hanging such murderers had no preventative effect, for that sent them straight to heaven, the place they desired to go to. Our authorities at last invented the plan of hanging them with their heads tied up in the skin of a pig, the abomination of Mohammedanism. This prevented the soul from going upwards; to avoid the pigskin it went down, and found its way to Jehenam. No Europeans had been attacked in this way at Jellalabad, but it was feared that crimes of the kind might occur, for some grass-cutters and camp followers had been killed, and some severely wounded. A Hindu, being an infidel in Mohammedan eyes, serves a Ghazee's purpose as well as a European. These facts explain General Macpherson's order of an escort.

We had gone first to Darunta, where the Kabul river flows through a rocky gorge of the north end of the Siah Koh range. From that we came back to where the Surkhab joins the Kabul river. At Darunta there is a ferry, and we sailed back in the ferry-man's boat or raft. Our purpose was to visit a remarkable group of caves on the north bank, which the natives called the "Bazaar." We had some lunch in these caves, and I made a sketch or two; then we ascended the heights behind, on which were mounds, and remains of the "Pheel Khana Tope." Masson had in his time made an excavation of the Pheel Khana Tope, and we were scrambling on the boulders he had thrown out, when we heard the crack of a gun, and a bullet whistled past very close to us. On looking in the direction the sound came from, we could still see the smoke; but no one was visible. A great cliff descended behind the tope, forming a chasm; we hurried down from the exposed position on the débris of the tope, so as to find cover. Adye and Rose, seizing the muskets of the Goorkhas, lay down ready to fire if any one could be seen. At last an Afghan with a gun, a jesail, appeared running round a corner. Adye and Rose fired. I saw the bullets knock up the dust within a yard or two of the man's feet; but he was untouched, and we saw no more of him. We could not follow him owing to the deep chasm that lay in front, and to have made the attempt to chase an Afghan among the hills would have been a waste of time. As no one lived near the place, this man must have followed us all the way from Darunta, a distance of about two miles. As we, with the two Goorkhas, made a group of five persons, all standing pretty close together, the wonder is that the Afghan missed us.

During the first Afghan war Major Bailey of the Rifles had been a non-commissioned officer in the 13th Infantry, and had been all through the "illustratious defence" of Jellalabad by Sale. One day he took us to the spots that were connected with events in the siege. First we went to the Kabul gate, and he pointed out the spot where Dr. Bryden, the solitary survivor of an army, was first seen as he approached Jellalabad. He took us to the spot where Elphinstone was buried, and where Colonel Monteath was swallowed up in a rent of the mud wall at the time of the earthquake. Bailey described to me the costume worn by Dr. Bryden on his coming in, and I made one or two sketches till I satisfied him of the likeness.

Some one reported Buddhist remains up the Kunar valley, and Major Cavagnari arranged that I was to go one day with Major Stewart of the Guides and an escort to visit them. We went up the valley about fourteen miles, as far as a place called Islamabad. The principal remains were at a place called Kona Deh, the old village. Here we found a ruined tope, with some walls of Buddhist masonry, which I supposed had been the Vihara. These were picturesquely situated on a height with a fine view of the valley. Amed Khan of Shewa treated us to fowls, cake and sugar, and talked about the ark being seen on the top of the Ram Koond. When I expressed a wish to go up and see it, he said it could only be seen on the Mohammedan Sunday, which is our Friday. At Islamabad we were opposite the valley by which the Ram Koond is ascended. On the maps it is called Dur Noor, but according to Ahmed Khan it ought to be the Durra-Nooh, or Valley of Noah, for he and all that were in the ark descended by this route. General Van Cortlandt told me that the Mohammedans make pilgrimages to the Takhti Sulieman, on the Sulieman Range, where they see a supposed piece of the ark, which they believe rested on the top of that mountain after the Deluge. It is difficult to understand how the Mohammedans managed to transfer and fix legends like these into the new regions they had conquered. The only guess I can make is, that there may have been a previous Hindu myth which the Mohammedans modified to suit their own ideas. The words Vishnu or Satyavrata would convey no meaning to the new-comers, and they substituted names like Noah, which they were familiar with. In the same way Jellalabad—which means the "Abode of Splendour"—had not that meaning to our soldiers' ears, so they called it "Jolly-be-dad." In the Punjab and Afghanistan there are a number of large tombs to which the Mohammedans, and in some cases the Hindus also, do pilgrimage. The smaller kind of these are called "Nan Gudge Wallahs," or "Nine Yard Fellows." A larger kind are known as "Chalis Gudge Wallahs," or "Forty Yard Fellows." These, according to my guess, were originally monuments of the sleeping Buddha, or Buddha attaining to Nirvana. Such monuments were often formed of colossal figures in a recumbent position. The Chinese pilgrim, Hionen Tshang, describes one at Bamian as 1,000 feet in length. No doubt this is an exaggeration.

After we went on to Gundamuck in April I made a reconnaissance as far as the bridge over the Surkhab. On the way we saw the spot where the 44th Regiment, in the unfortunate retreat from Kabul, made their last stand. It is a small hill on the right-hand side of the Kabul road. The only man that escaped from this spot was Dr. Bryden, already mentioned as arriving at Jellalabad. One day afterwards I went with Major Cavagnari and one or two others to the base of the Suffaid Koh. As we had ascended to some height we had a fine view towards the Hindu Kush. Cavagnari sat down beside me while I sketched. Some Afghans from the villages were with us, and one old man sitting beside Cavagnari, said he was a youth at the time of the former war, but he remembered the events and the final struggle of the 44th. He described it to Cavagnari, and said that the British fought like Shaitans.

In the beginning of June the troops began to move south. At Ali Musjid, which is two marches from Peshawur, I parted from my friends of the 4th Goorkhas. I gave, with the officers' permission, thirty rupees as a present to the men of the regiment, on account of their having attended me when I went sketching, as a guard. This, Captain Mercer suggested, should be employed to purchase two silver cups or measures for the canteen, with an inscription as a memento of my long connection with the regiment. On the last march, after proceeding a few miles, as daylight appeared—we started at 4 a.m.—I bade goodbye to the officers, and rode ahead. As I passed along, the regiment gave me a parting cheer. It was taken up along the whole line by the sturdy little Goorkhas, and echoed among the hills of the Khyber that early morning. The Rev. Mr. Male, an army chaplain, had arranged to ride on to Peshawur with me, and we arrived there about 7 a.m. I had been about six months with this regiment, and my connection with it is a pleasing memory.

At Bombay, along with Mr. Geary, of the *Times of India*, I called on the party of Theosophists that had lately come from America. This party was composed of Madame Blavatsky, Colonel H. S. Olcott, a Mr. Wimbridge, and a Miss Bates. When we sent in our cards a tall, thin man rushed in and shook hands with me, saying, "How do you do, Mr. Simpson?" As I looked surprised, he said, "Perhaps you have forgotten me, my name is Wimbridge." Then I recollected him as an architectural draughtsman who had been connected with Day & Son. We were invited to remain to tiffin, and we smoked cigarettes with Madame Blavatsky afterwards. At that time the sect had not developed into tricksters and jugglers. They were supposed to be studying the old religions of India; they were inquirers and not teachers. It was about a year afterwards when Madame Blavatsky shone forth, and obtained celebrity by her spiritual and occult powers. Then it was that the Maha Atma, Hoot Koomi, of Tibet, came to her aid. By that time my friend Wimbridge and Miss Bates, seeing the new development, had left. Wimbridge started the making of artistic furniture in Bombay. A year or so later Miss Bates came home, and from her I learned a good deal as to how the tricks were performed.

When we were in Afghanistan I had hopes of getting to Kabul, and, if I reached Kabul, of being able to visit Bamian, with its caves and colossal statues which have not as yet, while I write, been properly illustrated. I expected Major Cavagnari to go to Kabul with Yakoob Khan, and as he knew my wishes, and had had from my explorations practical proof of my knowledge of the archæology of the country, I felt sure he would allow me to go with him. But he was ordered back to Simla to consult and receive instructions from the Viceroy, and as it would be a month or perhaps two before he proceeded to the Afghan capital, I could not wait, and had to come home with a kind of grumble in my mind at my bad luck. When in September following, the news came home of the massacre of the British Mission, including Cavagnari, Jenkyns, Lieutenant Hamilton, and Dr. Kelly, all of whom I knew, I began to change my mind about the luck, and to think I had made a very narrow escape. For I could scarcely, had I gone to Kabul, have visited Bamian and come back again in time to get away before the massacre took place.

This massacre led to what might be termed "Part II" of the Afghan War. The *Illustrated London News*, however, did not send out any one to act for them, but trusted to sketches sent home by officers.*

* [After his return Simpson read a paper on Afghanistan before the Geographical Section of the British Association, which met that year at Sheffield.]

PORTRAIT OF SIMPSON.
From a photograph.

To face p. 288.

CHAPTER XXXI

ROYAL INSTITUTE OF PAINTERS IN WATER-COLOURS

I HAD been elected a member of the Institute of Painters in Water-Colours in 1874. John Tenniel, now Sir John, of *Punch*, Oakes, Syer, Hardy, Houston, and Woolf, were all elected at the same time, as known artists, without having to send in pictures as specimens of their work. In 1880 the Crown Princess of Germany became an honorary member, and as it was through my action that this took place, I propose here to tell something about it.

Carrick and I were in the habit of going over to Haghe's house in Brixton every Friday evening. In summer we played at croquet in the garden, and in winter we had a game at whist. The "Old Society," as the now "Royal Society of Painters in Water-Colours," was then familiarly called, had elected H.R.H. the Princess Louise as an honorary member. This was naturally a subject of conversation at our meeting on the next Friday evening. Haghe, I may mention, was president of the "New Society," as the Institute was generally called. Carrick and myself being members, we were all interested in the event. It ought to be mentioned that there was a good deal of rivalry between the two Societies. While we were talking about it I said to Haghe, "I do not see why we should not have a princess in the Institute as well as the other society." I explained that the Crown Princess of Germany was a much superior artist to the Princess Louise, and a possible empress in the future, and if we could secure her as an honorary member, we should be a long way ahead of the old Society. The more I thought of it, the more I felt sure that if I wrote to Count Seckendorff, with whom I was on sufficiently intimate terms, asking if the Crown Princess would become an honorary member, the enterprise would be crowned with success. Haghe was doubtful, but I asked him as president to let me do it. At last he consented. I wrote, and received a reply stating that the Princess would be "much honoured and flattered" at becoming a member. Mr. Haghe then, as president, wrote an official letter, asking for permission to elect Her Imperial Highness, and on his receiving an affirmative answer, the election took place at the next meeting. Princess Beatrice and Prince Louis of Battenberg also became honorary members.

The "Old Society" procured the title of "Royal," or it was rumoured that they had applied for it, so, with the success achieved already, I thought we were as well entitled to have this distinctive honour. I wrote to Seckendorff asking the good offices of the Crown Princess to procure the title from the Queen. We were then in the midst of many difficulties about the building of the new galleries in Piccadilly, and the union of the two Water-colour Societies was being urged by us. Feeling ran high on this question. The old Society was the first, or original Water-colour Society, and it had been most successful. The younger Society had had many struggles to pass through. The old Society, instead of considering the advantages to be derived from union, talked only of its superior position, and the proposal came to nothing. While efforts were being made to achieve this union, it was thought that if the Queen could be influenced to express a wish in favour of it, her desire might produce some effect. With this object in view Mr. W. L. Thomas had written to Sir Henry Ponsonby, and while writing had touched upon the title of "Royal." The Crown Princess of Germany was over here at the time, and she must have moved in the matter. My letter and that of Mr. Thomas had been both in Sir Henry Ponsonby's hands, and he was unable to make out what it was we wanted. He wrote a chaffing letter to Seckendorff, saying that we should make up our minds regarding our requests, and Seckendorff sent Sir Henry's letter and the others on to me. I called on Mr.

Thomas, and he left the matter in my hands to put right. In the end we were told that for the Queen to interfere between the two Societies was out of the question; but the title of "Royal" was granted.

This was not the end of these diplomatic movements. The president of the old Society received the honour of knighthood from the Queen, and became Sir John Gilbert. Louis Haghe died in 1885, but he had resigned his presidency the year before, and James D. Linton had been elected. Of course, there was a natural desire that we should not be behind in the matter of such honours. It was thought that the Crown Prince of Germany might be asked to use influence with the Queen. It was arranged that Mr. James Orrock and I should go to Berlin and see Count Seckendorff. This we did in June, 1885. We had to go to Potsdam. I had written out a document with a statement of our case, giving the claims on which we founded our request that the president should receive the honour of knighthood. We gave some verbal explanations and left the document with Seckendorff to be shown to the Princess. Again we were successful. On August 1, 1885, Linton went to Osborne and was dubbed Sir James.

For the kind assistance which Seckendorff gave in all these transactions, he also was elected an honorary member.

CHAPTER XXXII

THE MARRIAGE OF PRINCE WILLIAM OF PRUSSIA

PRINCE WILLIAM, son of the Crown Prince and Princess of Germany, was to be married on February 27th, at Berlin, and the editor asked me to attend and illustrate the event. On my journey to India at the time of the Prince of Wales's visit it was thought necessary to provide me with a court dress. On my visit to Berlin I took this dress with me, and by the kindness of Count Seckendorff I was admitted to the ceremonies of the marriage, among those who "assisted," and did not require to go with the other correspondents, who only saw the ceremony from a top gallery.

On the second day after my arrival in Berlin I went out to the palace of the Crown Prince, and saw the Princess. I showed her a sketch I had made the day before of the Marble Palace of Potsdam, the future home of the young couple. She said it was the best she had seen of it. She then congratulated me on my marriage, and asked if the lady was Scottish. I said, "No; she is an artist, and paints miniatures, and has exhibited at the Royal Academy for a number of years." She asked me to take my sketch in to the Crown Prince. I found him dressed in a military coat, unbuttoned in front. He showed me over some of his rooms, and let me see Angeli's very beautiful portrait of the Princess—a small oil painting, almost a miniature. Three days later I attended the State Ball at the Schloss, and saw the Emperor and Empress. He was eighty-four and she seventy-two, but she looked the elder. Seckendorff told me that after I had gone she asked after me, and inquired whether I had got all the details of the chapel for my picture of the marriage ceremony. On the Friday before the wedding, I attended the rehearsal of the fancy dress quadrilles in the White Saloon, and saw the Prince of Wales arrive; and next day from Count Redern's palace at the Brandenburg gate I saw the entry of the bride.

The marriage itself took place on Sunday, February 27th. Seckendorff arranged that I should go with the British Embassy. The ceremony in the chapel, the march past and obeisance, the dinner in the Rittersaal, and the Fackel Tanz, took a long time, and it was not till about half past eleven at night that the whole thing ended. While the wedding was going on I stood only about a yard from Count Moltke. When he made his obeisance the young couple and the others all more or less rose and returned the salute. Next morning Seckendorff called and told me the Empress wished to see me. I was to go at one o'clock to the Palais des Kaisers, Behren Strasse, and ask for Baron Knesebeck, private secretary to the Empress. I managed to knock off a sketch of the Fackel Tanz, and took it with me. The Empress was very kind, and asked if I had had every facility given me for my purpose. I told Her Majesty that the last Imperial marriage I had attended had been that of the Emperor of China at Pekin, and I recounted a few of the leading incidents of that occasion. The Emperor came in and asked if I had been present at the wedding of the Princess Charlotte. To which I had to answer No. The honour of this interview I believe I owed entirely to the kindness of the Crown Princess.

Before I left Berlin, Seckendorff gave me one of the bride's garters—a survival, I suppose, of an old German custom, probably allied to the acquisition of the bride's stocking at marriages in Scotland a hundred years ago.

CHAPTER XXXIII

WITH THE PRINCE OF WALES AT ABERGELDIE

IN 1881 it was arranged that there should be two grand reviews of the Volunteers before the Queen. One was to take place at Windsor, and the other at Edinburgh. The former was for the English, and the latter for the Scottish Corps. I received a commission from the Queen to make pictures of both. The *Illustrated London News* had been giving a series of seats of dukes and noble lords, and Mr. Jackson suggested that I should go north in time to make sketches of Balmoral as one of this set. It was further suggested that when at Balmoral I should make sketches of Abergeldie, where the Prince of Wales went every autumn. I communicated with Sir Francis Knollys for permission to sketch at Abergeldie, and the answer came that the Prince would be there on the 10th of September, and that I was to come then as his guest. To comply with this royal command as well as the previous one required a rather complicated series of movements, for one of the conditions of permission to sketch at Balmoral was, that it had to be done before the Queen arrived there, and the review was to take place in Edinburgh, as the Queen passed through to her Highland home on the 25th of August. I went first to Balmoral, where I found lodgings at Balnacroft, near Abergeldie, and made the necessary sketches, returning to Edinburgh for the review. This event came off in the Queen's Park, close to Holyrood, and the day turned out very wet. It rained heavily while the review was going on, and the ground of the march past became so deep with mud, that this part of the evolutions was known as "the wade past." On the 10th September I started for Abergeldie.

This was my first visit to a royal residence, and naturally there was a slight feeling of nervousness as to details. On my arrival the question was put as to whether I had a servant or not. This being answered in the negative, a gorgeous creature in blue plush breeches, a red coat, powdered hair, and silk stockings was told off for me, and he made a request for the key of my portmanteau. This was an ordeal I had not been prepared for, but without hesitation I gave the keys. While doing so, there flashed through my mind the thought that some of my stockings might have darning upon them, and an internal shudder seized me as I imagined this magnificent being turning over and transferring them from the portmanteau to a chest of drawers, which he as a matter of fact did. I imagine that the guests of the Prince of Wales are not likely to wear socks till there are holes in them. Such guests generally carry about with them a valuable dressing-case, filled with gold-stoppered bottles. What was this very superior individual to think when he turned out my simple, old, well-worn leather case, which had only a couple of very common hair brushes and a comb in it? It is perhaps well that what he thought, or what he said, was never revealed to me.

After this first initial trial I found Abergeldie a very pleasant place, and I had no difficulty in conforming to the conditions of the establishment. My old friend Teesdale was on duty as equerry, and I had no hesitation in consulting him about any point regarding which I had doubts. It would not have surprised me if a poor artist had been overlooked among more important people, but this was not the case. I was included in every day's proceedings, and the same arrangements were made for me as for the other guests and members of the Prince's establishment. After about a week, I found that I had been out every day and had done no sketching. I spoke to Teesdale about it. "When can I remain here and do my work?" was the question I asked. This was at breakfast, and I said I hoped nothing would come off that day, and I should go and get my sketching things, and begin to do something. The Prince had gone out shooting that morning, which had given me hopes that

I might have the day for myself. Before I got the portfolio out, Teesdale came to my room grinning. "The Princess," he said, "is going over to Altnaguisach, the Prince's shooting lodge." He himself was to go, and my name was down. He had hopes of some fishing, and he consoled me with the suggestion that I might find a sketch. We were to lunch at the lodge.

I had arrived at Abergeldie on a Saturday. On the Sunday afternoon the Queen drove over from Balmoral to visit the Prince. Hearing that she was coming I thought it best to keep out of the way, so I went to my room; but the Prince sent for me, and I was presented to her Majesty in the garden, where they had all gathered. Something chanced to be said about Cavagnari, and the short conversation was principally about him. I think the Queen told me that his little dog had escaped the massacre, and had ultimately been sent home to Lady Cavagnari. On the Monday we all went off to Mackenzie of Glenmuick's to shoot grouse, and we lunched on the moor. One day Teesdale drove Colonel Stephens and me to Altnaguisach, where we lunched, and Stephens and I went on to Glassalt Shiel and the Dhu Loch. Another day in the afternoon the Duke of Albany invited Colonel Stephens and me to a drive to the Falls of Garrawalt, where we made tea on the banks of the stream in picnic fashion. The Hon. Alex. York was with us. There was some fun in this, for the kettle capsized once or twice, and put the fire out, and it was only when I showed the Prince how a native of India makes his chula or fire to cook his food, that we managed to produce hot water. One evening the Duke of Edinburgh and the Duchess came to dinner. The Duke brought his violin, and after dinner he played upon it, while the Duchess accompanied him on the piano. In the Highlands the gentlemen of the royal family wear kilts both for morning and evening dress.

The day before I left, the Prince went deer-stalking, and took me with him. We first drove in a trap past Balmoral, where we met the Queen walking on the grass. The Prince stopped the trap, and I remember that the conversation was about President Garfield. The Queen had had a telegram that morning announcing his death, and the two royal personages spoke very feelingly about the event. After driving some distance to the west of the Castle, we had ponies to go up part of the hill. At last we left the ponies, and the stalking began. Some deer were seen, and a shot or two were fired. As we walked over the moor the Prince picked up a bit of white heather, and presenting it to me, said, "There's a piece of white heather to you for good luck." We lunched high up, near the summit of Loch-na-gar. Afterwards we went on, and at last came down upon Altnaguisach, where we had tea. Letters and telegrams were here waiting the Prince. There was only one large trap to bring us back to Abergeldie, and into it the Prince, myself, and the gillies went. We were rather crammed. His Royal Highness started me to tell the gillies about the tiger-shooting when the Prince was in India, which interested them very much.

When we set out in the morning a stick, a long one with a crook at the end, such as deer-stalkers use in the hills, had been lent to me. On my return in the evening the Prince told me to preserve it as a souvenir of the day. I afterwards had a silver ring put on it with an inscription.

It may be worth recording that on the morning on which I left, breakfast had been ordered for me at an earlier hour than usual. Somehow I went into the room by accident where breakfast was laid for the three young princesses. They had not come in, but everything was ready for them, and I saw three plates of oatmeal porridge, which was evidently intended as the first dish of the morning repast.

CHAPTER XXXIV

ROYAL AND OTHER EVENTS

IN 1882 the great sale took place at Hamilton Palace, and I went there and made sketches. In October also I went down to Manchester, and made sketches on the route of the great Ship Canal about to be begun. Next year, on the evening of January 4th, I was shot off at a few minutes' notice to Paris to make sketches of Gambetta's funeral. I left immediately after the funeral and got back to the office early on the following morning with my sketches. It was a Sunday morning, but the artists who were to draw the sketches on the wood came in, and by this means the pictures were enabled to appear in the paper on the following Saturday.

In the end of the same month I went to Berlin on the occasion of the silver wedding of the Crown Prince and Princess of Germany. Count Seckendorff took me in to the Princess, and Her Imperial Highness showed me her private sitting-room and her studio with the wedding presents, and gave me liberty to sketch them. The death of Prince Charles, however, brother of the Emperor, and father of the Red Prince, stopped the celebration. I had gone to a wedding, and found I had to attend a funeral. It was whispered that the Crown Princess and Prince Charles had never been very amicable, and the Princess was reported to have said that even in his death the Prince was still unfriendly, for by dying at that time he stopped all the arrangements for a bright and joyful event. The Princess gave me a gold scarf pin, with a medallion of herself and the Crown Prince, as a souvenir.

The same year, 1883, saw the coronation of the

THE GOLDEN HALL IN THE KREMLIN, MOSCOW.

To face p. 298.

Emperor of Russia at Moscow. My wife went with me, as she had a brother at St. Petersburg, and we reached Moscow on May 21st. The Emperor entered the city next day, and I saw him dismount at the Voskresenski Gate to pay his respects to the Iberian Mother of God. The Duke of Edinburgh, whom I saw at the Kremlin, recommended Sala and myself to get places in the Uspenski Sobor. Prince Dolgorouki, to whom I had a letter, asked me to call, and told me it was all but impossible to get into the cathedral, but got me a good place outside. The coronation ceremony, on May 27th, lasted from ten o'clock till about half-past twelve, and I got off my sketch in the evening. Next night I went to the ball in the Kremlin, and saw the Imperial party go through a polonaise. Among the notables from whom I had sittings before I left the city were the Ameer of Bokhara, the Lama of the Don, the Khan of Khiva, and sons of the Tekke chiefs. I also sketched the House of the Romanoffs, and scenes at the popular fête. At St. Petersburg there were fireworks and illuminations on the Emperor's return from Moscow, and I made sketches of the new Cronstadt Canal, of the palace at Peterhoff, and of the beautiful country residence of the Grand Duke Constantine at Strelna. We visited also the tombs of the Russian Emperors, Peter the Great's cottage, the Summer Gardens, and the spot where Alexander II. was killed. As we came home by Stockholm, to see the grave of Thomas Burt, my wife's father, we saw the sailors dress the ship with branches of birch on St. John's Day.

In November of the same year I attended the Luther Quartenary celebrations, and made sketches of the ceremonies at Worms and Wittenberg, as well as of Luther's house and tomb in the Schloss Kirche at Wittenberg, and of the room in which he was born at Eisleben. Luther was born November 10, 1483. I saw the unveiling of his statue, and the historical procession representing his arrival at Eisleben in 1546, to die a few weeks afterwards. This was on Saturday. On Monday the 12th I was at the *Illustrated London News* office a little after 6 a.m., so the illustrations were ready for the next Saturday's paper.

WILLIAM SIMPSON, R.I.

The Duke of Albany died very suddenly at Cannes at the end of March, 1884, and on April 2nd I went to Portsmouth, where the body was to arrive. Prince Edward of Saxe-Weimar had then the military command at Portsmouth, and I dined with him at night. The Prince of Wales went to Cannes, and came back with the body. When the *Osborne* arrived from Cherbourg, Prince Louis of Battenberg took me on board and told the Prince of Wales that I had come. The Prince himself took me into the mortuary chapel, which had been fitted up on deck for the coffin, and made arrangements for me to sketch. It was late in the afternoon, and he invited me to remain on board and dine. Next morning I was permitted to go with the train that took the body to Windsor.

CHAPTER XXXV

THE AFGHAN BOUNDARY COMMISSION

RUSSIA'S conquests in Central Asia, but more particularly her occupation of Merve and Sarrakhs, which brought her frontier on to Afghan Turkestan, made it necessary that the boundary between Russian and Afghan territory should be properly defined. From our relations with the Kabul Government, it was considered necessary that this matter should be carried out by the British authorities, and a Commission was appointed to proceed to the region for this purpose. A few weeks before the Commission started Mr. Ingram asked me if I should like to go with it, and if I could get permission to do so. The first of these questions I could answer, but the second could only be replied to by making inquiries. General Sir Peter S. Lumsden was an old Indian friend, so I called upon him at the India Office, and stated the case. Sir Peter told me that there had been many applications from gentlemen of the press to accompany the Commission, but all had been refused. He said, however, that for himself, he should be very pleased if I were allowed to go, and he would do all that lay in his power to procure the necessary permission. A few days afterwards I had a letter from him stating that I was to be one of the party.

General Lumsden was the head of the Commission, which consisted of himself and three others. These were Alexander Condie Stephen, of the Diplomatic service, and Colonel C. E. Stewart and Colonel Ridgeway, Indian officers. The latter was in India, and came from there with the escort and camp. Colonel Stewart did not start with us. Sir Peter, Condie Stephen, Captain Barrow, the Nawab

Mirza Hasan Khan, a Persian gentleman attached to the Commission, and myself, started from London.

We went by Vienna, Odessa, and Batoum, to Tiflis, thence by Baku and Retch to Teheran. Sir Ronald Thomson, our Minister, was at Gulahek, the summer quarters, a few miles out of Teheran, and there we put up till our camp was formed for the journey eastward.

Sir Peter made a ceremonial call upon the Shah. I asked to be allowed to accompany it, and permission had to be obtained, particularly as I wished to sketch. When we were received I kept behind, and slightly in a corner, so that I might see and use my pencil. They all noticed that the eyes of the Shah were upon me during the whole of the interview, and at the end the interest His Majesty had taken in my doings was shown by his asking to see what I had sketched. This rather took me by surprise, for the interview had not lasted above ten minutes, and my sketches were of the slightest—they could not be otherwise in such a short time. So I asked Sir Ronald to explain that they were only shorthand notes, to be finished afterwards. The Shah took so much interest in the subject that Sir Ronald told him of a few of the wars I had been in and the travels I had made. His Majesty seemed pleased, and gave orders that I should receive every facility while I was in Teheran. Particularly I was to be given an opportunity of seeing the ceremonies of the Corban Bairam, which would take place in two or three days. When we retired, all said that my "face had been whitened," a figurative phrase meaning that I had found favour in the eyes of the "Centre of the Universe." This interview took place in the palace of Sultanabad. Coffee was not served to us in the Shah's presence, but we went to another house in the gardens, where this was done.

Next morning the Shah sent me his photograph, that I might do justice to his portrait. The letter which accompanied it was written by Aboul Kassem Khan, son of Mahmoud Khan, the Foreign Minister. The son had been educated in England, and could speak and write our language.

THE GREAT HIGHWAY OF CENTRAL ASIA.

To face p. 302.

On the morning of the Corban Bairam we had come into Teheran, to make the final preparations for our journey. While we were at breakfast a Persian, gorgeous in blue and silver lace, entered the room, bearing a long silver mace in his hand, and stated in Persian that he had brought a carriage for the "Naksha Basha." One of the Churchills—sons of Colonel Churchill who had been with General Williams in Kars—at table, was said to be particularly well up in Persian, but at first he could not see what was meant. I was familiar with the word *naksha*, a "plan," or "picture," in India. It caught my ear at once, and I made a guess that it applied to myself. The man meant that he had been sent by the Shah for the "great artist." I was driven in a carriage and four to the palace of Sultanabad, where the ceremony took place. It was what would have been called a Durbar in India. In Persia it is called the Salaam. All the high officials of State, officers, and troops, occupy the ground in front of the palace, and the Shah sits at an arched opening. There are no presents, as at an Indian Durbar. The Shah makes a number of statements about the country, and other countries, and the officials say, "Bali, bali"—yes, yes. A khatib, or reader, repeated some words, a poet recited some verses in praise of the Shah, the troops marched past, and the ceremony was ended.

We left Teheran on our march eastward on the 2nd of October, and it took us a month to reach Meshed. Our route lay along the great highway between Western Asia and Turkestan. It is the route that armies must have taken in the past, for on our left was the great Elburz chain of mountains, and on our right the great Salt Desert that extends over nearly all the central part of Persia.

The first day's march from Teheran brought us to Kabud Gumbaz, "Blue Dome." There is no blue dome at the place, though blue domes are common in Persia. Close to Dowlutabad, which we passed on the way, are the remains of an old city called by the Mohammedans Rey, and by the Christians Rajis, a name in the Bible. Parts of the walls remain, but they are only mud. An old kind of pottery is found in fragments on the site. It is white with a purple colour which has a very fine metallic lustre. Churchill showed me a small cup of it. This kind of pottery has not been made in Persia for seven or eight centuries. Lasgird, four marches further on, is a remarkable place, and illustrates the condition of the country in the times when the Turkomans made raids upon it. *Las* or *Last* was a son of Noah, and he first traced the circle of the village—*Gird* means "circle" or "round." The place might have been copied from the Ark, for it is in three storeys. In the lowest are vaulted cellars in which all the grain is placed. In the second storey are the animals; and in the highest are the human inhabitants. Below are a number of wells, which are kept in good order in case of an attack by the Turkomans. The entrance is by a very small stone door about 45 × 37 × 7½ inches, which works on sockets. The place now belongs to the Shrine of Meshed, and has to pay 100 kurrwas of grain and 1,000 bomans a year. I saw sheep and goats high up in the balconies. Mud, I should think, has always been the building material of this part of the world. Water is the thing of value. Wherever there is water there are villages. On the road, in the dark of the early morning, we passed long groups of pilgrims on the way to Meshed. Their salutation was, "Eltimasa dua"—"Pray for us all!" On Sir Peter's entry to some of the villages a sheep was sacrificed, till he stopped the practice.

At Sabzawar I went in the evening to see the crowd that had collected in a kubberistan, or burial-ground, close to our camp. Crowds of men and women had gathered to pray or perform other ceremonies at the graves. It was the festival of the Mohurrum, which I think must be a survival of an older faith. A crowd came past, bearing a cone ten or twelve feet long, painted red, green, and gold, surmounted by a brass ornament of peculiar form, on the top of which was a long flexible piece of steel like a sword, but broadened at the point, which swayed in the air. On the cone were letters, no doubt from the Koran. In the crowd were a number of lads and boys who sang or shouted, jumping into the air every half minute or so, and striking together two round pieces of wood they held in each hand.

THE TOMB OF OMAR

At Nishapur Sir Peter arranged that the mehmander should take us to the tomb of Omar Khayam, the astronomer poet of Persia, as it was only half a farsach or hour's journey from the town. As we neared the spot we noticed the mounds of old mud walls, which turned out to be those of the original Nishapur. This had been a large place. The mehmander pointed out a blue dome as the tomb. It used to be in the outskirts, and was close to the old walls. There were trees round the building, and it appeared an important place. I was rather astonished to find so magnificent a monument in a country where everything is mud, and all is poor and primitive. On dismounting we passed through a doorway and found a walled-in garden in front of the tomb. The arrangement reminded me of the Taj and other Indian tombs, but of course the materials and condition of the monument were far inferior. A path led up through the garden. In this was a tank with water, and we had to ascend a few steps to a platform on which the tomb stands. I looked at the coloured tiles with which the tomb was decorated, regretting that some of those on the dome had fallen off, but saying to myself that Omar Khayam must be thought highly of to enjoy such a monument, when I heard it explained that the building was an Imamzadah—the tomb of an imam's son. The central part of the monument, that under the blue dome, contains the body of Mohammed Marook, brother of the Imam Reza, the eighth imam. It was built in the time of the Shah Sultan Hassan Suffawer. There are two wings in the front, and we were led to the left, where, in a recess formed by the wing, is a plain oblong mass of brick, plastered, with no ornament. This was the tomb of Omar Khayam. Here, as at Westminster, was the "Poets' Corner." On the platform in front are small stones, marking graves, and behind the building lies an extensive *kubberistan*, or burial-ground. The roof over Omar Khayam's tomb was falling to pieces, and the plaster on the walls was breaking off. The spot looked neglected. After I had made my sketch I looked about to find some flowers or plants, a green leaf, or anything growing on the spot, to take away as a souvenir.

The few plants growing through the bricks were all poor, and undesirable as relics. I looked into the garden in front of the tomb, and to my delight I found a row of rose-bushes. At that season the flowers were gone, and even the leaves were brown and withered. Still, I found a few that were green, and there were three hips, which I secured. On returning to camp I wrote to Mr. Quaritch, and enclosed the seeds and some of the rose-leaves. The seeds have since been cultivated at Kew, and a cutting has been planted on the grave of Edward Fitzgerald, the translator of Omar.*

Four days later we were received at Meshed with much ceremony and lodged in gorgeous tents by the Governor-General of Khorassan. I sketched the shrine of the Imam Reza. The tomb is of stone, about six feet long, and it has three railings, the first or inner one of sandal-wood, the second of gold and jewels, and the outer one of steel. There is a space of a foot or so between each. Over the tomb is a canopy of gold, with five pear-shaped ornaments. Abbas Khan, the British representative at Meshed, told me Haroun al Raschid is buried in the shrine, and that he began the gilding of it. He also said the shrine was believed to stand on the site of an older temple of the pre-Mohammedan period, some of its foundations being as old as the time of Alexander. The pilgrims move round the shrine, making certain specified prayers at each side.

From Meshed we marched to Sarrakhs, where there was a grand turn-out—first the Governor, Ali Mardan Khan, with a large group of what might be called Central Asian Horse, carrying a long pole covered with red cloth, and surmounted with yak tails and a gilt ball; then, near

* [In a communication to Miss Franklin, an intimate friend, Simpson remarked, "I cannot speak for certain about the person who first brought Fitzgerald's edition of Omar before the public. The legend is that it was Rossetti or Swinburne, but I am inclined to believe it was my old friend T. W. Hinchliff, so long my neighbour at 64, Lincoln's Inn Fields. He published a notice in *Fraser's Magazine.* I do not know the date of it, but my guess is that that was the magazine article which is credited with the calling attention. Quaritch was Fitzgerald's publisher."]

THE TOMB OF OMAR KHAYYAM AT NISHAPUR.

To face p. 306.

Sarrakhs, some infantry in line, a queer lot, looking as if recruited from a workhouse. New Sarrakhs is Persian, Old Sarrakhs is Russian. Stephen and Barrow went over to Old Sarrakhs on the part of the General. After breakfast I went over on the part of myself. My passport, *viséd* for Russia, served as an introduction. General Komaroff invited me into his tent, where a large party were sitting at breakfast. Afterwards we all went outside, where there were carpets and chairs, and we had coffee, wine, and cigarettes, while the soldiers danced and sang. Old Sarrakhs is a mound, a gathering most probably of the *débris* of a succession of cities, one on the other. On the top of all are the hollows of the houses of the last Sarrakhs. The walls of one house stand, and one of the Turkoman guides said it was the house of the Wuzzeer of Haroun al Raschid. A hawk on one of the ruined walls was the only life I saw in Old Sarrakhs. North-east lies the Sarrakhs of the present day, a scattered collection of reed huts. On the plain rise the tombs of Avil and Kavil, the two sons of Adam and Hava, or Eve.

From Sarrakhs I sent a telegram to the *Daily News* telling of our arrival, and of the occupation of Pul-i-Khatun by the Russians. General Komaroff sent to explain that the occupation had taken place because the Afghans had advanced beyond the frontier at Penjdeh and at Sariaz, and because troops were coming from India. This was an allusion to our Indian escort. We discovered later that the Russian officer in command at Pul-i-Khatun had been disgraced because he either had not seen or had not reported the passage of the escort—Wali Mohammed Khan and his hundred sowars—to join Sir Peter.

From Sarrakhs we came south along the Heri Rud, which is the boundary here between Russia and Persia, to Kuhsan, where we found the Indian camp and escort. Thence a party of us struck off north-east to Penjdeh, and the camp settled at Bala Murghab for the winter, moving after February to a place called Gubran. From this place I began my homeward journey. I had illustrated the region sufficiently well, and there was nothing more for me to do.

The fighting between the Russians and Afghans took place after I left, but I had sent home sketches of the locality, which the editor luckily had ready to appear when the news reached London.

On my return to Meshed I came by Turbat-i-Shaik Jami, so I can claim to have visited the tombs of two celebrated Persian poets. I remained about a week in Meshed, and saw a good deal of that holy place. From this I travelled back to Shahrad, on the way we had come from Teheran, but at Shahrad I struck off to the north for Asterabad, and then to the Caspian at Bunder Gez, where I found a steamer to Baku.

In this journey back we put up every night in caravanserais. My man Abbas and I had horses, and there were horses for the baggage, and a man to look after them. Abbas and I started in the early morning, and he carried my breakfast in bags or receptacles on his horse. When we got about half-way, or at some place we thought was suitable, we stopped, a fire was lighted, on which the kettle was boiled, and the substantial part of the breakfast was warmed up. This, with the eating of the meal, generally occupied about hour. We then finished the march. On arriving at the an caravanserai, we looked round to see which was the cleanest of the rooms, or pens, as they might be called. On one being chosen, Abbas swept it out, laid down a piece of carpet, set my small camp-table and stool, and made my bed (which was of iron and folded up), so that I felt very comfortable even in such rough accommodation. The curious thing in these caravanserais is the strange neighbours one has. Next door to me on one side might be a travelling dervish, on the other a camel driver; or it might be pilgrims to the holy tomb of the Imam Reza at Meshed. To see a European eating with a knife and fork was a great attraction to these people. The rooms in the caravanserais were simply open, arched recesses, so that my doings could be seen. Abbas at times put up a cloth to serve as a screen, but it kept out the light. A dervish from Herat came along part of the way with me; that is, he turned up every evening at the caravanserai. He was bound for Kerkella, and carried an iron rod with the figure of a hand, the *Panja*, at the end of it. He had a few words of English, and some Hindostani, so we could manage some slight conversation. He was quite young, and carried a begging bowl, which reminded me of Buddha's ascetic outfit.

After all this rough kind of travelling—and the last two marches, from Asterabad to the Caspian, had bad roads and vile caravanserais — when I found myself on board the steamer, and sitting in the cabin with cushioned seats and a white table-cloth before me, it seemed as if my journey was ended. The steamer, *The Grand Duke Constantine*, Captain Hack (a Norwegian who could speak English), called at a port called Mashad-i-Sar, on the south coast of the Caspian, west of Bunder Gez, so I took Abbas on board and landed him at this place. This saved him more than a week's travelling in getting back to Teheran. I handed all my camp traps over to him, as they were now useless to me. He had seen a photograph of my little daughter, which had been sent out to me, and he gave me a gold coin, or rather token, for her. It is one of the tokens sold in Meshed, which are worn by those who visit the tomb of the Imam Reza at that place. There are one or two old coins with it. The British Museum Authorities expressed a wish to have one of three small copper coins, so I sent it to the Museum in the name of "Anne Penelope Simpson."

In Persia I had seen the children and young folk playing with eggs dyed red, as part of the New Year ceremony. At Baku, I found them playing with similar eggs, as part of the Easter celebration. This is a good illustration of the theory that a ceremony is older than the legend that grows up to explain it. The playing with the dyed eggs has probably the same origin in both cases, but it has different significations at the present day.

I had a letter of introduction to Mr. Törnudd, the head of Messrs. Nobel's establishment at Baku. One of Mr. Nobel's sons went with me to the oil-wells and the Fire Temple at Sarakhani; this I found was a Hindu temple. I made sketches of it, and managed to make a rough squeeze of one or two of the Devanagari inscriptions.

The British Consul-General at Odessa asked me to take a packet of dispatches home with me to the Foreign Office, and gave me a special passport. The events on the Afghan frontier were critical, and the chances of war were serious, so it was considered unsafe to trust the documents to the Russian Post Office.

After two nights and days in the train, with little food, I felt very tired when I reached Berlin, so I determined to have a night's rest. In the morning I called on Count Seckendorff, and he asked me to call again after breakfast to see the Crown Princess. This I did. When she came in she had a pretty young girl with her, whom she introduced to me as her grand-daughter. I believe she was the daughter of the eldest daughter of the Crown Princess, the Princess or Duchess of Saxe-Meiningen. I said, "Is this your grand-daughter?" giving a slight emphasis on the word "your." The intonation meant, "Are you already a grandmother?" She caught the meaning quickly, for she at once replied, "Yes, my granddaughter," giving a repetition of my emphasis on the word "my." I then mentioned that I recollected the announcement of her own birth. I asked if the young lady could speak English, and the Princess replied, "Yes; nothing but English here." This was the only indication I ever had from her of the strong English proclivities she has been credited with. I then told her about the Afghan frontier, regarding which she was evidently much interested, and made some strong remarks. Then she asked me if I would oblige her by calling on Colonel Swaine, the Military Attaché to our Embassy (she wrote out his address for me on a piece of paper), and telling him all I knew. On my leaving, Seckendorff went with me to the Embassy, where I saw Sir Edward Malet. Then I went to Colonel Swaine's house, and saw him, telling him important points, and answering questions he put to me. I did all this and was in time for the midday train, which brought me to Willesden on the evening of the next day, the 29th of April, 1885. I had been away close upon eight months.

The dispatches I brought home were sent to Lord

Granville, who was then Foreign Minister, and this led to an invitation to lunch in his house in Carlton Terrace. I did not take my sketches, so had to go another day soon afterwards, to show them to Lord and Lady Granville.

The action of the Russians at Penjdeh, which so nearly led to war, seemed to have given the Queen a great interest in the locality, for at the end of May I received a message from Sir Henry Ponsonby that I was to come to Balmoral, where Her Majesty was, and bring my sketches with me. I started on the 1st of June, and arrived at Balmoral next day. Sir Henry told me that I was to remain two nights in the Castle. I had my meals with the suite. In the evening, just as dinner was coming to a close, a message came in from the Queen asking if my sketches could be shown at night. I said "Yes," and went to my room to bring them. I was taken into the drawing-room, where the Queen sat with some ladies. One was the Marchioness of Lorne, and another was the Princess of Leiningen. I had with me some silver ornaments which I had brought from Central Asia, as well as a child's cap I had brought from Penjdeh. These were first looked at, and the Queen appeared to be delighted with the jaunty look of the little cap, for she held it up as high as her hand could reach, and called the attention of the other ladies to it. Her Majesty looked carefully over all the drawings, while I stood at the table and gave explanations of each.

Next evening the suite were invited to the drawing-room, a proceeding known as "joining the royal circle." But I found the word "circle" very far from correct geometrically. I should prefer to call the figure a very irregular polygon, for on entering the drawing-room, we each took a place anywhere round the room, as near to the wall as the furniture would permit. The Queen went round chatting for a longer or shorter time to each. When she came to me the conversation chanced to turn upon Lady Canning in India. She was a great friend of the Queen, and the details I was able to give of Lady Canning, of the camp life of which I had seen so much, how Lady Canning devoted her time to sketching, how a number of her sketches were burned by a fire in her tent—all this so interested Her

Majesty, that she stood talking to me for about half an hour. When at last the Queen retired and we were all going out, Dr. Reid said, "Why, Simpson, you kept the Queen all to yourself to-night."

Next day, before I left, Miss Stopford, one of the ladies in attendance, brought me the two volumes of "The Queen's Life in the Highlands," with Her Majesty's signature in them; and I had to write my name in two small books of names Miss Stopford produced. One of them was an old and very shabby volume, but I saw a number of important names in it. I assumed that every visitor or guest of the Queen would write his or her name in this well-worn little book.

About a week afterwards I was called to Marlborough House to show my sketches of Central Asia to H.R.H. the Prince of Wales. The Princess of Wales and one of her daughters, with Prince Victor and Prince George, also came in to see them. This was in the Prince's own room. I took the silver ornaments with me on this occasion also, and the ladies were much interested in them. One of the ornaments, which is worn on the breast, I placed on the breast of one of the Princesses to show the manner it was worn on the Afghan frontier. It was much admired. I had lost the small medal of the Prince's visit to India which he had given me in the Terai. It had dropped off the chain on which it hung in one of the marches, the third beyond Meshed, during my expedition, and on this visit to Marlborough House the Prince most kindly gave me another to take its place. I was invited to stay to lunch on this occasion.

CHAPTER XXXVI

THE SILVER WEDDING OF THE PRINCE OF WALES

THE Prince of Wales' silver wedding was to be celebrated on the 10th of March of this year. A special number of the *Illustrated London News* was to be published, and in order to give something of the home life of the Prince and his family, sketches were wanted of the inside of Sandringham. I was asked if I could manage this, so I applied to Sir Francis Knollys. I was requested to call at Marlborough House, and there I saw the Prince himself, who invited me to Sandringham. I was instructed to telegraph to the equerry-in-waiting from the station when leaving London, and a brougham would be waiting for me at Wolferton station on my arrival.

I was quartered in what was then known as the "Bachelor's Cottage," where Teesdale, who chanced to be the equerry at the time, and Sir Francis Knollys slept. This house was afterwards enlarged, and, as "York Lodge," became the Sandringham residence of the Duke and Duchess of York. We had a brougham to take us to the great house to dinner, and the same to take us back. On the first evening, which was a Monday, the Turkish Ambassador and Canon Duckworth were of the party. There is an American bowling-alley in the house, and I played with Canon Duckworth while the Prince kept count for us. This was a complicated matter, and His Royal Highness seemed the only one who understood it. I believe the Canon and I were equally strange to the game, but the clerical eye was not so good as the artistic, and the Church got beaten by Art. The Rev. John Mitchell, vicar of Wolferton, was there that evening, and he and I tried a game. The Church, judging from first results, would have come off badly again, but H.R.H. stopped marking, as he had to attend to some letters which arrived by the post, and we had to stop, as we could not mark what we had gained.

Next day the Prince had to go to London, and his secretary and equerry went with him. I was alone at lunch that day, and in the evening I dined with Sir Dighton and Lady Probyn at their house. The Prince returned next day, bringing with him a large party, including Lord and Lady Downe, Mr. Chaplin, Lord Amherst of Hackney (then Mr. Tyson Amherst), and others. I found it very pleasant, and might have extended my stay, but I knew time was pressing with the editor, so I had to hurry on my work.

The day I was sketching the drawing-room the two young Princesses chanced to come in, and on looking at my sketch they expressed wonder regarding the perspective. This told me they must have been bothered with perspective in their efforts at drawing. The Princess of Wales also came in, and she expressed herself about the difficulty of drawing all the details; for the rooms may be described as littered all over with nick-nacks. She said this, however, was nothing to her own room, which she took me upstairs to see. Every chair, sofa, and table was covered, as if a shower of articles had come down upon the room. The only spaces uncovered were the writing-pad on the table, and the small chair the Princess sat on when writing. It certainly had not the appearance of a comfortable room. When we were in this room she again expressed her doubts about the possibility of drawing such a mass of objects. I said it must be done, but I really managed to avoid most of them, by limiting my subject to the corner with the table and chair occupied by Her Royal Highness.

I managed to have all done that was necessary on the Thursday evening, and I asked Teesdale how I should act. He asked if I had my sketches ready to show. This was at dinner. I said, "Yes, I have them hid in a corner of the drawing-room." "Well," he said, "catch the Prince as soon as we leave the dinner-table, and tell him you wish to go in the morning." This I did, producing the sketches, which

His Royal Highness looked over. He then said, "Leave your address with Teesdale; I want to send you some game." Next morning there was a brougham ready for me, and the hamper of game was also ready, so I brought it on. There was a big label on it with the words, "From H.R.H. the Prince of Wales, Sandringham." I gave the hamper a wide berth at the stations where we had to change, for I had no exact notion of the amount of backsheesh it would be necessary to offer to a railway porter for moving a hamper bearing such an important piece of information. At one place I saw quite a crowd round the hamper reading the label. This will show that I kept my eye on it, and took care it came safely home.

Having received so many kind attentions from the Prince of Wales, I thought I was justified in sending something on the occasion of the Silver Wedding. So I had a sketch, done when at Abergeldie, framed in a silver frame, and sent it to Marlborough House. This was graciously accepted. I know this was not the case with every present sent. One at least I know was rejected, and in this I learned one great difficulty such a personage as the Prince of Wales has to encounter. All sorts of people would send presents, whether they were justified or not in doing so, and His Royal Highness has to be careful in accepting. I learned of one instance in which Sir Francis Knollys wrote to Sir James Linton, to ask who a certain person was, for he had sent a picture as a present. The fact that the man was unknown at Marlborough House was enough in itself to show the act a piece of presumption.

CHAPTER XXXVII

THE SPECIAL ARTIST: LAST YEARS

THE Emperor William I. died in Berlin on the 9th of March, 1888, and I left London the same evening to make sketches of the funeral. The diary of my journey may give some idea of the details of a correspondent's experience. I give it *in extenso*.

Friday, March 9th.—Left Victoria at 8 p.m. for Berlin. Slept most of the way across the Channel. Had a sleeping berth on rail to Cologne. Got into Cologne late, so my luggage was allowed to go without the bother of opening. Just caught the train. Had dejeuner, to me it was dejeuner and dinner, in the train between Dortmund and Hamm. Got into Berlin—due at 10.40.

Saturday 10th.—After breakfast I went about ten o'clock to the Embassy, and saw Sir Edward Malet, who kindly gave me a letter of introduction to Count Gulenberg, Ober Ceremonien Meister, Seiner Maj. des Kaiser und Konigs, who promised me every facility. Sir Edward, in the letter, said I was well known to the Emperor and Empress (the new Emperor and Empress). Sent off three sketches, very rough ones, of what I saw in the streets. I waited to-night to see the body of the Emperor carried to the Dom. It came on to snow, and continued all night. At 11.45 I went out and stood till about one o'clock, when the procession went past.

Monday 12th.—Called on Count Gulenberg, who does nothing for me. Met there an artist of a Frankfort paper, and we went to the Chamberlain's office, and I got a ticket which let me into the Dom. Made sketches and sent them off to-night. Prince William was in the Dom when I went in, and I put him into the sketch.

Tuesday 13*th*.—At work on carrying body of Emperor from Palace to Dom. Lowe dined with me.

Wednesday 14*th*.—Went with Lowe this morning to Charlottenburg. Saw Seckendorff, who sent a man with us to the Mausoleum. As we left Mausoleum two ladies in mourning were coming down the walk. As we passed, one of them used my name, and on looking round, I found it was the Empress. She was very kind, and asked after Mrs. Simpson. She looked sad and worn.

Thursday 15*th*.—Sir Edward Malet sent me an invitation from Count Redern to go to his house and see the funeral procession. Lunched with Lowe at the Berlin Club. Met his *confrère*, Brinsley Sheridan, *Times* correspondent from Vienna; Mr. Smalley, *New York Tribune*, and Mr. Charles Williams, who had been in the Soudan.

Friday 16*th*.—Went to the royal stables, and saw funeral car, and then to Count Redern's, where I saw the procession. The curious thing is that Seckendorff arranged that I saw Prince William's bride arrive in Berlin from the same windows—that was when the present Count's father was living. Got back to hotel, and got a sketch ready in time for post same evening.

Saturday 17*th*.—Went to Charlottenberg, and saw Seckendorff about making sketches at the Palace. Came back and paid a visit to the Museum. Dined at Lowe's in the evening. Smalley, Charles Williams, Mr. Saunders, *Pall Mall Gazette*, and Rederick were of the party.

Sunday 18*th*.—Went to Charlottenberg, and Seckendorff sent me into the chapel, where service was performed by Dr. Koegel before the Emperor and Empress and household. Returned and wrought at the sketch in afternoon. It had been snowing all night, and was bitterly cold all day. Had a fire in my room in the evening.

Monday 19*th*.—Breakfasted at 11.30 with C. Williams in the Kaiserhof. Lowe and Rederick formed the party. A young man who is here for the *Morning Post* came in later. Finished sketch of the chapel this day, and posted it in the afternoon. Went out and made some purchases.

Tuesday 20th.—Went to Charlottenberg, and made sketches of the Orangerie. The Empress was in the Orangerie when I went in, and she shook hands and talked for about ten minutes. She said the Emperor was better. The Princess Victoria was with her, and I found the other two Princesses also walking in the place. On returning to Brandenburg Gate, I left a card on Count Redern. Went back to hotel and packed up. Left by the 9.41 p.m. train. It snowed all day, and I had fears of being blocked up on the way.

Wednesday 21st.—Got into Cologne about 7.5 a.m. Had a cup of coffee in railway restaurant, and went off to see a little of Cologne. The Cathedral is overdone with spires, pinnacles, and crockets. Noticed that some of the small pinnacles were held in their places by iron bars, and the golden cross on roof over altar had what a sailor would call two "stays" to keep it secure. To the south, and nearer the river, I came upon the Church of St. Martin, a fine old place, Romanesque. The interior had been lately done up. Service was going on, and I waited till it was finished. Walked about for some time, but the snow made the streets slushy, so I returned to the restaurant, had something to eat, and left at 1.13 p.m. The companion I found in the carriage was an Englishman, and he turned out to be an old friend of Hinchliff's, Mr. Hedges, in whose mother's house we dined on the 20th of November, 1879, when I gave a lecture to the Streatham and Tulse Hill Institute. We parted at Brussels. Had something to eat and left at 8.13 p.m. Snow on the ground all the way from Berlin, but it was much thinner in Belgium.

Thursday 22nd.—I slept most of the way across the Channel. Got to Victoria about 6.30 a.m. The Custom House Officer passed the big box with court dress, when I showed him that I was a special artist from Berlin. Got home about 8 a.m.

In this same year I attended the great International Exhibition at Glasgow, and the funeral of the Emperor

Frederick at Berlin. In the year following, by royal command, I attended at St. George's Chapel, Windsor, the christening of the third child of Princess Beatrice, for a picture of the ceremony, and on the announcement of the marriage of the Princess Louise of Wales to Lord Fife, I went and made sketches at Duff House, Banff, and Mar Lodge, Braemar, Lord Fife's residences in Scotland. I also made some sketches of the Shah's visit to Balmoral.

The Forth Bridge was to be opened or finished, by the Prince of Wales putting in the last rivet, on the 4th of March, 1890. This was a Tuesday, and it was necessary to have the event in the paper on the Saturday following. This necessity indicates a great change in the history of the *Illustrated London News*, as well as in the history of illustrated journalism. When the paper was first started, and for many years afterwards, what is called the "make up" was arranged on the Thursday week before the issue appeared. From improvements in the printing press, which produced greater speed in printing, events that took place on the Friday became possible. Later on, events on a Saturday could be produced within the time. And at last, owing principally to greater speed in printing, important events taking place on the Monday were possible. Rivalry with the *Graphic* may have had something to do with these efforts at rapidity of production. One device which helped in such cases, was to give the late event in a supplement, which, being a smaller sheet than the body of the paper, could be run more quickly through the press. The floating of the *Daily Graphic* brought a new necessity for speed. It produced or intensified the feeling that if an event could not be given till the Saturday week after its occurrence, it had become "ancient history," which in these days of fast living, would be all but forgotten. So extra pressure has since been put upon the speed in producing illustrations of events of importance. To produce on the Saturday an event like the opening of the Forth Bridge, which was to take place on a Tuesday, was a difficult task, and all the more so, as there would be ten hours lost in passing the distance from Edinburgh to London. I promised to use every endeavour to accomplish it. It was arranged that Mr. Forrestier should go down with me a few days before, to see the spot, procure the details, and as we had a block with us, get as much as possible done before the event.

On the morning after our arrival in Edinburgh Forrestier and I started for the bridge. Most luckily at the station we found the Marquis of Tweedale, Lord Colville, of Culross, and Sir John Fowler, on their way to the bridge also. They were going to see about the final arrangements for the coming ceremony, and on our explaining to them our purpose, they gave us every facility. We were shown every detail, and had the ceremony explained, so that on our return to Edinburgh Forrestier was able to begin the block, and it was all but finished before the event came off. I attended the ceremony, and returned immediately after to correct any details that were wrong, and we were able to leave for London with the night train, bringing the finished block ready to begin engraving in the morning. The picture, therefore, was in time for appearing in the paper on Saturday.

It had been snowing some days before the ceremony, and the ground was white. It blew a strong gale on the 4th of March, and there was no protection from it on the bridge, so that we had to hold on to our hats while the Prince performed his part of the work. The royal party sailed under the bridge that they might see it. The Marquis of Tweedale, who was chairman of directors of the Bridge Company, invited me on board the steamer. Colonel Colville was present in attendance on the Duke of Edinburgh, and he introduced me to M. Eiffel, the designer of the Eiffel Tower in Paris, who was with the royal party. Lord Rosebery was also there; the royal party were being entertained at Dalmeny during the visit. Dr. Russell was at the ceremony, but so lame, he could not leave the train. Hearing I was there, he sent a message by Colville that he would like to see me; we had not met for many years. I looked out for him after the ceremony, and was sorry to find him such a cripple, but he had not lost his old cheery spirit. I had to forego the luncheon that followed, as it was necessary for me to return with details to have the block finished.

This year I received an invitation to attend a garden party at Marlborough House, but I was at the Forth Bridge at the time, and could not attend. Mr. Jackson, the editor of the *Illustrated London News*, wrote to ask if he might not send another artist, as he wished to have sketches of the party. Sir Francis Knollys wrote in answer that I had been invited as the "personal friend of the Prince of Wales," and no other artist could attend. In 1891 I again received an invitation, and was able to be present. The Queen, with the Emperor and Empress of Germany, was present. On these occasions the Queen, with the Prince, walked round the garden, to see and be seen by every one present. As they passed where I was standing, I heard the Prince say to the Queen, "Mr. Simpson, the artist."

There was a split this year among those who had the management of the Congress of Orientalists, and in September one section, under the leadership of Dr. Leitner, held what they claimed to be the "Ninth Congress" in London Not knowing of the quarrel, I gave in my name to this meeting, believing it was the regular Congress, and as Leitner was an old friend I did not care to withdraw. He placed me at the head of a section, and on the 5th September I went down to the Oriental Institute at Woking, and in the Museum opened the section with an address, the principal part of which was on the Graeco-Buddhist architecture of the Indus region and Afghanistan.

The other section of Orientalists held their Ninth Congress in London, in September, 1892. As I had, although unintentionally, been a member of Leitner's Congress, I supposed I should not have been welcome to this gathering. On the contrary I was invited, and asked to read a paper, which I did, on Indian Architecture.

In January I had read a paper to the Society of Arts on "Lithography as a Chapter in the History of Illustrative

Art;" and in November the Society presented me with their silver medal for it. The principal value of the medal lies, to my own mind, in the fact that the same Society gave Sennefelder, the inventor of lithography, the same medal for his invention.

On the 14th of January, 1892, at Sandringham, the eldest son of the Prince of Wales, the Duke of Clarence and Avondale, died. The death took place in the morning, and by the evening I was in Dersingham at "The Feathers," the nearest place of accommodation to Sandringham. I found the house filled with correspondents, and I had to double up with one of these in one of the bedrooms. These gentlemen of the Press were all in a despondent state, because the police had orders to admit none of them within the gates, and no news was allowed to be sent out. This did not look hopeful, but I sent a short note to the house addressed to Sir Dighton Probyn. A note came down next morning in answer, telling me to come up at once with my sketching materials. I was taken up to the room in which the dead Prince lay. It was the bedroom he had occupied since his boyhood. When I went into the bedroom at first the Princess Victoria was sitting alone beside the bed. She told me she had arranged the flowers round the pillow, and could not realise that the Prince was dead. The Prince of Wales came in shortly after my arrival. He shook hands with me, and called me his "dear old friend." I felt quite overcome by the warmth of the kindness he manifested towards me. After a few minutes his voice began to falter; his feelings were getting the better of him, and he suddenly turned and left the room. He came in again, some time afterwards, and said he would like to have my sketch, but again, after a few minutes, he began to lose his voice, and left. The Princess of Wales came in once or twice during the day. Her eyes looked watery, but she showed more command of herself than the Prince did. The Duke of York's room was close to that of his brother, and he came in at times. I was in the room from about ten in the morning till nearly 4 p.m., and I made a fairly good drawing in pencil of the head, as

Sketch for Medal of the Abyssinian Expedition, made by Simpson on the march from Magdala (p. 197).

Simpson's Grave in Highgate Cemetery.

To face p. 323.

well as a more general sketch of the bed and its surroundings. I was asked down about the middle of the day to lunch. Sir Dighton Probyn gave me a card to admit me to the grounds and the house at any time, and told the head of the police that I was not a "correspondent," but "a friend of the Prince of Wales." I waited till the day of the funeral, and did sketches of the service in the church on Sunday, and of the funeral procession from Sandringham to the railway station at Wolferton.

This year, 1892, being the 50th, or Jubilee year, of the *Illustrated London News*, Mr. Ingram invited all connected with the paper to a dinner at Margate, which I attended, on the 16th of July.

As the great exhibition at Chicago was to open in 1893, the editor spoke to me about going there for the paper. On consulting with the doctor about this he advised me not to go, a piece of advice in which I think he was quite right. I am now close on the end of my 70th year, and for the last thirty-nine years I have been a sort of Wandering Jew, but now at last I begin to feel the effects of age. After so many years spent in this way, it is not without a feeling of regret I at last realise that at least one part of my career has come to an end. Here these pages must close.

["Finished" was written on the last page of these "Notes and Recollections" by their author on September 17, 1893. Six years later, on August 17, 1899, he died. An attack of bronchitis, caught at the opening of the Forth Bridge, laid him aside, more or less, during these last years, and proved fatal in the end. He died at Willesden, early in the autumn morning, his wife and his beloved daughter by his side. His grave is in Highgate Cemetery.]

APPENDIX

GLASGOW SEVENTY YEARS AGO

THE locality in which I spent these early years is now very much changed. I remember the making of Parliamentary Road. On the north of it, bounded on the east by the ground of the Royal Lunatic Asylum, on the west by the Port Dundas Road, and as far north as the present Buchanan Street station, was a space which had been quarried out, and was still being worked within my recollection. On the south, between Parliamentary Road and Cathedral Street—the space where Holmhead Street is now—was a green field called Bell's Park. At the top of Frederick Street this was used as a bleaching-green. At the south-west corner there was a quarry. This was very deep, with a great precipice on the side from the park. Part of this quarry was on the south side of what was then known as Love Loan, and behind the house of James Ewing the rock was left like a great wall, with perpendicular sides, along the top of which Love Loan passed to the head of Buchanan Street. Through this rock was a tunnel communicating between the two portions of the quarry. There was a great traffic with carts taking coals from the "town-head"—the Monkland Canal—to the Broomielaw. Love Loan was a very narrow lane, and at the quarries it had a stone wall. Not far from the head of North Hanover Street was an artificial mound, formed of earth heaped up from the quarry. This was known among the boys by the word "Humplucks." It was a favourite spot for flying "dragons," or kites, and was a sort of Akropolis to the boys of the "Bay"—meaning "Botany Bay." This was the name by which Dempster Street was known, and was supposed to express the social and moral condition of those living there. It was a narrow, dirty place, with very poor houses. The boys were at constant war with the boys of the Cowcaddens, who from that word were called "The Cuddies." The Humplucks were the central point of the war, and were often taken and retaken in an afternoon, stones being the projectiles used in the warfare.

The levelling of Bell's Park for the purpose of building on it took place when we were in Frederick Street, and was a work of years. The earth—most of it a blueish-grey clay, with boulders—was used to fill up the quarry. There was an old engine-house, with red tiles and a brick chimney, in the quarry, which was left and covered over. I often wonder if that house still remains buried, or if it has been removed in the extension of Queen Street station. The making, but more particularly the widening and extension of the station under Cathedral Street must have required the removal of a great part of the soil of Bell's Park which I saw in my boyhood thrown in with so much trouble. The north end of Queen Street was a kind of recess, or *cul de sac*, with a railing and a gate. This was the entrance to the house of James Ewing, well known in my boyhood as "Craw Jamie." His house was surrounded by fine old trees, which the crows were partial to, and their nests as well as their cawing were a marked feature of the spot. The house itself was in the style common at that time, such as Kirkman Finlay's in Queen Street, and others now disappearing. Dr. Wardlaw, Independent, had his church at the corner of George Street and Dundas Street.

When the "Lords," *i.e.*, the judges, came to the town for the Circuit Courts, they generally put up at the George Hotel, at the south-east corner of George Square. This hotel disappeared when the new City Chambers required the ground. To us boys the coming in of the "Lords" was an important event. They were escorted with cavalry, and sentries walked in front of the hotel while the judges were in town. On the day of their arrival there was a crowd, and we boys generally found a point of vantage on the railings with which the square was then surrounded.

The square was our Olympia, or rather our Stadium; it

was our recognised space for races. Many a race I have run, and won, round George's Square. The square was well filled at that period with trees and bushes, and only those living in the square had access. Sir John Moore's monument was in the square from my earliest recollection; and I remember the putting up of Sir Walter Scott's statue, and the pictures of the monument, lithographs, which appeared. Both Allan & Ferguson and Maclure & Macdonald published prints at the time. I am under the impression that it was not till after I came to London, in 1851, that the railings of the Square were removed. One great feature connected with George Square was a steam-carriage that plied between Glasgow and Paisley. It made one journey to Paisley and back in the day, starting from George Street, at the foot of North Frederick Street, and such a novelty, I need scarcely state, attracted the boys for some distance round. It was built on the model of an ordinary stage coach, with a small funnel projecting from the top, and the engines were low down behind, where the engineer stood. A man on the front seat steered the vehicle by means of a wheel. This carriage ran for some weeks, but its career came to a sudden end from the boiler bursting at the "half-way house," when a number of people were severely injured. I forget whether any were killed or not.*

An early association of my boyhood is connected with the word ".Burkers." This word came from the man Burke, of Burke and Hare notoriety, whose crimes had startled the world only a few years before. On the winter evenings we used to recount wonderful stories to each other about Burkers, how they went about with large cloaks and a plaster in their hands, and how, when they managed to catch a little boy, the plaster was clapped on his mouth to serve the double purpose of suffocation and silence, as the boy was being carried off to some dissecting room. Some of the tales had for their basis the giving of a boy a note, and a sixpence to deliver the note where there was a dark "close"

* [The engine of this coach, a somewhat cumbrous affair, is now in possession of the Corporation of Glasgow, and was shown at the Exhibition of 1901.]

—this word meaning a court or passage—and a dark stair, from which he never returned. Or he was invited into a room where the man who received the letter "burked" the boy. One terrible version of this story was that of a boy who delivered the note, and the man told the boy to sit down on a chair in the room, and then went out. Luckily the boy did not sit down, as in a few minutes the chair sank through the floor. The "Burke" fever was so strong that there was no story too improbable for our minds. When out on messages in the winter nights we kept an open eye for men with big cloaks. The Burkers were generally supposed to be medical students who required "subjects" to dissect. At that time there were no legal arrangements by which bodies could be procured from the hospitals, and the "subjects" had to go through a resurrection process in churchyards at night. The inhabitants were in consequence requisitioned in turn to attend and watch the churchyards. I remember the requisition coming to our house, and my father had either to pass the night watching or pay for a substitute.

Our games at that time were "hide and seek," "robbers and rangers," and "high spy." These were all games with running and hiding. "Prisoner's base" came in, introduced, I think, from England. Other games were "rounders" and "housie," which was rounders played without a bat. We threw the ball with the hand, and then ran round the "dulls," as we called the stones forming the stations. At the place where we struck the ball at rounders, or threw it at housie there was a hole about a foot wide—this was the "mug." Three stones placed some fifty yards apart, forming a shape like a lozenge, were the "dulls." We also played cricket. "Bools"—the Scottish word for marbles—implied a number of peculiar and ingenious games. We had marble "bools," and "whinnies," made from what was understood to be some kind of whinstone. But the common kind were only of baked clay. We had two games called "muggie" and "target," in which the losers had to suffer the penalty of "nags." That was having a "bool" projected against the knuckles. The gambling games were two. In one a "mug" or hole, at the foot of a wall, was used. One boy took one or more "bools" in his hand, and, according to the number, said to the other boy, "Set us one," or "two," or whatever was the number in his hand, the other boy placed an equal number, and the boy standing at the "hail," made a step forward, throwing all the bools into the mug. If they all went in he won, or if an even number chanced to remain in the mug, he won. But if an odd number remained, he lost. I still remember one boy who had a wonderful knack of throwing two marbles into a very small mug. This was important when there were only two, for if one came out the thrower lost.

The great gambling game was called "kep and smash." A ring was marked about a foot from a wall, on a pavement, each boy placed in it a similar number of "bools." The burnt clay ones only were used in this game, except the "plunker," which was large, and made of the same clay as glazed jars. Each boy had his turn: he stood at the hail, and threw his plunker; if it knocked any of the "bools" out of the ring they were his, but his principal object was to throw the plunker so that it first struck the pavement, then the wall, and thus rebounded, and he ran in, caught it, and then made a smash in the ring, knocking out as many of the "bools" as he could, which became his. "Kep and Smash" expresses the process of the game. "Buttons" was another favourite game, and must have disappeared since from the change in costume. At that time brass buttons were worn on coats and waistcoats—a blue coat with brass buttons was the fashionable style. We boys called the coat buttons "tosters," as they were used for tossing, and the smaller ones on waistcoats were dubbed "singlers." Two singlers were valued as equal to one toster. Pitch-and-toss and simple tossing, "head or tails," were the two games at buttons.

There was a curious word in use among Glasgow boys at that time; it was "bauchee." I never saw the word in print, but it can be easily pronounced from the way it is here written. I have no idea of the origin of this word.

It was used in this sense: When any game was going on that had two "sides," or two sets of boys playing against each other, and two boys wanted to join, they retired a bit, and one said, "You will be a gun and I'll be a pistol." Other words might be used. The two then came forward; the question was put to those playing, "A gun or a pistol?" The captain of one side uttered one of these words, and the side he belonged to got the boy to whom that word had been assigned.

We had at that time, from 1830 to 1840, a language among the boys which was so common that we scarce spoke in any other way among ourselves. This I know has been the case among boys at school in many parts of the world, but I have never heard specimens of another that equalled ours for facility of speaking. We called it "Stockwell Gaelic." I do not know who gave it that name, nor who invented the peculiar manner of speaking. It was done by putting the end of a word at the beginning, or the end syllable at the beginning As an illustration—"At-wha are oo-yu aying-sa?" is "What are you saying?" "The an-ma ookit-too": "the man took it." There were very few boys in Glasgow at that time, or even for ten years later, who did not understand this curious jargon. It has long since died out; but if I meet a Glasgow man anywhere who belonged to that date as a boy I have no hesitation in addressing him in Stockwell Gaelic.*

"Pallall" or "peevor" was the girls' game. Both these names were given to what is known in England as "hop-scotch." The piece of flat stone, slate, or marble that was kicked from bed to bed marked on the ground was called "peevor." "Pallall" and "peevor" are other two words requiring the philologist to explain. A writer not long ago in a Glasgow paper announced a conclusion he had come to that the kicking of the peevor round the beds was in imitation of the course of the sun, and was a survival of the solar myth. The beds were numbered, and, in commencing, the girl stood in the semicircle outside, and threw the

* ["Stockwell Gaelic" was still a current form of speech among the boys of Glasgow High School as late as 1877.]

peevor into bed one. She then stood up, and lifting one foot began to hop from the semicircle; she had to hop and kick the peevor all round and into the semicircle. She next lifted the peevor and slid it along into bed number two. She then hopped from the semicircle into bed one, then to bed two, and pushed the peevor round as before. Next time she had to slide the peevor to bed three, and so on till she got to bed eight, and that was a game. If the peevor was kicked so that it stopped on any of the "scores" or lines forming the beds, the girl was "out." I was an adept at this game, as well as at most of the lassies' games. The "jumping-rope," or skipping-rope, I was perfect at, and could do all the fancy movements with it, such as "crossing" both forwards and backwards.

As I grew up what I might perhaps call my first efforts in art were manifested on "Halloween neeps," or turnips for Halloween. Boys brought their turnips to me to "howk," or hollow out, my recompense in such cases being that I could eat as much as I liked of the turnip that was dug out. The idea was to make the turnip into a kind of lantern, in which a candle-end was placed, and the boys carried these lanterns about after dark on Halloween. After being sufficiently hollowed out, I had to ornament them by cutting on the outside rude outlines of faces and other forms. Other boys could do the "howking," as we called it, but I excelled in this artistic department. Among our other games the most elaborate was "Galatians," a survival of one of the mystery plays of early days.*

The Broomielaw Quay extended then from Glasgow Bridge to near Napier's wet dock, which was only a recess at the side of the river, with a yard walled in round it, so that the public at this point could not pass along except by a narrow roadway outside. Napier had a large crane here for putting boilers and engines into steamers. It has only been from a comparatively late period that the river steamers started from Glasgow Bridge. The Greenock railway had

* [A full version of "Galatians," as it was performed at Peebles in 1809, is given by Chambers in his *Popular Rhymes of Scotland*. That author assigns its origin to the time of the Plantagenet kings.]

its termination on the south side of the river at the bridge, and when the railway was opened the steamers were brought up to compete with the new rival. Previous to this the passenger steamers all started from the lower end of the quay below Clyde Street Ferry. Parkholm was on the south side of the river, opposite the end of the steamboat quay of that time, just where the Kinning—I think it used to be called the Kinning House—burn ran into the Clyde. Probably the water of that stream was used in the printing. It was not a sewer then.* About a quarter of a mile to the west of Parkholm, again, was a small bay, which was a fishing station. I remember the fishermen's hut, and their cobles, and have often seen them hauling in the nets with salmon in them. Windmill Croft was then a large field surrounded by a wall. Tradeston extended only to West Street. The river was embanked with stones on the south side, but this embankment did not at first extend up to Glasgow Bridge. My first recollection is of a green bank along the water's edge from the bridge westward. It was the old Glasgow Bridge with holes—circular tunnels in shape—over each pier.

When I was a boy a season seldom passed without a "spate" that flooded the Briggate and the lower end of the Saltmarket. The Goosedubs and lower end of Stockwell Street also were liable to these visitations. The "Bottle-house lum" was a marked feature in those days. It was the chimney of a work where bottles were made, and it stood where the Custom House now stands, near the north end of Glasgow Bridge.

About 2 p.m. the *Caledonia* was generally coming up the river. What a contrast between her and the later style of steamer on the Clyde. She had a bluff bow, each side of which was rounded like the chubby cheeks of a country boy, and her small paddles were well forward. She was one of the river passenger steamers built in 1815, the year after the *Industry* and *Trusty*. She disappeared at an early date,

* [Sketches of the locality by Simpson, showing the various erections, &c., of that time, are to be seen in the now somewhat scarce volume, *Views and Notices of Glasgow in Former Times*.]

but the *Industry* and *Trusty* remained for a long time on the river as luggage boats.

About 1832 my father was employed at Barrowfield turkey-red print-work. This very large establishment belonged to Henry Monteith. There was a Mr. Hervey in it, either as a partner or as one of the principal managers. He was brother to George Hervey the artist, afterwards Sir George, and President of the Royal Scottish Academy. Alexander Rodger the poet, author of many Scottish songs, was also an employé at Barrowfield at the time. My father knew him then, and at a later date I was familiar with his round, short figure, when he was connected with the *Loyal Reformer's Gazette,* Peter Mackenzie's paper. I used to see him regularly about Argyle Street, and I have often heard him sing his own songs at the Saturday Evening Concerts. This he did in a genial, " pawkie " way.

INDEX

INDEX

INDEX

INDEX

D

INDEX

INDEX

INDEX

INDEX

INDEX

INDEX

INDEX

INDEX

INDEX

INDEX

T

INDEX

INDEX